GARLAND STUDIES IN

THE HISTORY OF AMERICAN LABOR

edited by
STUART BRUCHEY
UNIVERSITY OF MAINE

A GARLAND SERIES

A HISTORY OF WORKMEN'S COMPENSATION 1898–1915

FROM COURTROOM TO BOARDROOM

PAUL B. BELLAMY

GARLAND PUBLISHING, INC.
NEW YORK & LONDON / 1997

Library of Congress Cataloging-in-Publication Data

Bellamy, Paul B., 1951–
   A history of workmen's compensation, 1898–1915 : from
courtroom to boardroom / Paul B. Bellamy.
        p.   cm. — (Garland studies in the history of American
labor)
   Includes bibliographical references and index.
   ISBN 0-8153-2827-3 (alk. paper)
   1. Workers' compensation—United States—History.   I. Title.
II. Series.
HD7103.65.U6B45 1997
368.4'1'00973—dc21
                                                      96-28933

Printed on acid-free, 250-year-life paper
Manufactured in the United States of America

To Wendy, Carlye and Michael

Contents

List of Figures

List of Tables

Preface

No less a sceptic of reform impulses than Richard Hofstadter referred to workmen's compensation as "one of our finest inheritances from the Progressive movement." Excluding fault-based worker lawsuits from the courts and moving the injury claims to a newly created administrative system for processing and   settlement was, in Hofstadter's view, a genuinely munificent, worker-favoring development that reflected the very best of Progressive thinking. As he put it in the *Age of Reform*:

> Today it is perhaps necessary to make a strong effort of imagination
> to recall the industrial barbarism that was being tamed—to realize
> how much, for instance, workmen's compensation meant at a time
> when every year some 16,000 or 17,000 trainmen (about one out
> of every ten or twelve workers so classified) were injured.[1]

Hofstadter's characterization of workmen's compensation as a benign accommodation to the harsh realities of a modern industrial state is the same explanation offered by most of the reform's promoters: "changed conditions" in the workplace, the new "factory system" of manufacturing with its maiming steam and electric-powered machinery, required a new social welfare system to protect the inevitable numbers of incidentally injured workers who were daily exposed to the increased hazards of the new and more efficient workplace. However, this version of the reform begs a question as to the extraordinary national consensus that prevailed in support of workmen's compensation, notwithstanding its obvious "socialistic" aspects.

So, when this project first began to take form it was going to address the question raised by the unacknowledged but implicit contradictions within that generally accepted version of the history of workmen's compensation. That paradox can be stated this way: If the common law of employers' liability was so overwhelmingly unfavorable towards injured workers seeking redress in the courts against their employers,[2] why did large American business corporations[3] play a leading role in the workmen's compensation reform effort?[4]

As between the two competing historical propositions, the corporate leadership phenomenon seemed the stronger, more thoroughly and recently examined historical premise. The characterization of the courts as consistently worker-oppressive seemed based upon older, more suspect, and sketchy evidence,[5] and I decided to test that received wisdom by doing a limited quantitative survey of trial level, worker-initiated injury cases in the local state courts in Cleveland, Ohio. The target defendant of that litigation survey was the Cleveland-based United States Steel Corporation[6] subsidiary, the American Steel and Wire Company, and the period of the survey was from 1898-1915. That exploratory work cast the Eastmanesque view of the courts as worker-oppressive in serious doubt. In fact, the survey of 127 work injury cases clearly demonstrated quite the opposite was true. In the Cuyahoga County Common Pleas Court, the American Steel and Wire Company did not win a single judge or jury verdict against a worker in the eighteen years of litigation examined.

There was, and is, a curious paucity of sustained scholarly interest in the phenomenon of workmen's compensation.[7] There are no published monographs on the reform that treat it solely as a historical subject. Robert Asher, who has written extensively on workmen's compensation,[8] occupational safety and health,[9] and corporate welfare programs,[10] wrote his dissertation on the national reform movement but organized it around individual states, dwelling upon the consensus building process within each state's unique political context.[11] Usually, workmen's compensation is treated as a chapter in a larger work[12] or in journal articles.[13]

There is a more substantial legal literature addressed to workmen's compensation, but again, the historical aspects are often de-emphasized in favor of doctrinal or theoretical treatments of competing notions concerning the evolving law of torts.[14] While the work of legal historians is leading to a better understanding of the negligence doctrine's responsiveness to the burgeoning problems of an industrializing economy and is beginning to fill embarrassingly large holes in our historical understanding, I felt that certain crucial aspects of the reform have been either misunderstood, de-emphasized or buried altogether under the oppressive "industrial dreariness" of the subject. This work will try to revive some of the important issues that were trampled under in the national reform stampede to pass compensation legislation or that were simply subsumed in the shadow of the funereal gloom inevitably associated with the subject of industrial injury.

About the same time this project began taking shape, legal historians started to revisit their long held notions that nineteenth century negligence doctrines generally, and employer liability doctrines in particular, shifted the burden of industrial accidents onto the victims of those accidents and away from the industries whose remunerative activities caused the accidents.[15] Although the literature is still far from settled, the trend of recent research seems to be coalescing into a view of the courts in this period as far more victim-oriented than was formerly believed to be the case.[16]

When examined from Cleveland's historical vantage point, a prominent feature of the story behind workmen's compensation involves the large scale, new immigrant migration to the jobs available in the city's prospering heavy industries. I believe that one of the effects of that immigration, or more directly stated, the "new" Catholic, southern and eastern European immigration, was to provide a conceptual "window of opportunity" for passage of the workmen's compensation reform. The new immigrant groups that swarmed to the low skilled and hazardous jobs available in Cleveland's factories both exacerbated the work injury problem and provided an opportunity for that problem to be treated in a way that might well have been unthinkable had the issue been confined to "real American" natives. So long as the work injury problem was perceived as one that predominately affected the newest arrivals to America, it was easier to consider radical, even constitutional, adjustments to the existing social order. The perception of the affected new immigrant workers as "dependent," helpless even to the point of not being able to speak English, contributed to the complacency surrounding the suspension of their constitutionally protected right to jury trial.[17] In a phrase, they weren't yet Americans. It would be some generations before the new arrivals would rank as nominal equals in the social order,[18] and until that time, there would be greater flexibility to deal with them as dependent, not-quite-Americans.

It would be a misleading overstatement of the case to claim that new immigrants "caused" the American compensation reform. The point, rather, is that when they arrived and effectively displaced the former, old immigrant workforce in American steel production,[19] they labored in an industry that employed over 200,000 people nationwide and assumed a national leadership role in advocating for the compensation reform. The consolidation, merger and verticalization of the steel industry leading up to and overlapping with the period of this study, also saw the ascendance of a business enterprise form, the large finance capital corporation, that institutionalized rigid, hierarchical management systems.[20] The social, cultural and economic gap between the old immigrant and native born managers[21] of the newly transformed steel industry and the industry's predominately new immigrant workers, tended to nominalize the putative civil rights of that industrial workforce and encourage the wholesale abandonment of their formerly "inviolate" right to seek redress in the courts.[22]

This constitutional readjustment of the political economy formally institutionalized an American proletariat class.[23] That is not to say that workmen's compensation created the American industrial worker. But it did provide the legal and moral authority for treating the industrial worker differently than all other citizens, in all other relations. This wholesale abandonment of the republican ideal is, I think, the only instance in American history of one economic class (call it the corporate constituency or the "owners of capital") depriving another economic class (call it wage-earning labor or "the proletariat") of its constitutional inheritance—simple civil equality—to serve the ends of administrative convenience and social efficiency.[24] Viewed in this manner, workmen's compensation was an anti-democratic development within the larger political economy that darkened and obscured the American vision of individual autonomy and democratic control over the most basic social and economic equities affecting American life.[25]

Prominent too, will be the pre-compensation role juries played in formulating the evolving common law response to industrial injuries. Although it is less clearly understood, much of what led to the adoption of compensation had to do with the modern business corporation's patent and abiding aversion to the jury trial system of the American civil law. In a very real sense, the workmen's compensation reform was one of the opening (and withering) volleys from the corporate sector directed to disestablishing the jury and its apparently capricious power within the American political economy. That struggle has become more open and explicit recently, but attempts at what has come to be known as "tort reform" should be understood as merely recent, not new.

Interrelated with the role juries played in the era leading up to compensation was the clear distinction between the state and federal courts during the period examined. Although most of the suits against the company were filed and prosecuted in the state courts, the federal courts, or more accurately, the federal judiciary, played a signal role in the litigation faced by American Steel and Wire, a "foreign" corporation. Their function up until about 1907 was to preserve the despised employer defenses and provide some succor to the large national corporations from the onslaught of worker litigation. Indeed, the federal courts enforced a very stringent set of legal doctrines against workers, but as we shall see, they handled only a small (albeit significant) fraction of the total work injuries in the Cleveland area.[26]

Moreover, workmen's compensation was not a wholesale change in the manner of compensating work-injured employees. Rather, I believe that the compensation reform is more accurately conceived of as a successful effort on the part of the reformers to "freeze" the organic common law of negligence into a static statutory framework that would supplant the relatively dynamic tort law with comparatively stable contract law, thereby providing employers with the predictability they sought for their ongoing business concerns. What appears is that this period experienced a radical transformation of the American "ethos of injury"[27] causing an ever upward recalculation of the true costs of industrial injury to both the worker and the larger community. The compensation reform stultified that dynamism with a constitutionally mandated statutory scheme that has, to this day, prevented any reinvigoration of that still evolving injury ethos, at least as it affects that uniquely disfavored class—American workers.

Although it is generally accepted that the corporate sector provided leadership in creating and maintaining compensation schemes in lieu of worker lawsuits (and this work is fully in alignment with that view), what is not so well understood is that having done the crucial actuarial spade-work to set up the compensation system, the corporate sector still dominates the realm of workers' compensation by way of an insurance industry that administers over 80% of the national compensation bureaucracy. Workers' compensation is not social insurance nor even, as has been suggested, a precursor to social insurance. Rather, it is a corporately administered solution to a corporate problem.[28]

While this book looks at a unique reform development during the Progressive period, it attempts to take the reader further and more broadly afield into the era than a strict adherence to the "facts" of workmen's compensation might allow. In a sense, what this book really concerns is how the modern (post 1900) American commonweal pie has been apportioned. Moreover, how the pie is sliced concerns not only the distribution of wealth, but the risks and responsibilities that are borne attendant to wealth creation. Looking at the American compensation reform, it is clear that one class was required to bear an abundance of the risks and responsibilities without sharing in a commensurately equitable portion of the wealth that was created by those terrible burdens.

All of this and more lies within the developments of the period studied here, 1898-1915. I have struggled to present a fresh (and hopefully, by turns even entertaining) look at what has been too long considered an irredeemably stale and dreary topic. Hopefully, this work will elucidate and inform the determined and patient reader, and suggest new ways of thinking about the present as well as the past.

Notes

1. Richard Hofstadter, *The Age of Reform* (New York: Vintage, 1965), 242.

2. The orthodox view of the compelling need to revamp the worker-oppressive common law of employer liability was forcefully presented in Crystal Eastman's classic *Work Accidents and the Law* (New York: Russell Sage Foundation, 1910). In the appendix of that book, her landmark contribution to the Pittsburgh Survey, Eastman included a summary of the findings of the New York State Employers' Liability Commission. According to the Commission, the court-administered common law system for providing compensation to injured workmen was "objectionable" for four reasons: uncertainty of substantial recovery by the injured workman; wasteful expenditure of money and resources in lawyer fees and court costs; delay of from 6 months to 6 years for resolution of litigation; and finally, the inevitable and abiding antagonism between workman and employer bred by the adversary court system. Eastman's work was a reform classic when published and her conception of the harsh common law rules of negligence and the oppressive court system that discriminated against injured workers in applying those rules, remains essentially intact as our historical explanation for the workmen's compensation reform movement.

3. The ground breaking reinterpretation of the Progressive period generally, was Gabriel Kolko's *The Triumph of Conservatism* (London: Free Press of Glencoe, 1963). Building on Kolko, James Weinstein's *The Corporate Ideal and the Liberal State* (Boston: Beacon Press, 1968) argued that the principal vehicle of the liberal corporate interests, the National Civic Federation, was instrumental in molding the national consensus and marshaling the support of the business community in favor of reform of industrial accident compensation. Leading corporations, including the United States Steel Corporation, were establishing voluntary compensation schemes that entitled workers to collect directly from the company even though no "legal liability" was established. Small employers could not afford such schemes, but the Civic Federation promoted the idea of large funds established on a state-wide basis in which smaller concerns could participate. See also: Roy Lubove, *The Struggle for Social Security, 1900-1935* (Cambridge: Harvard University Press, 1968) and Edward Berkowitz and Kim McQuaid, *Creating the Welfare State* (New York: Praeger, 1980).

4. As phrased the question assumes that agents of change perceive their economic self interest as being served by whatever readjustment they are seeking through reform of the existing order. Admittedly, this assumption rules out the possibility of altruistic motives as an explanatory tool. However, given that the question posed concerns actors within an economic realm, and that business corporations are and were, by definition and law, purely economically self-interested entities, altruism seems an unlikely and unpersuasive explanation.

5. The problem with accepting Eastman's portrayal of the common law of employer liability is that she was a committed reformer who actively sought over the course of her career to take the problem of industrial injuries out of the courts. Aside from her obvious bias, the statistics usually cited by the compensation reformers were, in essence, temporal "snap shots" and did not look for trends or focus upon any positive aspects of the court system. The statisticians who did the studies for the various reform-minded state Commissions, were not hired to "discover" that the existing law of employer liability was well serving the larger social order.

6. Focusing on the American Steel and Wire Company was suggested by the Kolko-Weinstein-Lubove "business school" of historiography which pointed to the United States Steel Corporation's Voluntary Accident Relief Plan as a precursor to, and model for, the many state compensation laws adopted between 1911 and 1920.

7. I can attest that the phrase "workmen's compensation" has a predictable and pronounced soporific effect upon most people, except perhaps to provoke an occasional scolding for eschewing the modern usage of "work*ers*'" rather than "work*men's*". Inasmuch as the reform was universally referred to as work*men's* compensation during the period of this study, I shall be using that historically correct, and meaningful, term throughout.

8. Robert Asher, "Radicalism and Reform: State Insurance of Workmen's Compensation In Minnesota, 1910-1933," *Labor History*, Winter 1973, 19-41; Robert Asher, "Ignored Precedent: Samuel Gompers and Workmen's Compensation" *New Labor Review* (Fall 1982): 51-77; Robert Asher, "Failure and Fulfillment: Agitation for Employers' Liability Legislation and the Origins of Workmen's Compensation in New York State, 1876-1910," *Labor History*, Spring 1983, 198-222; Robert Asher "A Flawed Precedent: The Legacy of the Original Workmen's Compensation Laws," unpublished paper presented to the annual meeting of the Organization of American Historians, April 12, 1986.

9. Robert Asher, "Organized Labor and the Origins of the Occupational Safety and Health Act" *Labor's Heritage* 3, no. 1 (January 1991): 54.

10. Robert Asher, "Business and Workers' Welfare in the Progressive Era," *Business History Review* XLIII (Winter 1969): 452-75; Robert Asher, "The Limits of Big Business Paternalism: Relief for Injured Workers in the Years Before Workmen's Compensation," in *Dying For Work: Workers' Safety and Health in Twentieth-Century America*, ed. David Rosner and Gerald Markowitz (Bloomington: Indiana University Press, 1987), 19-33.

11. Robert Asher, "Workmen's Compensation in the United States, 1880-1935," Ph.D. Diss. (University of Minnesota, 1971).

12. Ibid., Berkowitz & McQuaid; Weinstein; Lubove.

13. Most of the journal articles focus upon individual state legislative battles. Robert F. Wesser, "Conflict and Compromise: The Workmen's Compensation Movement in New York 1890-1913," *Labor History*, Summer 1971, 345-72; Patrick D. Reagan, "The Ideology of Social Harmony and Efficiency: Workmen's Compensation in Ohio, 1904-1919," *Ohio History*, Autumn 1981, 317-331; Joseph F. Tripp, "Progressive Jurisprudence in the West: The Washington Supreme Court, Labor Law, and the Problem of Industrial Accidents," *Labor History*, Fall 1983, 342-65.

14. Richard Posner has written extensively on economic theory and negligence doctrines. Other theorists include: Richard A. Epstein, "A Theory of Strict Liability" *Journal of Legal Studies,* 2, (1973):151; John Prather Brown, "Toward and Economic Theory of Liability," *Journal of Legal Studies,* 2 (1973): 323; James R. Chelius, "Liability for Industrial Accidents: A Comparison of Negligence and Strict Liability Systems," *Journal of Legal Studies,* (1978): 293-309.

15. A classic statement of the former vision of the courts' tendency to protect infant American industries is presented by Lawrence M. Friedman and Jack Ladinsky in "Social Change and the Law of Industrial Accidents," *Columbia Law Review* 67, no.1 (January 1967): 50-82; see also: Lawrence M. Friedman, *A History of American Law*, (New York: Simon and Schuster, 2nd Ed., 1985). For a related view of the nineteenth century's common law see Morton Horwitz *The Transformation of American Law, 1780-1860* (Cambridge: Harvard University Press, 1977). In a piece that used a unique appellate case sampling methodology, Richard A. Posner's "A Theory of Negligence," *Journal of Legal Studies* 1, no. 1 (1972): 29-96, argued that the courts were probably more victim sympathetic and economically rational than the doctrinal law suggested, although as has been observed, Posner does not explain exactly how this was so. However, that emerging historical

notion was confirmed by James L. Croyle in "Industrial Accident Liability Policy of the Early Twentieth Century," in *Journal of Legal Studies* 7, no. 2 (June 1978): 279-98, where he suggested that statistical analysis demonstrated that plaintiffs' lawyers did add value to worker claims, rather than just syphon off money from injured workers as was repeatedly suggested by the reformers. Gary T. Schwartz, in "Tort Law and the Economy in Nineteenth-Century America: A Reinterpretation," *Yale Law Journal* 90, no. 8 (July 1981): 1717-75, examined the case law of California and New Hampshire and found that the courts were far more receptive to claimants than previously believed. Schwartz notes however, that the doctrines of employers' liability law still seemed perniciously vital within the published opinions he reviewed, 1768-72. Robert A. Silverman, *Law and Urban Growth: Civil Litigation in the Boston Trial Courts, 1880-1900* (Princeton: Princeton University Press, 1981) looked at litigation in the Boston courts and found that negligence claims were increasing in volume during the two decades examined, and that overall, plaintiffs prevailed about 60% of the time. Frank W. Munger reviewed the litigation from three West Virginia counties in a longitudinal trial court study and found that employees were beginning to fare better against both coal mine owners and railroads beginning around the turn of the century, in "Social Change and Tort Litigation: Industrialization, Accidents, and Trial Courts in Southern West Virginia, 1871-1940" *Buffalo Law Review* 36, (1987): 75-118.

16. Randolph E. Bergstrom, *Courting Danger: Injury Law in New York City 1870-1910* (Ithaca: Cornell University Press, 1992). G. Edward White *Tort Law in America: An Intellectual History* (New York: Oxford University Press, 1980), 51; Anthony Bale, "America's First Compensation Crisis: Conflict over the Value and Meaning of Workplace Injuries Under the Employers' Liability System," in *Dying For Work: Workers' Safety and Health in Twentieth-Century America*, eds. David Rosner; Gerald Markowitz (Bloomington: Indiana University Press, 1987), 34-52. See also Schwartz and Posner.

17. Significantly, when the new compensation statute was challenged in an "arranged" appeal before the Ohio Supreme Court to so as test its constitutional validity, the permanent deprivation of the injured workers' due process right to bring suit against their employers for a civil jury trial was dismissed by the court as a claim for *"mere negligence"* (emphasis the court's) and "a most unsubstantial thing." The property rights of employers', on the other hand, received far more extensive analysis and consideration from the court. *Yaple v. Creamer*, 85 Ohio St. 349 (1912).

18. John Bodnar, *Immigration and Industrialization: Ethnicity in an American Mill Town, 1870-1940* (Pittsburgh, 1977).

19. David Brody, *Steelworkers In America: The Non-Union Era,* (Cambridge: Harvard University Press, 1960).

20. Alfred D. Chandler's study of the organizational systems and the management transformations that evolved in American business before, during and following the period of this study in *The Visible Hand: The Managerial Revolution in American Business* (Cambridge: Belknap Press, 1977) outlines some of managerial contributions to the developing corporate culture. The railroads were seedbeds for the development of compensation alternatives. See Walter Licht, *Working for the Railroad: The Organization of Work in the Nineteenth Century* (Princeton: Princeton University Press, 1983), for a discussion of mid-nineteenth century experimentation with employee injury relief systems.

21. Gerald G. Eggart's biography of William Brown Dickson, *Steelmasters and Labor Reform, 1886-1923* (Pittsburgh: University of Pittsburgh Press, 1981) provides an excellent discussion of Steel Corporation's home office politics and the Morgan banker contingent's attitudes towards labor. John N. Ingham's *The Iron Barons: A Social Analysis of an American Urban Elite, 1874-1965* (Westport, Conn.: Greenwood Press) includes an interesting social profile of the Cleveland steel industry's managerial elites.

22. "The right of trial by jury shall be inviolate . . ." Article I, Section 5, Constitution of Ohio (1912).

23. The term is used simply because its common meaning best evokes and describes what I take to be the dominant forces driving, and populations most affected by, the compensation reform. Injured workers, to the extent they were at a disadvantage with their employers, found themselves so disadvantaged primarily because of their "relation to the means of production," that is, they were employee wage earners. Work injury policy simply "fits" better into a straightforward Marxist paradigm than most issues of American political economy, and it was, at least in part, that potentially inflammatory aspect of the problem that fueled the often strident urgency of the reform's many promoters.

24. See Schwartz, 1771.

25. It should always be borne in mind that workmen's compensation developed within the larger context of the American employment relationship. That relationship was still being discussed and analyzed in the American legal literature as one between "masters" and "servants," and that

vocabulary connoted deeply ingrained ways of thinking as much as it served to distinguish the actors within the relationship. What appears in Ohio (and I believe nationally) is that organized labor played a muted role in the policy debates and formulations that led to workmen's compensation, following, albeit reluctantly, the lead of the innovating corporate sector. And too, this was not a period of union predominance in the steel producing (or any other industrial) enterprise. A recent study of the evolving employment relationship, Robert J. Steinfeld's *The Invention of Free Labor: The Employment Relation in English and American Law and Culture, 1350-1870* (Chapel Hill: University of North Carolina Press, 1991) suggests interesting ways of thinking about the "mix of freedom and unfreedom" in employment that emerged just prior to the period addressed here. Two recent studies of the American labor movement focus particularly on the effect of law on American labor relations. Christopher L. Tomlins' *The State and the Unions: Labor Relations, Law and the Organized Labor Movement in America, 1880-1960* (Cambridge: Cambridge University Press, 1985) and William E. Forbath's *Law and the Shaping of the American Labor Movement* (Cambridge: Harvard University Press, 1991) both subscribe to an "instrumentalist" notion of the role of law in the larger American political economy. While this study necessarily focuses upon the law of employers' liability, I do not consider law, nor corporate lawyers, nor even judges, to be the instigators of change, even legal change. Rather, the agents of change here were juries and the corporate managers in the large finance capital organizations who developed the "actuarial self awareness" that led, in turn, to a broader understanding of a compensation system's potential savings to the corporate enterprise. In short, I think that at least as concerns the reform of workmen's compensation, the lawyers and judges did not give the orders, but rather, they accommodated and legitimated them.

26. This federal sanctuary for large interstate business corporations has been extensively documented in Edward A. Purcell's *Litigation and Inequality: Federal Diversity Jurisdiction in Industrial America, 1870-1948* (New York: Oxford University Press, 1992). Discussing the role of the federal courts as a refuge for national corporations from state tort common law, Purcell argues:

> . . . the federal common law was a major factor only from the mid 1880s to world War I, and it reached its peak of importance in the years between 1893 and 1908. During those years it regularly confronted injured workers with fatal obstacles to recovery by giving sweeping defenses to employers and by imposing exacting

evidentiary burdens on employees. The rules weighed heavily, too, because during those same years a number of state courts developed innovative ways to ameliorate the harshness of their own common law rules and thereby widened the divergence between federal and state law.

Purcell, 264. As will appear at length in this study, in Ohio, juries (acting with the tacit acquiescence of an elected judiciary) were the primary innovators ameliorating the harsh common law rules of employer liability.

27. The phrase is borrowed from G. Edward White, *Tort Law in America, An Intellectual History* (New York: Oxford University Press, 1980), xvi.

28. Bergstrom posits a turn of the century change in the "practical" theory of tort law that occurred, or was at least evidenced, in the New York trial courts. The transformation seemed to be responding to a changing popular notion of injury, its causes, and responsible actors. He refers to the new conception as transforming accidents themselves, formerly "private events," into "public events." Ibid, 195. Arguably, workmen's compensation acted to "re-transform" a special type of increasingly visible and problematic "public event"—injuries to workers—back into "private events," matters of contract, defined and resolved according to the terms of the employment relationship between companies and their workers.

Acknowledgments

My thanks to Michael Grossberg, Carl Ubbelohde, David Hammack, and David Van Tassel (The Patient Ones) for taking me into the History of Social Policy program and their unflagging support throughout my extended, and sometimes tortuous, term at Case Western Reserve. I hope you find what follows worth the wait, if not worth claiming, in some sense, as your own. The good stuff, that is. For the rest, that is mine, all mine. For the genuine enthusiasm, encouragement and assistance my thanks to Michael Altschul and Robert Strassfeld; for the rooms with a view to Any Katan; for the patient assistance and good humoring—to all librarians and archivists everywhere; to my brothers, Ned and Mike, for their adamant encouragement that spring morning on a rolling (and fishless) Lake Erie; to my wife, Wendy, for everything, and much more; to my father, Richard, for his input, patient and exacting proofreading, and his ringing caution to me, "Hey, this is for the record," when my own precision and enthusiasm failed; to Ezra Brudno, upon whose narrative coattails this study shamelessly rides; and finally, to Perez Hamlin, for the inspiration to revisit the verities.

A History of Workmen's Compensation, 1898–1915

I

A Bird In The Bush

. . . it would be like telling which shot out of a gun hit a bird . . . [1]

O n the afternoon of March 23, 1900, Joseph Letmenski, a twenty-nine
year old wire drawer at the Newburgh Works of the American Steel
and Wire Company, noticed that a troublesome belt connecting his wire
drawing mill to the whirring array of overhead shafts and pulleys had, yet
again, jumped from its track. Deprived of the power supplied by the rotating
overhead pulley, his machine stopped "drawing"—pulling really—the strand
of wire through the draw plate and created dangerous, potentially entangling,
slack in the wire. Letmenski had repeatedly discussed this chronic
belt-slipping with his foreman, who demonstrated a way to slip the belt back
on the spinning pulley above the machine. The makeshift procedure he
showed Letmenski got the wire drawing mill back on line without having to
disengage the main, steam-driven power shaft which would, in turn, cause
a shut down of all the wire drawing operations for the whole department.
When Letmenski suggested that the belt and pulley needed to be adjusted, he
was instructed by his foreman to get back to work and "not bother him so
much about the belt slipping."

As had been demonstrated by his foreman, Letmenski grabbed a five
foot long 2"x4" board and, hooking the errant belt on the inside with the end
of the board, shoved it back in place on the spinning, overhead pulley.
Apparently, the board got pinched between the belt and the whirling pulley
and jumped out of Letmenski's grasp. The board whipped around the shaft
of the pulley with deadly force and smashed into Letmenski's forehead,
leaving him slumped and unconscious on the floor next to his now revived,
but unattended, wire drawing machine. Andrew Balzer, a plant laborer who

3

witnessed the accident, thought Letmenski was dead, and so informed his co-workers.

Letmenski only looked dead. He was taken to St. Alexis Hospital where the doctors removed an inch and one half square of shattered bone from his skull. The surgery left a permanent, bluish depression in the center of his forehead, where only a thin tissue of skin covered throbbing blood vessels. Letmenski spent three months confined in the hospital, and then at home, recuperating. He could no longer perform physical labor. As is not uncommon in frontal lobe injuries, he suffered constantly from severe and debilitating headaches along with occasional bouts of "crazed and deranged" behavior, causing ". . . his wife . . . to confine him in a room, under lock and key, to prevent his doing her and his children bodily injury."

In January of 1901, Letmenski's lawyers filed suit in the Cuyahoga County Common Pleas Court against the American Steel and Wire Company seeking damages in the sum of $20,000. The company's lawyers filed a pro forma motion for removal alleging *inter alia*: that American Steel and Wire Company was a "citizen" of New Jersey (where the company was incorporated) and that Letmenski was a citizen of Ohio; that Letmenski had requested more than $2,000 in damages from the company; that together these two facts entitled the company to invoke the "diversity jurisdiction" of the federal Circuit Court for the Sixth Circuit and required the Common Pleas Court of Cuyahoga County to surrender its jurisdiction over the case to the federal court.

Upon removal to the federal court, American Steel and Wire filed its Answer to the plaintiff's petition, denying all the allegations save that it was a corporation duly organized under the laws of the State of New Jersey. Further, the American Steel and Wire Company averred that ". . . if plaintiff were injured as alleged . . . his own negligence contributed thereto."

Trial commenced before a jury in the federal court on Friday, October 18, 1901. Among plaintiff's list of witnesses subpoenaed for trial was a co-worker by the name of "T. Sieracki," who, Letmenski believed, could testify as to the full particulars of the accident at the drawing machine. Although the court file confirms that the United States Marshal served the subpoena on Sieracki (notwithstanding the vague address the plaintiff provided, "Cor. 3rd Ave. and Tod St.") Sieracki failed to show up to testify on Letmenski's behalf. On Monday, October 21, 1901, at the urging of plaintiff's counsel, Judge Francis J. Wing issued an "Attachment for Contempt" (arrest warrant) that was duly executed by the marshals who "attached" the witness and brought him into court. Upon finally taking the stand, T. Sieracki, a very reluctant witness on behalf of the plaintiff, denied any knowledge of how the accident occurred.

Without Sieracki's testimony, Letmenski's lawyers were unable to prove their case. Reconstructing from the court files, it is unclear whether the company's lawyers were required to put on any evidence at the conclusion of the plaintiff's case. If it was necessary, they were certainly well prepared, having subpoenaed numerous American Steel and Wire employees to testify on behalf of the company—all of whom appeared without the necessity of being first arrested.

On Tuesday, October 22, 1901, Judge Wing directed the jury to return a verdict finding in favor of the American Steel and Wire Company of New Jersey. The jury did as the federal judge instructed. Joseph Letmenski lost his case against the company before it even got to the jury.

On November 11, 1901, counsel for Letmenski filed a motion for new trial. Counsel maintained that on the last day of trial after the close of proceedings, one Andrew Balzer, an employee of the defendant company who had been subpoenaed by the company, approached Letmenski and informed him that he could relate the entire set of circumstances leading to Letmenski's mishap. Counsels' motion for new trial emphasized their repeated efforts to locate an eye-witness to the accident and their total surprise when the recalcitrant Sieracki denied any knowledge concerning the accident. Counsels' brief along with the plaintiff's supporting affidavit makes no effort to disguise their suspicion that the company had effectively secreted the eye-witnesses in its employ and threatened them with their jobs should they cooperate with the plaintiff or his counsel. Thus, according to Letmenski's lawyers, it was only *after* the case was concluded in favor of the company that Letmenski's co-workers were willing to "tell all about it."

Pursuant to the post-trial motion, Letmenski's lawyers took Balzer's deposition in the presence of all counsel, the short-hand court reporter and an interpreter. Balzer's version of the facts and circumstances of the accident supported the plaintiff's allegations in the original petition, except regarding the exchanges between the Letmenski and his foreman, about which he had no knowledge.

Counsel for the American Steel and Wire Company asked Balzer:

Q.   Were you present in the courtroom when this case was tried a few weeks ago and had you been subpoenaed there as a witness?
A.   Yes.

On redirect examination by Letmenski's counsel, Balzer testified as follows:

Q. You were subpoenaed by the defendant (company) were you not?
A. Yes.
Q. Did you ever tell plaintiff that you saw him receive his injury complained of?
A. No!
Q. Didn't you tell plaintiff after the hearing in the U.S. Circuit Court that you saw him when he was hurt?
A. No.

On November 30, 1901, Judge Wing overruled the motion for a new trial, without opinion, leaving undisturbed the directed verdict in favor of the American Steel and Wire Company of New Jersey.

* * * * *

Cleveland lawyer cum novelist, Ezra Brudno, sets the scene for his Progressive Era satire and expose' of the legal profession, *The Jugglers*,[2] by describing the novel's turn of the century urban locale principally in terms of its atmospheric charms:

> One humid summer day I arrived in a mid-western city well fortified for conquest; world conquest, I then thought. My armor consisted of a college degree and a certificate attesting my right to practice law. I had chosen this city partly because a boyhood friend of my father lived here and partly because I had been impressed by the aphorism of a successful American—spoken of as a merchant prince—that success thrives on smoke, dirt and noise. The city of my choice embodied these three graces to a marked degree. Its inhabitants boasted of its smoke, of its dirt, of its noise. The local orators eloquently, if not elegantly, spoke of its vomiting chimneys, of its fire-spitting furnaces, of its sizzling thrift. The most widely circulated local newspaper, The *City Daily*, proclaimed with pride that a city with so much smoke and dirt and noise was bound to forge ahead of all of its rivals.

For Brudno it was the "three graces," the smoke, dirt and noise of the city that were synonymous with its promise, however oppressive the soot and din might have seemed to the casual observer. Cleveland was a boom town that depended on its basic smokestack industries to keep its heady prosperity afloat, or perhaps more appropriately, in the air.

Initially a slow growing and relatively insignificant settlement in Connecticut's Western Reserve, Cleveland's location on Lake Erie, at the mouth of the Cuyahoga River, helped assure its increasing economic and political significance following the opening of the Erie Canal in 1825. In 1827 the Ohio Canal opened, running 300 miles south into the state's interior, connecting Cleveland to the Ohio River at Portsmouth. Further bolstered by the provisioning needs of the Union Army during the Civil War and the seemingly insatiable requirements for iron rail necessitated by the national railroad building binge after the war, the city's marriage to the iron and steel industry (and the "in-law" transportation and extractive industries associated with the production of iron and steel) determined its essentially "industrial" character well through and beyond the period examined here. Cleveland was strategically located for steel making between the coal deposits to the south, and the iron ore deposits to the north and west at the head of the Great Lakes. After the first shipping locks were built at Sault St. Marie in 1855, permitting navigation between Lakes Huron and Superior, its convenient nexus assured Cleveland's continued prominence in the Ohio-Pennsylvania steel producing region.

Just as Cleveland was geographically well situated to serve its role as a center of the burgeoning steel industry, it was historically well situated to demonstrate social and economic changes of national significance during the period addressed here. As a regional center of commerce and industry, with very strong economic, social and political attachments to the East, it was an even more important, and typical, American city during the Progressive Era than is suggested by its rank of fifth among urban centers in the Census of 1910. The national transition from an entrepreneurial economy based upon family ties and simple business partnerships to a corporate, finance-capitalist dominated economy is wonderfully well portrayed throughout Cleveland's advance to the forefront among the young nation's urban centers. Cleveland's pantheon of prominent citizens reveals the extraordinary mettle of the local commercial and industrial leadership. Men such as John D. Rockefeller, Sr., Marcus Hanna, Jeptha Wade and Samuel Mather started in their diverse businesses as entrepreneurs and closed out their careers presiding over immense private corporations—hierarchical commercial organizations concocted by lawyers and administered by a new manager class of salaried overseers of incomprehensibly vast aggregations of productive wealth. These men were not just city fathers, they were nation builders.

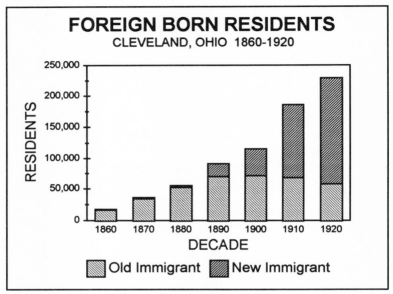

Figure 1   Source: Galford, *Foreign Born and Urban Growth*

It might not be overreaching, in a symbolic and metaphoric sense, to suggest that by 1900 Cleveland was just beginning to fulfill its destiny as a center of the Second Errand into the Second Wilderness. The city's elite, many of them lineal descendants of the original New England land speculators and settlers who migrated to the Western Reserve, were mostly Protestant and Anglo-Saxon and, if their control over the political affairs of the city was sometimes tenuous, the same cannot be said of their dominion over the city's commercial realm. Their preeminence was social as well as economic and stood in stark contrast to the waves of "new immigrant" arrivals who were fast displacing the prior Irish and German populations huddled in the city's teeming industrial-residential districts.

In Cleveland, as in other industrial cities between 1890 and 1920, the swelling new immigrant populations far outstripped the formerly predominant Irish and German groups. The period of greatest influx for these distinct, mostly Catholic, industrial migrants was from 1900 to 1920. And while the "old immigrant" migrations were tapering to a mere trickle, the rush of southern and eastern Europeans to the jobs beckoning in the prospering industries lining the murky Cuyahoga, was felt and feared by older native citizens who perceived the agrarian Catholics as somehow "more foreign" than the mostly Protestant northern and western Europeans who preceded them. The exotic, minaret-evoking domes of the Eastern Orthodox churches that sprouted, mushroom-like, adjacent to the furnace stacks, stoves and ovens of the local steel plants only served to confirm the strangeness, the disquieting "otherness" of the shawled denizens who seemed to be—who were—pouring into the city. By the height of the migration in 1910, foreign born residents comprised 35% of the city's total population of over 560,000.[3]

Having introduced the reader to Cleveland's sooty atmospherics in the opening paragraph of *The Jugglers*, Ezra Brudno goes on to describe the turn of the century "urban gestalt" of the city that was home to his own legal practice for nearly two decades preceding his novel's publication in 1920:

> This was one of those fast growing cities that seem neither city nor village, with the unmistakable features of both. It had the appearance of a boy who has outgrown his breeches. Dilapidated two-story shacks were wedged in between towering skyscrapers; beautifully laid avenues intersected uneven country roads; colossal billboards spanned vacant lots within a stone's throw from the business centre; hoosiers, who could have stepped upon the stage of a burlesque theater without the slightest make-up, elbowed dandies, whose dress was patterned after Broadway models; saloons, with large foaming "schooners" painted in yellow on their windows, vied with the gaudy magnificence of cafes built after the style of the castle at Nurenburg. The Square was the heart of the city. Into it all the city's blood vessels flowed. In the center of the Square, as an eloquent specimen of the city's artistic aspect, stood a monument, which was a cross between a lighthouse and the Statue of Liberty—a monstrosity dedicated to the memory of the brave soldiers who laid their lives down in the cause of liberty.

Whatever thin disguise might have been affected by the generic "mid-western city" alluded to in the first paragraph of Brudno's satire is thus abandoned by the explicit reference to Cleveland's aesthetically notorious Soldier's and Sailor's Monument. But disguise would have proved quite pointless. Brudno did not use a pen name for *The Jugglers* and given his life-long law practice in Cleveland, it would have been impossible to mask the very local and autobiographical nature of the book. Whatever his motives for explicitly satirizing the Cleveland legal community, given the transparency of the fictional pretense, *The Jugglers* will serve well as a primary historical source for the purposes of this study.

We shall be relying upon *The Jugglers* and its graphic, if exaggerated, delineation of a work injury lawsuit to provide a dramatic narrative reenactment of the historical reality of pre-compensation litigation between workers and employers. Of the four hundred page novel, spanning a 15 to 20 year period, approximately eighty pages concern the sundry personal and legal misfortunes of the hapless and good-hearted recent Greek emigre, Nick Nikopopulos. (Brudno was fond of giving his characters allegorical names.) The novel's heroic protagonist, recently admitted lawyer and Yale graduate, Guy Stillwell, represents Nikopopulos in his struggles with a corrupt Justice of the Peace and in a Kafkaesque appearance before the "Delinquency Court" (read Cleveland's new and very "progressive" Juvenile Court) before Nikopopulos is injured on the job at the American Tool Company. In *The Jugglers* Brudno called upon his own experiences as a recent immigrant and practicing lawyer to imbue his fictional account of the immigrant experience in America with a Dickensonian vigor and fidelity. But it would be misleading to characterize *The Jugglers* as starkly naturalistic. Brudno was attempting to entertain and amuse his reader, and an unrelenting "realism" concerning the subjects that he chooses to parody in *The Jugglers* would undoubtedly have fallen far short of entertainment for most readers.

Born in Lithuania in 1877, Ezra Selig Brudno was an atypical Jewish emigre. He obtained his early education at a private European school. He came to the United States with his parents in 1891, when he was 14 years old, and finished his preparatory education at Central High School in Cleveland. He spent two years at Adelbert College, and two more at Yale where he began "reading the law" in addition to his academic studies. He returned to Cleveland in 1900, finished his legal studies at Western Reserve University and began practicing law in 1901. Brudno's legal career encompassed both solo private practice and an extended tenure as an assistant prosecuting attorney. He married Rose Hart Heiss in 1913 and lived in Cleveland Heights. He was a Republican and until 1915 a member of the corporate lawyer-dominated Cleveland Bar Association.[4]

In all, Brudno wrote and published five novels while continuing to practice law: *The Fugitive*, 1904; *The Little Conscript*, 1905; *The Tether*, 1908; *One Of Us*, 1912; and *The Jugglers*, 1920. It appears that his avocation as a novelist ended with the publication of *The Jugglers*, which met with neither critical nor popular success. He continued to publish magazine articles regularly in *Lippencott's* (also the publisher of his earlier novels) and the local *Jewish Review and Observer*. He published a non-fiction effort in 1935, breezily entitled *Ghost of Yesterday: A Reappraisal of Moral Values and of Accepted Standards in This Changing World*. He continued to practice law in the Cleveland area up until 1949 and died in 1954.

As clearly demonstrated in his most controversial novel, *The Tether*, Brudno felt many of the conflicting impulses of an elite first generation Jewish immigrant. An iconoclast within the Cleveland Jewish community, he held, and freely expressed, many controversial views, not the least of which was his belief in the efficacy of intermarriage between Jews and Gentiles. His novel, *The Tether*, is, in fact, one long argument in favor of intermarriage and the eventual assimilation of Jews into Western, Christian dominated culture and society. To be sure, *The Tether* was also a passionate and scathing condemnation of the ignorance, prejudice and hatred separating Jew from Gentile. However, Brudno accepts ignorance, prejudice and hatred as inevitable features of human social experience and proposed that as long as Judaism preserved its separateness from the Christian mainstream of western civilization, Jews would suffer the opprobrium of the ignorant, of the prejudiced, of the hateful. Implicit in Brudno's thinking, and undoubtedly what got him into trouble with many of his Jewish contemporaries, was the notion that there was little worth preserving in the separate Jewish experience of life and God. For Brudno, assimilation into the larger, more powerful mainstream was the key to dispensing with the Jewish heritage of suffering and persecution.

The theme of assimilation, or more accurately, lack of assimilation, looms large in Brudno's final fiction effort, *The Jugglers*. The novel's protagonist, young Guy Stillwell, has an extremely varied legal career that provides the principal dramatic focus of the book. An expose of the Cleveland legal profession, *The Jugglers* follows the Progressive Era legal career of the newly admitted, university-educated lawyer from about the turn of the century up until an Armistice Day epiphany in 1918 when Stillwell suddenly gives up his thriving law practice to become an architect/contractor and build new suburban homes. In that almost two decade span, Guy Stillwell hangs out his shingle for a short, but eventful, albeit unsuccessful solo practice; works as an associate with the notorious and wildly successful personal injury attorney, Mark Leffingwell (the portion of the novel with which we shall be mainly concerned); takes a job as an associate for the large corporate firm, Nixon, Wright, Croak & Powers (and marries a partner's niece); works as an assistant county prosecutor; and finally, gets elected to the state legislature (and serves during a session when the "Compensation Bill" is under consideration). Stillwell is idealistic, naive and unrelentingly stuffy and officious—and is consequently largely ineffectual during his short-lived, initial solo practice. Fresh out of Yale with a head full of professorial delusions concerning the pristine majesty of "The Law," he is as long on righteous indignation as he is short on discretion and good judgment. New to both the city and the profession, his university education has evidently failed to provide our hero with any grasp of the practical considerations of lawyering. It is this conflict between the ideal and the real which Brudno plays for most of *The Jugglers* comic effect.

Clearly, Stillwell served as Brudno's fictional alter ego. Throughout the novel Stillwell takes time from his legal practice to pursue his avocation as a writer—just as Brudno did during his early law/writing career. Like Brudno, Stillwell went to school "back East" and takes time from his practice to travel to Europe after his first published novel meets with some modest success. Finally, as was true of his creator, Guy Stillwell works an eye-opening stint as an assistant county prosecutor.

Having a small stake from his father to begin a legal practice, Stillwell rents office space, hires a "typist who could not type" (appropriate for a "counselor who could not counsel") and waits for his first client to appear. When Nick Nikopopulos finally arrives, bloodied and bruised from a confrontation with a "constable" serving a creditor's attachment, the gross injustice of Nikopopulos' plight stirs young Stillwell to immediate and righteous—if ill-considered—action. It seems that his new client, a hot tempered and recently emigrated Greek, had just opened a shoe repair shop in the city. The constable, dispatched by a local Justice of the Peace, had mistakenly assumed that Nikopopulos was the "dago" who formerly occupied the shoemaker's shop and owed money to the City Machine Company. When Nikopopulos attempted to explain the mistake and dissuade the constable from taking his tools, a fisticuffs ensued with Nikopopulos ending up much the worse for his intercession. So begins Guy Stillwell's first case.

Having determined the Greek's problem was at once both simple and compelling, he instructs Nick to take him to the offending Justice of the Peace. Following his client through the city they turn up an alleyway that ends in a cul-de-sac containing a smelly kitchen attached to a saloon, the back of an old melodrama playhouse, a seedy barber shop and a chop-suey place "where one was served by an opium smelling Chinaman." Loitering outside the kitchen, "like dogs near a slaughter house" were the "ragged tramps and the scum that claim fealty to political leaders." Here, One Eye Smith, the Justice of the Peace who issued the writ of attachment against Nick's tools, held "court" on the second floor of the same dilapidated wood frame building that housed the barber shop and "chop-suey den."

Notwithstanding his undeniably righteous client and cause, "Mr. Lawyer" (as the needful Greek was wont to call his young counsel) is singularly unsuccessful in his appeals to Charlie, the constable who had taken the shoemaker's tools in the first place. When the "Squire," One Eye Smith (a very busy man[5]), interrupts his constable to inquire as to the nature of the young lawyer's urgent protestations, matters turn from simply awful to even worse. The constable's justification for the levy prevails:

> "The City Machine Co. ordered execution against a dago who keeps that store—that's good law enough for me!"
> "Specuzza, he move out two mon'," struck in the son of antiquity. "The other fellow was an Italian and this man is a Greek, as their names indicate." I made another attempt to clinch the argument . . .

But to no noticeable effect. Ever earnest Guy Stillwell's first court appearance was not only unsuccessful, the young lawyer comes within a hair's breadth of being held in contempt by the increasingly restive Squire One Eye Smith.

Regrouping at his office, Stillwell pours through the law books and divines the next move in furtherance of his client's cause. Our hero locates a procedural countermeasure to the bogus tool attachment. Of course, Nikopopulos would have to post a bond with *another* Justice of the Peace, who would in turn issue "process" effectively negating the attachment order from the ill-tempered Squire One Eye. This bond would have the further beneficial effect of requiring the City Machine Company to return the tools to the Greek, at least until such time as the matter could be set for a hearing . . . Unless, of course, the City Machine Company were to file what Stillwell (later) learned was called a "re-delivery bond." Not, as yet, comprehending the convolutions of the re-delivery bond, and still after all, a *very* new lawyer, Guy lends his client the money for the bond, convinced of his ability to eventually prevail. The City Machine Company immediately posts a re-delivery bond. Stillwell is out the bond money and his client remains tool-less and idle until the matter is eventually set down for hearing.

Finally the hearing day before Stillwell's "Squire" (highly recommended by the bondsman) arrives. One-Leg-Jones was also known as the "Marrying Squire" because of the great number of marriages he performed. At the entrance to his "court" hung a conspicuous, if indecorous, overhead sign:

STOP — LOOK — GET MARRIED
COME INSIDE
Squire Jones Will Marry
You At Cut Rate Prices

Notwithstanding all Stillwell's exacting preparations in anticipation of the hearing, things end up even worse for the star-crossed "descendant of Homer" and his earnest young attorney.

At the hearing, the skulking and nefarious Pat Keegan, counsel for the City Machine Company and "fixer" for the "party in power" (read Democratic), arranges for the testimony of three "disinterested freeholders" to the effect that the cobbler's tools, whether taken from the Greek rightfully or no, had, in any event, a fair market value of no more than $5.00. To Stillwell the "freeholders" look suspiciously like the "ragged tramps and scum" previously noted to loiter outside One Eye's "chambers." However, focusing on the matter at hand, rightful possession of the tools, our callow counsel doesn't elect to trifle with a matter as irrelevant as their purported market value. In short, Stillwell doesn't see the ruse until it is too late. He wins a favorable decision from "his" Squire ordering the return of Nick's tools, but when Guy demands the tools back from the surly constable Charlie, he is informed that the tools "can't be found" so his client will have to settle for their cash value, already established by uncontradicted testimony to be $5.00! Unable to contain his humiliation and indignation, Stillwell causes a scene, is assaulted by the constable and thrown out into the street.

It was time to regroup, again:

> When I found myself in the open air, mopping the blood off my face, I realized what had happened. Nick Nikopopulos was by my side, sympathizing with me, and holding my hat. For I was bare-headed. The Greek was swearing in his native tongue. I knew that nothing but utterances of vengeance could be hissing in the manner that the words escaped his lips.
>
> Yes, I, too, craved vengeance. So I wended my way to the Police Court. Nikopopulos, with the courageous instinct of his

ancestors, seemed to have forgotten his sorrows in mine. He
followed me. I was as yet unfamiliar with police court methods . . .

As one might expect, things do not go well in Police Court either. Pat
Keegan is spotted lurking about the Judge's chambers prior to the court
session and the Judge soon takes the side of the pugnacious constable,
chiding the young lawyer for defaming the integrity of Squire One Eye's
"court." The charge against Charlie is dismissed.

"Its all right, Nikopopulos," I managed to say, swallowing a
lump, "we are not licked yet. I'll appeal."
I was not quite clear about this appeal business . . .

The next day a dark-skinned young woman appears at Stillwell's office
and informs him that her man, Nick Nikopopulos, was arrested at their home
the night before. Stillwell follows his client's wife to the Sheriff's office
where, upon interviewing Nick, he learns that his client was arrested for
"neglecting his children."

. . . I learned that the night before the constable (Charlie) and
another officer called at the place he called home and informed him
that he must not live in such small quarters with a family of six;
they had told him it was against the law. Whereupon, Nikopopulos
told the constable that if he had not robbed him of his machine and
tools he might be able to move to larger quarters. And while the
Greek and officers were arguing the children began to cry for food.
"We'll have to arrest you for neglecting your children," the officers
had told him. Nikopopulos thought they were joking but when they
laid hands on him he showed fight. The result was too plainly
written on his countenance.

The hearing on this new litigation was down at the "Delinquency
Court." As was true of the Justice of the Peace and Police Courts, the
Juvenile Court was crowded with the litigation-oppressed, in this instance,
mostly women and children:

. . . The air was heavy, mildewy with the stench of rags soaked in
rainwater. Mothers with babes at their breasts, fathers with the fear
of Russian despotism indelibly written on their faces, boys and girls
of all ages and sizes—crippled and maimed, unwashed and

> unkempt—were herded together at the entrance . . . Bareheaded
> women, shawled women, bewigged women, women with infants in
> rags, with scratched faced urchins . . .

Here Judge Joshua Balaam (nicknamed Balaam's Ass by the local bar) held
court with the aid of his probation officer, Miss Potipher, a spinster type
Stillwell notices, "the kind that knows most about the raising of children and
the handling of husbands." Sitting in the gallery were gentle ladies,
"uplifters," who nodded approval of the good Judge Balaam's wisdom "in
the manner of faithful devotees."

What transpires before Judge Balaam (whom Stillwell nicknames "The
Oracle" owing to the apparent thrall in which he holds the "uplifters") is a
scathing indictment of many of the reforms Juvenile Court ushered onto the
Progressive legal scene. Cleveland boasted one of the first juvenile courts in
the nation and Brudno was, judging from his portrayal of the Delinquency
Court, more than a little skeptical of what he perceived to be the dangerous
short cuts used to informalize its hearing procedures.

Nikopopulos is brought before Balaam who turns to his probation
officer, Miss Potipher, for background on the case. Miss Potipher who stands
sternly before the Judge, steps forward to whisper into the Judge's ear.
(Readers familiar with the Old Testament may recognize Potiphar, the
Pharaoh's chief officer, who purchased Joseph as a slave.) Stillwell
immediately and vehemently objects to the secretive procedure. After the
startled Judge Balaam determines that Stillwell is Nick's lawyer, he chides
the young counsel that he will have his turn. Miss Potipher resumes, this
time loud enough for counsel to hear. She reports that Nick and his wife and
five children live in the most congested part of the "Dumps," with a boarder,
and it had been over two weeks since he had worked. When she asked Nick
about his delinquency he made an excuse about his tools having been taken
from him. At this juncture she requests that Officer Corrigan (Charlie's
accomplice) take over the narrative of Nick's delinquency case.

Stillwell again objects on the grounds of hearsay evidence. The Oracle,
Judge Balaam, informs counsel that he will "sort the wheat from the chaff"
and to stop interrupting the proceedings. Stillwell then requests a court
stenographer and is informed by Judge Balaam that, "we have no need for all
this red tape in this court." Having again silenced Stillwell, the Judge
requests that Officer Corrigan tell what he knows about the case. What
follows is a trial lawyer's worst nightmare:

"Your honor, there is a dago neighbor who told me that this here dago is a very dangerous man. He said that a friend of his'n in the Old Country told him that a mother-in-law of his'n knew a pal of this here dago, and he said that this here defendant once killed a man in the Old Country—"

"I object! I object!" I shouted losing control of my temper. "The witness is prejudicing the court's mind by hearsay evidence."

"None of your gab," thundered the Judge, his eyes fixed upon me threateningly. "We don't try cases here your law school way—"

Officer Corrigan continues with his "evidence":

"Yes, your honor; and the man told me that he knows it for a fact that this here defendant skipped the Old Country—"

"Me no skeep ole' country," Nikopopulos struck in, at last having evidently grasped the meaning of the policeman's testimony. "Me no keel nobody—"

"Yes, he did," continued the officer. "And he also attacked the constable who attached his machine for which he didn't pay nothin'."

Finally, Nikopopulos is permitted to speak. He states the facts of his recent misfortunes in broken and abbreviated English phrases, denying that he killed anyone, insisting he did pay for the tools, but that they were taken from him nonetheless.

The Oracle again consults with Miss Potipher in whispered tones, ponders a moment, and then rules with a flourish:

"The court is satisfied beyond all reasonable doubt that the defendant is a dangerous man. I know the officer wouldn't fabricate his story. Nor would Miss Potipher prevaricate. He is an idler as anybody can see by looking at him. (The uplifters nodded their heads. They evidently saw this very clearly.) I'll recommend that Miss Potipher look after the family, and the defendant is sentenced to three months confinement in the workhouse and pay the costs."

Nikopopulos stared blankly from me to the others in the room, turned this way and that, when the officer tapped him on the shoulder and said, "Come along, Macaroni . . ."

Stillwell again researches the law and determines that he will seek a writ of habeas corpus— from yet another, higher tribunal.

Judge Silas Screech, who is to hear the petition for habeas corpus, is, alas, yet another friend and associate of Pat Keegan's. This time, Stillwell *is* held in contempt. But not before he presents a compelling case and impresses some newspaper reporters— providently seated in the rear of the courtroom—even as our impetuous young hero is dragged away to serve his sentence for contempt. The *City Daily* runs a glowing account of feisty Guy Stillwell's artful pleading before the cantankerous and intemperate Screech on the front page of the morning edition. Stillwell is an instant hero, and the voter-sensitive Screech, realizing his miscalculation (and on the eve of an election!) purges Stillwell of his contempt and grants the writ of habeas corpus, finally releasing poor Nikopopulos from the long, gaunt arm of the law.

It is from this point in the narrative line that Brudno begins his portrayal of urban industrial work injury litigation. Nikopopulos will reappear, no longer as an independent, albeit struggling, artisan, but now reduced to a tool-less, machine-tending wage-slave employed at the American Tool Company. One day, under disputed circumstances, he is caught up in a large machine and severely injured. Broke from his faltering solo practice, Guy Stillwell begins employment as an associate with the renowned personal injury attorney, Mark Leffingwell, and is taught the personal injury "game" by the Fagin-like Henk, Mark Leffingwell's runner. Counsel for the tool company, the prestigious corporate firm of Nixon, Wright, Croak & Powers, likewise makes its first appearance during Nikopopulos' unfolding work injury lawsuit. And it is in the Nikopopulos case that we first meet Tim, the crooked Jury Commissioner, whose favor is so eagerly sought by both sides of the personal injury bar.

* * * * *

A shining star in the constellation of Cleveland's leading corporate citizens, and a prime local target of employee litigation, was the American Steel and Wire Company of New Jersey, one of the subsidiary companies of the behemoth United States Steel Corporation. Even before joining the Steel Trust in 1901, American Steel and Wire was a virtual paragon of the consolidation, integration and verticalization tendencies that swept American industry in the 1890's and early twentieth century. By the time American Steel and Wire joined the massive Steel Corporation, it had already subsumed all the previously independent wire mills and much of the basic iron and steel producing facilities that had theretofore been separately owned and managed by individual Cleveland-based partnerships and entrepreneurs. How those separate Cleveland facilities joined together with other wire producing plants across the country to form what was, by the time U.S. Steel was founded, a monopoly of the wire manufacturing business in the United States, is a story that primarily focuses upon a traveling salesman-turned-stock speculator and pioneer corporate raider, one "Bet-A-Million" John Warner Gates.

Gates was an early and successful barbed wire "drummer" credited by his biographers[6] with almost single-handedly bringing barbed wire to the formerly open cattle ranges of Texas. An extremely enthusiastic man, he was able through demonstrations, promotions and sometimes pure bluster, to overcome the ranchers' strong attachment to the open range method of cattle raising. Although small town Illinois born and bred, his legendary penchant for gambling[7] was encouraged and well served in the wide open "cow towns" that he worked in his territory on the Texas frontier of the late 1870's. He had a good product that would finally permit fencing off of the vast grazing ranges previously left open, simply because there was no other way to fence it with a material that was both cheap enough and strong enough to frustrate hungry, roving steers. Perceiving the vast fortunes to be made sharing in the profits of the wire firms, instead of the mere commissions from his wire sales, Gates returned to the home office of the firm he sold for and demanded a partnership share in the business—a concern that he felt he was responsible for having made so prosperous. When he was refused, Gates quit and went into competition with his former employers.

The temper of the man is best captured by the following story, widely circulated at the time of his entrance into the "moonshine" end of the wire business. Gates had started a small wire manufacturing concern in St. Louis not long after quitting the sales end of the business. However, most of the wire trade was at that time controlled by Gates' former employer, Col. Isaac Leonard Ellwood who, in partnership with the Washburn and Moen Company of Worcester, Massachusetts, controlled most of the patents for the wire drawing machines needed to cost effectively manufacture barbed wire. Gates knew he couldn't make the kind of money he was interested in if he had to pay license fees and royalties to his former boss. For a time he was able to slide by the problem while Col. Ellwood and his partners were engaged in litigating against larger competitors over the rights to the patents. Finally, in 1880, the United States Circuit Court for the Northern District of Illinois decided the patent suits in favor of Col. Ellwood and the Washburn and Moen Company. Soon thereafter, Gates and his partner were named as defendants in an injunction and patent suit filed in the federal court in St. Louis by Ellwood and Washburn and Moen, still flush with success from the decision giving them control of more than 220 wire drawing patents. The suit demanded that Gates and his partner cease manufacturing operations and pay $100,000 in damages. Anyone in the wire business was going to pay tribute thenceforth to Washburn and Moen and Ellwood.

Gates and his partner were already over-extended and could ill afford the disruption of an injunction proceeding, much less the extended, probably meritorious, patent litigation filed against them. Hiding by day to avoid court process servers, Gates crossed the Mississippi after nightfall to rent a building on the riverfront of *East* St. Louis, Illinois, where he was able to move his machines and stock the following night, resuming full blown manufacturing operations the very next day. At that time, the Mississippi formed the eastern boundary to the St. Louis federal court's venue. Thus, the moonlit foray across the river freed Gates and his partner from the patent litigation against them now pending, impotently, across the Mississippi. Safely ensconced beyond the reach of process servers from St. Louis, Gates and company resumed manufacturing wire, at least until a new suit could be mounted against them in the proper venue across the river. It was, to be sure, a stop-gap measure, but then Gates was a makeshift man.

Floating in and out of partnerships, pools, gentlemen's agreements and such other loose and passing commercial alliances, Gates not only survived, but prospered. Matters in the wire business took a decided turn for the worse however, when, in 1892, the United States Supreme Court upheld Washburn and Moen's patents, yet again triggering waves of litigation and uncertainty in the wire business. Finding himself abandoned by some of his fainthearted associates, Gates declared his intention to expand his operations in the unsettled industry. "Done fooling with pikers," he retained the services of a boyhood acquaintance, a clever and stolid Chicago corporate lawyer, who, unlike Gates, was given to following legal niceties and attending to the minutest organizational details. Little did Gates suspect that Elbert H. Gary, whose devoutly Methodist style so grated with Gates' own 'devil take it' approach to business, would, within the decade, preside as President and Chairman of the Board over the largest aggregation of private capital the world had ever known, the United States Steel Corporation. Starting small, Gary laid the legal foundation and Gates set about to gather the necessary backing.

Their object, to build a wire making monopoly, began with the formation of the Consolidated Steel Company, capitalized at $4 million.

Gates and Gary brought together plants from around the country, including in this first round of acquisitions the Baackes Nail Company of Cleveland, Ohio. Observers in the industry fully expected Gates and Gary to continue to make moves to acquire other wire producing facilities, and indeed, at a much reduced but steady pace, consolidation continued after 1892. Soon Gates and Gary became primarily interested in the Illinois Steel Company, and Gates was personally involved in managing that operation throughout much of the decade. However, the wire trade continued to prosper (annual returns of twenty-seven percent on invested capital were reported) and the dream to corner the wire market was not forsaken.[8]

In 1898, Gates approached J. P. Morgan, the reknown investment banker, with a proposal to consolidate the bulk of all the wire producing facilities in the United States under Gates' and Gary's tutelage. Morgan was interested (he was impressed with Gary's abilities, anyway) and intended to set about raising the money for the proposed consolidation, when the battleship *Maine* blew up in the harbor at Havana. The ensuing war with Spain caused Morgan to back out of any commitment to Gates, at least temporarily.

Nearly simultaneous with the Morgan deal for the second consolidation falling through, Gary was, unbeknownst to Gates, engaged in different albeit related negotiations with Morgan. Gary sought to merge the Illinois Steel Corporation, in which Gates still had a considerable interest, with the Morgan steel companies in a corporate hybrid to be known as the Federal Steel Company. Because of Gates' reputation as a rank speculator and a reliably unreliable business associate, Gates was, at Morgan's insistence, excluded from the negotiations. Although he was eventually handsomely paid for his interests when Federal Steel was finally formed, after discovering his exclusion from the deal Gates was no fan of either the House of Morgan or Judge Gary.

Later that same year, without Morgan's involvement, Gates and Gary (whose dealings with Morgan over Federal Steel were still unknown to Gates) and Gates' old nemesis, Col. Ellwood, put together a more modest venture than originally proposed to Morgan. Capitalized at $24 million, the American Steel and Wire Company of Illinois brought two more Cleveland wire making concerns into the snowballing conglomerate. In addition to the Cleveland-based H.P. Nail Company and American Wire Company, the Illinois-chartered corporation brought the Salem Wire and Nail Company of Salem, Ohio, into the nascent monopoly's fold. Soon after putting the new corporation together, Gary's developing covert alliance with Morgan came to light, and thereafter Gates and Gary forever parted their business ways.

John W. Gates was not yet done. His technique for amassing the widely scattered wire concerns could be best described as "buy and bad mouth." While he was setting about to purchase or take options on wire facilities across the country, he would simultaneously spread rumors and make official sounding gloomy pronouncements about how depressed the wire business was. This approach, transparent though it may seem (recall the massive returns on investment his own concerns were posting) succeeded in reducing the value and prices for the firms he wanted to purchase by undermining investor and lender confidence in the wire market.

Without his dour Methodist counsel, who now stood squarely with Morgan, Gates sought a new lawyer to help him in his further consolidations. Max Pam, with his extensive connections with the larger investment banking houses back East, proved an able replacement for the "betrayer" Gary. Pam convinced the conservative investment banking firm of J. & W. Seligman to underwrite Gates in his final gambit to corral the wire trade. With Seligman's backing the last consolidation occurred in 1899 with a total capitalization of $90 million. The American Steel and Wire Company of Illinois was transformed into the American Steel and Wire Company of New Jersey. It was at this point in time that the largest Cleveland concern, the Cleveland Rolling Mill Company, with its basic steel production facilities, joined the combine to give Gates effective control over all the wire production in the United States. The Cleveland Rolling Mill Company included the Newburgh Steel Works, the Newburgh Wire Works and dock properties on the Cuyahoga River, enabling Gates to produce the raw iron and steel, as well as fabricate the finished products in the Cleveland wire winding and rail rolling mills. The American Steel and Wire Company of New Jersey was now ripe for joining the Steel Trust in 1901.

Gates persisted in his unconventional—some might say patently dishonest—methods, issuing contradictory pronouncements concerning the wildly alternating vigor and demise of the domestic wire trade. Apparently up to his neck in a scheme to "sell short" his considerable stock in the newly formed American Steel and Wire Company, Gates summarily closed ten plants around the country (including one in Cleveland) claiming the general depression in the wire business required draconian measures. When asked how matters could have taken such a sudden turn for the worse only two months following his glowing annual statement to stockholders—announcing record surpluses and his confident anticipation of even better to come—Gates insisted that:

... the wire and steel business is in bad shape. It has been getting worse constantly and the mills of every sort have been running on orders that they obtained six or more months ago. The demand today in our line, at least, and I think proportionately in the other departments of the steel trade is only about 30 per cent of the volume it should be.[9]

Thereupon the entire steel industry was thrown into a panic. Stock prices fell, not just for American Steel and Wire, but for all the publicly traded concerns. Gates, of course, had only to wait for the prices of American Steel and Wire stock to tumble. And fall they did, well below the prices he got when he sold large blocks of company stock not one month previously. At that time the company's stock traded at an all time high, the final surge in prices coming soon after his confidently bullish annual statement.[10]

As might be anticipated, these gross and irresponsible market manipulations led to considerable unpleasantness with his bankers who, after all, saw their collateral being precipitously devalued by Gates' unfounded pronouncements concerning the "depression" in the wire business. Repeatedly, Seligman's representatives on the American Steel and Wire board of directors demanded Gates' resignation. Gates refused, ultimately leading to a criminal prosecution in the New York courts under a penal statute proscribing false and derogatory pronouncements on the part of an officer of a corporation concerning the condition of that corporation. The prosecution was unsuccessful.

Gates, on the other hand, was very successful. Beginning in 1892 with the initial consolidation capitalized at a mere $4 million, the American Steel and Wire Company of New Jersey sold nine years later to the Morgan syndicate for $98 million. Morgan wanted the Steel Corporation to control the wire end of the business and purchasing American Steel and Wire gave him 90% of the country's productive capacity.

The American Steel and Wire Company, thereafter headquartered in Cleveland, became the wire subsidiary of the Steel Trust. While it began as a speculative effort on the part of a "drummer" turned corporate promoter to dominate a limited portion of the American steel manufacturing business, it was to end up as a semi-autonomous, bureaucratically administered entity with broad dominance over not only the American wire and rod markets but whole communities,[11] effectuating policies, both public and private, that were to carry on in their effects long past the demise of John W. "Bet-A-Million" Gates.

For the purposes of this study the American Steel and Wire Company merits further consideration because of its leadership role within the Steel Trust as the subsidiary that structured an "in house" compensation plan by 1910 that not only anticipated the legislative response to work injury litigation by four years in Ohio (and nearly ten years in other industrial states) but formed a national model for most of the legislative acts that were to follow. This explicit, ground-breaking corporate policy making is cause enough to justify dwelling upon American Steel and Wire. The company's legal disenfranchisement of its injured workers as a pre-condition to recovery under the Plan (by the Plan's terms, a worker could not recover for his injuries if he filed suit *or* was represented by a lawyer) arguably belies the true wellspring of, as well as the social sectors most munificently served by, the workmen's compensation reform.

But there is another reason, aside from its leadership role among subsidiaries in the Steel Corporation, to focus upon the American Steel and Wire Company. The firm was headquartered in Cleveland, Ohio, (although its diverse plant facilities were scattered from coast to coast) and the records of work injury suits filed against the company in the Cleveland area are readily available in the federal and state court records. Between 1898 and 1915, there were over 125 work injury suits filed against the company arising from accidents in its Cleveland facilities. The majority of those suits were settled without a public record of how much was paid to the injured employee, but over 50 cases either went to trial, where a verdict was entered, or were settled for a worker's death (as opposed to injury). The "wrongful death" cases then surfaced in the county probate files as record of the settlement distribution made to the heirs of the deceased worker. The records that exist, in both the state and federal courts, provide a rich qualitative, as well as quantitative, primary source for the broader examination of the dynamic forces that led to the national adoption of the workmen's compensation reform.

It is important to bear in mind that for the duration of the period under study (1898-1915), organized labor activity at American Steel and Wire had effectively ceased.[12] When the firm joined with seven other steel companies to form the United States Steel Corporation in 1901, one of the first orders of business for the new mega-corporation was to break the already enfeebled Amalgamated Association of Iron, Steel and Tin Workers. There was a short strike called at some of the corporation's facilities in 1901, it was summarily crushed, and the steel combination was not again burdened with organized labor activity until the famous steel strike of 1919, four years beyond the ken of this study. Consequently, the work injury cases that were filed against the company provided one of the only vehicles for the expression of work place dissent. This sometimes stridently expressed employee dissatisfaction was formalized in the plaintiffs' lawsuit pleadings and is consistently revealed in the court files as an underlying social subtext to the legal dynamics of the workers' suits. Usually the resentments surface most explicitly against the immediate supervisors whose near constant refrain to the worker before the accident was, "Get back to work." Union or no, all was far from well in the massive and scattered facilities of the company, and every suit filed by an injured worker was on some level a public declaration that working for the behemoth and indifferent Steel Corporation was, at once, personally unrewarding, sometimes degrading, and unrelentingly dangerous.

* * * * *

The front page newspaper story that cinched the victory for Stillwell and Nikopopulos led to waves of impecunious clients with "principled," albeit meritless, causes seeking out the services of the stalwart Stillwell, newly heralded champion of the oppressed. It was a very busy summer for young Stillwell . . . and by October he had gone through the stake from his father and was as destitute as his clients. Circumstances being what they were, Guy reluctantly resolved to look for a job . . .

On the day I decided to look for employment, I received a telephone call from the office of Mark Leffingwell. I had heard of Mark Leffingwell before. He was the envy of all the young lawyers and the despair of the older ones. His earnings were said to be fabulous. He was a thorn in the flesh of the "corporation lawyers." The verdicts he had won at the hands of juries were staggering.

I entered the large waiting room of Leffingwell's offices, and paused with unconcealed bewilderment. People on crutches, people with bandaged heads, people with arms in slings, legless people in invalid chairs, armless people, people in every deformity filled the spacious room. I stepped back into the hallway to make sure I was in the office of Mark Leffingwell. No, I had made no mistake. I was not in a surgeon's office. On the door, in letters as big life, was inscribed his name and his calling.

"Do you want to see Mark?"

Here we meet Henk, Leffingwell's best runner. Tough, crude, boisterous and street wise to a fault, Henk will show Guy "the ropes" in the personal injury business. A dramatic foil for (and welcomed relief from) Stillwell's unrelenting and officious naivete, Henk will advance in both moral and social stature as the novel's narrative unfolds. But for now . . .

I turned around and beheld a short, weazen faced fellow of an indeterminable age—he could have been 45 and just as likely 25—with a bulging upper lip that curved slightly to the left and seemed to form an aperture just large enough for a cigarette, which was then protruding from that corner of his mouth. A stiff hat, resting upon his oblong head at a sharp angle, made him look shorter than he actually was. Two streaks of smoke were emerging from his nostrils as he faced me . . .

Henk ushers Guy in to meet the fabulously successful Mark Leffingwell. Leffingwell is seated in a sumptuous office with a magnificent bouquet of "American Beauty" roses brightening the room. Their meeting goes well, and he is taken on as an associate at a salary of $100 a month.

"Henk," he presently turned to the fellow with the shrunken face, "Guy can have Frank's desk. I won't need you in court today, and you can show him the ropes," (my heart skipped a beat as this poetical lawyer lapsed into slang).

Shortly Leffingwell went to Court while Henk took charge of me.

"That's a good one on me," laughed Henk. "I mistook you for a dago who used to "run" for Kelly and Cohn. You don't look like a lawyer. You ain't shrewd enough, I guess. But you'll learn the game if you stay in this office awhile." And he snickered, showing a row of rotten teeth and what I supposed was a black tooth was the vacant space of a missing one.

His reference to my noble profession as "the game" jarred upon me.

Our talk was soon interrupted by the entrance of a man known as Twist (because, as I later learned, one of his arms, due to an accident, was twisted and the hand cut off at the wrist), who carried on a short whispered conversation with Henk.

"Is it all set?" Henk asked.

"Yep," replied Twist, and disappeared.

Then Henk turned to me and said "You come along with me, and I'll learn you the tricks of the trade quick enough." His tiny, snappy blue eyes winked ingratiatingly . . .

At that period, the automobile was still a novelty and the sight of Henk cranking a machine gave me a thrill of the mysterious (I felt the plot was thickening). "Jump in," he said as he, panting, threw the crank into the car.

The next moment we were off on our mission, Henk's tongue keeping a steady pace with the rattle of his automobile. He was enlightening me on some of the points of law pertaining to "the personal injury business."

"Are you a lawyer"? I asked.

"Naw"—there was disgust in his voice—"I ain't no lawyer. But I'll bet I've made more money this year than many a lawyer that's practiced 20 years. Mark will tell you, I'm his best runner." There was pride in his voice.

"Runner? What's a runner?"

He glanced up at me, eyed me queerly, and gave an inner chuckle.

"Say, when was you born? Did you say you was a lawyer?"

"I don't know much about the lawyer's business," I owned modestly.

"I should say you don't."

He suddenly grew absent minded. We reached the part of the city known as The Dumps, the factory district, with dingy, smoke-coated, dilapidated frame houses everywhere, and he had just made a turn into a narrow alley . . .

Notes

1. Deposition testimony of Andrew Balzer, given November 13, 1901, as translated by John Gander, interpreter and Notary Public. The deposition was taken in the case of *Joseph Letmenski vs. The American Steel and Wire Company*, originally filed in the Common Pleas Court of Cuyahoga County, Ohio (Case No. 73,363). On the company's motion the case was removed to the federal Circuit Court of the United States, Northern District of Ohio, Eastern Division (Case No. 6,192). The recounting of the work injury case that follows was gathered from the pleadings and available federal court files from Letmenski's suit.

2. Ezra Brudno, *The Jugglers* (New York: Moffet, Yard & Company, 1920).

3. Justin Galford, *The Foreign Born and Urban Growth in the Great Lakes, 1850-1950*, Ph.D. Diss. (New York University, 1957).

4. *Encyclopedia of Cleveland History*, ed. David D. Van Tassel and John J. Grabowski (Bloomington: Indiana University Press, 1987); *Book of Clevelanders* (Cleveland: The Burrows Brothers Company, 1914); *Representative Clevelanders: A Biographical Directory of Leading Men & Women in Present Day Cleveland* (Cleveland: The Cleveland Topics Company, 1927).

5. Brudno's description of a Justice of the Peace court's harried, but efficient, administration is worth reproducing here:

> We elbowed our way into the "court." Two lawyers were seated on the edge of the table, discussing the prognostications of the coming election. The constable was explaining why a certain candidate, whom he was opposing, could not be elected, while One Eye Smith was running back and forth, like a busy stage shifter, from one partitioned room to the other, panting, apologizing, administering oaths, solemnizing marriages, signing "attachments," with the thrift and cunning of a stall keeper at a Persian bazaar.

6. Robert Irving Warshow, *Bet-A-Million Gates, The Story of a Plunger* (New York, 1932); Lloyd Wendt and Herman Kogan, *Bet-A-Million! The Story of John W. Gates* (New York, 1948). Most of what follows is gathered from these two sources. Both biographies emphasize Gates' reckless and

often irresponsible bravura, oddly alternating in tone between the extremes of admiration and contempt.

7. His honorific moniker, "Bet-A-Million" derived from a storied poker game at the Waldorf Astoria, following his rise in New York financial circles. A member of his staff, reacting to local press reports of Gates' rumored losses in the card game, compensated by bragging to a reporter about his employer's recent, and highly speculative, stock market successes. The boast caused Gates considerable embarrassment in the stodgy investment banking community where he was already held in low esteem as a vulgar and rapacious speculator and heedless business associate. Ibid., Wendt & Kogan, 160.

8. Gates and his agents were often spotted in Cleveland, holding "secret" negotiations with local wire and rod mill owners. "Will Sell," *Cleveland Leader*, 5 December 1897, 1; "A Mystery," *Cleveland Leader*, 20 December 1897, 1.

9. William T. Hogan, S.J., *Economic History of the Iron and Steel Industry in the United States* (Lexington, Massachusetts: D.C. Heath and Company, 1978), 261.

10. Ibid., Wendt & Kogan, 175.

11. At the time the Steel Trust was founded, American Steel and Wire employed an estimated 36,000 people nationwide. Horace L. Wilgus, *A Study of the United States Steel Corporation* (Chicago: Callaghan & Company, 1901).

12. David Brody, *Steelworkers In America, The Nonunion Era* (New York: Harper & Row, 1960).

I I

The Rules Of The Game

Mr. John Sykes: . . . Personally, I am thoroughly interested in a compensation act, and also the employers' liability act, because one of my sons, a minor at that time, between the years of 19 and 20, met with an accident that took his right hand off, and he was at that time working for the Standard Lighting Company of this city. The Company offered to give me $100 and the insurance company offered me another $150—if my memory serves me right—but I flatly refused it. I took this view of it: That the boy, when he grew up to manhood, he would look at his wrist and say: "My father said that $250 was enough for that right hand." I says, "No," I took the chances in the court, and from that day to this, neither me nor my son has received one cent. He is still a member of this community, without a right hand, now 23 years old . . .

Mr. Harry Thomas (Representing the Cleveland Federation of Labor): Is it not a fact, that the accident to your boy, was directly caused by the negligence of the foreman of the plant?

Mr. Sykes: Yes, that is my judgment. The boy was at the machine, called a press. The machine got out of order. He called the attention of the foreman to this fact, and he said, "All right, I will go and fix it. You go back to the machine." In his judgment it was not in the right order. He put his hand through, gave it a little touch so that it would trip through, but it did not trip through. The foreman touched and tripped the lever, and started the machine. It cut off Tom's hand, and he didn't get a cent for it . . .

Mr. Thomas: Is it not a fact, that the case was thrown out of the courts on account of the fellow-servant rule?

Mr. Sykes: Yes sir; the foreman was considered a fellow-servant—the foreman of the works was.[1]

By 1910 the workmen's compensation reform movement was approaching its heady zenith in most of the American industrial states. The starkly affecting testimony of men like John Sykes recounted the manifest injustice workmen (and boys) too often faced in the courts pursuing redress for debilitating injuries sustained in the service of their employers. Relying upon such simple and moving, if anecdotal, evidence, the compensation reformers sank a deep and sustaining taproot into what seemed a poisoned well of bitterness and frustration with both the courts and the common law's employer liability rules the courts applied to work place accidents. In the quintessentially progressive flourish of one of the movement's leading national figures:

> The law is behindhand, and the law makers have been blind. With their minds thoroughly steeped in the old ideas of theoretical equality and freedom of contract they have gone on, content with the 'logic of the law' oblivious to the obvious facts.[2]

In her classic contribution to the Russell Sage Foundation's Pittsburgh Survey, *Work Accidents and the Law*, Crystal Eastman reviewed the common law rules of employer liability in Pennsylvania and concluded:

> In regard to the existing law of employers' liability and its consequences, our findings, founded on the accident experience of one great industrial district, lead inexorably to certain conclusions. The law in many of its principles is unjust; in operation it uses up time, money and good will, to little purpose; it furnishes small incentive for the prevention of work-accidents, and leaves well-nigh the whole economic burden of work-accidents to be borne by the injured workman and his dependents, with consequent hardship and privation. It is to be condemned from the standpoints of justice, method, and practical utility.[3]

Eastman's worker-sympathetic analysis led her to condemn the common law and litigation because it proved such a consistently unlikely and problematic source of recovery for the injured, and usually impecunious, industrial worker. Her reformer's perspective, circa 1910, has since evolved into the generally accepted historical premise that the workmen's compensation movement grew out of the need to address the institutional failure of the American common law and court system to adapt to the new industrial order. Workmen's compensation, according to this view, was a worker-favoring transformation that revamped the "hidebound" common law by depriving the courts of jurisdiction over work injury cases and creating in their stead industrial commissions doling out compensation according to predictable, efficient and humane standards which litigation was incapable of achieving.

Inasmuch as the widespread disaffection with the common law's response to industrial accidents was a universal and unrelenting theme among those who successfully advocated for reform, the common law's scheme of rules and litigation practices suggests itself as the proper place for a history of the reform to begin. This chapter will revisit that generally accepted historical view of the courts and their application of the common law, not so much to contradict the prevailing reform-oriented version, as to supplement that essentially correct—but static, and therefore misleading—perspective. To the extent that the courts were dominated by judges, the law was molasses-slow in changing. But there were other policy brokers in the trial courts, "civilians" as it were, with whom the judiciary had to share power—the jury. And, in fact, the common law of juries was a very dynamic and responsive institution. Moreover, it will be suggested that it was the juries' very dynamism and responsiveness that primarily motivated many of the reform's corporate champions.

In the pre-compensation era, recovery for injuries sustained on the job required that the worker bring a lawsuit against his employer. Even if, as usually happened, the employee settled with his employer prior to actually bringing suit or prior, at least, to the suit going to trial, the amount paid to the worker for recompense hinged upon a complex network of substantive, procedural and jurisdictional rules that together governed work place injury litigation. Thus, even when a suit was not actually filed against the employer, the anticipated results of a threatened action determined what recovery, if any, the injured employee could negotiate with his employer. Typically, and problematically, the reformers' analysis of the "common law of unhallowed memory"[4] only focused upon the substantive law of tort[5] liability with particular reference to worker actions for "negligence" and the accompanying employer legal defenses of "contributory negligence," "assumption of the risk" and the "fellow servant rule."

Rarely did the reformers address the substantive law of tort damages or the procedural rules governing the conduct of lawsuits filed against employers and the trial process actually culminating the litigation. And almost never did the reformers review the esoteric jurisdictional law that governed which of the available courts, state or federal, would provide a final forum for the litigation. But the law of tort damages was crucial to the workers' litigation (and, in fact, defined the final parameters of the compensation reform) and it was the procedural and jurisdictional law that determined the often pivotal issue of whether a judge—or a jury—decided a worker's case. The arcane and often anomalous rules governing federal jurisdiction had an important role to play in the cases filed against very large, "multi-state" employers, such as the American Steel and Wire Company, and were, as will be touched upon here,[6] more often determinative of the success or failure of a worker's case than the incessantly recounted and manifestly unfair liability doctrines comprising the detested employer defenses to negligence actions. Whether an action was heard in the federal, as opposed to state, court had a great deal to do with the efficacy of the various employer-favoring liability doctrines of negligence actions. In short, federal variations on the procedural rules of litigation and trial practice tended to frustrate employee claims against those defendant employers who could successfully invoke federal court jurisdiction over the employee's suit. These less often addressed procedural rules and practices will be covered at greater length here to supplement and enlarge upon the reformers' view of the common law.

Ultimately, the substantive tort doctrines of liability and damages, litigation practice and procedures, and the jurisdictional nuances of the American common law created a grim but very real "market" for negligently inflicted personal injuries, work injuries included. When all the legal rules were considered together with the particular injuries sustained, the circumstances of the accident and the identity and relationship of the parties, it was usually possible to predict the approximate dollar value of any given "case" in the event it went to trial. If the worker's attorney and the company's attorney both predicted the same value for a work injury, the case was probably settled. That settlement amount then served to further define the larger work injury market. If the lawyers disagreed, the matter would proceed to trial and the verdict amount would further define the market. Moreover, this gruesome tort marketplace, awash in blood, pain, disfigurement and death, served as the benchmark from which the compensation promoters set their reform compass when they embarked upon passage of the various compensation statutes that proliferated in the second decade of this century.[7]

Finally, there were other important "rules" that governed the pre-compensation work injury recovery process. These rules were not doctrinal in nature, but were nonetheless determinative of the larger contextual "social gestalt" comprising work injury litigation. These "rules of the game" were the professional norms and patterns of practice within the developing legal specialty area of employers' liability. Unwritten, but very powerful, these norms were but hinted at in the compensation reformers' passing disdain for the greedy and unscrupulous "ambulance chaser" attorneys who plagued responsible employers and those shysters' corporate counterparts, the hardhearted (and equally unscrupulous) liability insurance and company claims agents who routinely took advantage of law-ignorant and often desperate injured workers.

So with the objective of understanding those patterns of professional culture, let us rejoin our green-horned young hero, Guy Stillwell, as he takes instruction from his new, snaggle-toothed mentor—Mark Leffingwell's best runner—Henk. Recall that while Stillwell awaited Leffingwell's return from court, the whispering and dismembered emissary, Twist,[8] had tipped off Henk to a new and very promising accident case. Now Henk and his eager charge have made their way (in a new-fangled automobile) to the industrial district, "The Dumps," in an effort to get the recently injured prospect "signed up" with Leffingwell's office.

Now Henk led the way, and I followed.

First we passed through a long smelly corridor, then we climbed a broken staircase, another dark stenchy corridor, after which Henk paused and rapped on a door. We could hear voices within but no one answered to his knock. Henk rapped again but without attracting attention. He finally lost patience, pounded on the door and opened it almost simultaneously. I followed timidly behind.

We now found ourselves in a room that seemed like a kitchen, although a bed stood against one of the walls. Henk's glances were flitting from one to the other of the gathering, and his glances were anything but pleasant. A woman, whose back was turned toward us, was waving her arms eloquently and saying something to three men facing her. (Her English was broken and the fragments scarcely gave any inkling of their origin.) Then a young man of unmistakable foreign nationality, who was evidently interpreting for the two men next to him, began to jabber, making frantic gestures and evidently endeavoring to drive home a convincing argument.

At this point, Henk broke through the line fiercely, like a football tackle, and, shoving the interpreter aside with undisputed authority, addressed the other men jeeringly—.

"What are you's guys doin' here? I've got the case. Had it signed up yesterday, and I have all the witnesses in my *mitt* (displaying his fist to them as if he had them in his hand literally)—see?"

"And who are you?" the interpreter launched a brazen counter-attack but without showing much confidence in his strength.

The two other men peered wrathfully at Henk.

"Who am I?" Henk flared up indignantly. "I am from Mark's office. We had it signed up half an hour after the accident happened." He glowered at them all with a look of dismissal.

I could see the name of Mark overawed them.

"She," pointing to the woman, whose head was covered with a large woolen shawl, evidently preparing to leave, "has just told me she didn't yet give the case to nobody," the interpreter protested.

Now the woman turned around and catching sight of me spread out her arms with a cry of joy, "Ah, Mr. Lawyer—he call your name all de time—my man he vant you."

"Mrs. Nikopopulos!" I also exclaimed, amazed at the strange coincidence.

Henk now stuck his thumbs in the armpits of his vest and eyed the three men before him slyly.

"Gaw-on," he jeered, "the show is over."

The interpreter spat on the floor and muttered an ugly oath as he turned to the door, and the other two shambled along after him, with disgust on their faces . . .

*   *   *   *   *

The doctrine of negligence governed the fault-oriented legal rules used to analyze and compensate for unintended personal injuries, and therefore, most work accidents. For the period under consideration here (between 1890 and 1915 unless otherwise stated) the doctrine of negligence was still evolving as an organizing principle of social relations. It was only in the beginning of the nineteenth century that the older and more rigid common law "forms of action" of trespass and trespass "on the case" began to evolve into a discrete new concept enforcing rights of recovery for damages sustained as a consequence of unintended, but careless, conduct.[9] One factor that distinguished this evolving negligence "form" from its doctrinal predecessors was that its jurisprudential vitality did not necessarily rest upon, or spring from, an injured individual's pre-existing right of property or contract. Many legal writers have noted a correlation between the emerging negligence form of action and the Industrial Revolution[10]. The bloody, ever rising toll of injuries from the new and dreadful steam-powered machinery (especially evident in the increasingly commonplace juggernaut railroads) helps explain the English and American courts' growing reliance upon negligence as an organizing legal concept. By 1890 negligence was well ensconced in the American common law of tort.[11]

For a worker to pursue an action for damages against his employer, he had to show that his employer was in some respect lacking in due care and that the employer's lack of care was the legal or "proximate" cause of the mishap injuring the worker. The employer had a generalized legal obligation to the worker to refrain from injuring him but that duty was no more or less stringent than if the worker was a total stranger to him. The duty was implied in law, and did not depend upon an explicit understanding or agreement between the parties or the contractual relation of master and servant. However, merely suffering an injury on the job, in and of itself, was not sufficient. Rather, the employer's lack of due care had to be the cause of the worker's injury. If the injured employee could overcome this initial hurdle by demonstrating his employer's negligence (and there were situations where he could not), the lawsuit then had to survive the gauntlet of the three notorious, employer-favoring legal "defenses" to the claim of negligence: the fellow servant rule; assumption of the risk; and contributory negligence.

During the period under consideration, the tort concept of negligence was expanding in the sense that it tended, over time, to encompass more and more activities within the purview of "carelessness." Petitions for injured workers often had only to allege that employers controlled the premises where the accident happened. The owner's or manager's personal involvement with the accident, or the machine that caused it, was not necessarily required to make out a *prima facie* case. As the concept of negligence grew, so too did the causal remoteness of the liability creating conduct. On the other hand, the employer defenses were contracting in their power and application. The loathed fellow servant rule or "rule of common employment" is a case in point.

First among and most notorious of the "unholy trinity," the fellow servant rule held that if the worker's injuries were caused by the negligence of a fellow employee, the employer could not be held liable for the mishap.[12] Technically, the fellow servant rule was an exception to the older and broader common law rule of agency known as *respondeat superior*. *Respondeat superior* imputed a servant's carelessness, while acting in the service of the master, to the master. In the context of an employment injury however, the fellow servant rule suspended *respondeat superior* from operation. To demonstrate how the doctrine worked to protect employers, suppose a contractor's employee, a mason, carelessly dropped a brick on a pedestrian strolling on a public sidewalk adjacent to a construction site. According to the rules of agency, the "master," or contractor, was liable for the injuries sustained by the passerby. However, if that same clumsy bricklayer dropped the brick on a fellow employee of the contractor—no liability. Under the "pure" formulation of the fellow servant rule the injured fellow employee of the bumbling bricklayer would be without a remedy. Part of the bitterness engendered by this, the most infamous of the employer defenses, devolved from the special immunity the law extended to the master so long as the injured person was "only help." And too, as a practical matter, most work place accidents were in some manner "caused" by a fellow worker's lack of care.

In many states exceptions to the fellow servant rule developed soon after its arrival upon the scene of the American common law in the late 1840's.[13] In 1856, the Ohio Supreme Court diluted the harshness of the doctrine by holding, in *Little Miami R.. Co. v. John Stevens*,[14] that the employer would still be liable so long as the worker was injured as a result of the negligence of a superior, or supervisory employee of the employer. In the state courts further exceptions developed. For example, if an employee from another "department" of the employer caused the injury, the employer was liable. This "exception to the exception" of the fellow servant rule was justified by the policy ostensibly underlying the rule: that a servant was in a better position to know the hazards of the work place, including the identity and propensities of careless fellow workers, and could therefore better guard against same, than an often absent or otherwise engaged employer. The "other department" exception crept into the case law and found its way into the statutory law by way of early state railroad regulations.[15] In Ohio, the earliest regulatory statute altering a road's liability to injured employees appeared in 1894.[16]

Finally, in 1910, the Ohio Legislature, responding to the growing public indignation over the now roundly condemned failings of employer liability law, passed the comprehensive "Norris Act."[17] The Norris Act transformed all the employer defenses, but particularly gutted the fellow servant rule by very broadly defining superior servants. The Norris bill extended employer liability to situations where an admittedly "fellow" servant caused an injury by following "immediate or preemptory instructions" from a superior servant, and where a worker was injured for "want of necessary and sufficient (employer) rules and regulations for the government of such employees and the operation and maintenance of such ways, works, boats, wharves, plant, machinery, appliances or tools." The Norris bill met with virulent employer opposition but passed relatively intact, and was one of the primary motivating factors responsible for Ohio's smaller employer interests finally accepting the full-blown workmen's compensation reform.

Assumption of the risk, second in the "unholy trinity," presented another formidable hurdle to the injured worker's suit. This rule provided that if the injured worker had prior knowledge of the hazard that caused his injury and yet "chose" to brave the hazard or "assume the risk" by continuing to work—the evident perils notwithstanding—he could not maintain a suit against his employer. Again, as a practical matter, how many workmen could claim that they had no knowledge of the hazards involved in their employment? Assumption of the risk was often condemned as an inappropriate derivative borrowed from the realm of contract law that naively presupposed an equality of bargaining power between an employer and prospective employee that would, ideally, enable the worker to dicker with his employer for a safer work place. As a corollary to this supposed equality of bargaining positions, the rule was also justified on the basis that if an employee worked a hazardous job he was presumably paid a premium wage by his employer "to assume the extra risks" inherent in the job. Unlike the fellow servant rule, assumption of the risk was not confined to work injury cases.[18]

One common ploy of the workers' attorneys trying to dodge both the fellow servant and assumption of the risk defenses was to have the machine-maimed employee allege that, prior to sustaining the injury, he informed the foreman (a superior employee) that the offending machine was defective or in need of maintenance. Typically, the suit papers recounted the irritated foreman either refusing to stop production to fix the machine or insisting to the skeptical, but duly obedient, worker that the contraption was operating well enough and to, "get back to work." (Recall the brain-damaged Letmenski's version of the exchange with his obdurate foreman just prior to being knocked insensible by the whirling 2"x4".) This oft-repeated recitation in the pleadings served to anticipate, and presumably outmaneuver, the employer's certain-to-be-summoned "doctrinal henchmen." By claiming to obey a direct order to return to the malfunctioning machine, the employee could insist that he did not assume the risk of injury but rather attempted to avoid the danger by notifying the employer's "agent" of the hazard and requesting that it be corrected. Further, the fellow servant who "caused" the worker's injury was a superior servant, whom the deferential "inferior" servant was bound to obey.[19]

Third of the nefarious triad was contributory negligence. This defense provided that if an employer could show that the worker was careless in any regard, then, no matter how negligent the employer was, he was not liable for the worker's injuries. The rule was absurdly lopsided. Even though a factual situation might demonstrate that an employer's lack of due care was 99% responsible for an accident, if the worker's own lack of care was even 1% responsible for the resulting mishap, the employer was not liable. Contributory negligence was all or nothing: damages were not apportioned according to the parties' comparative degrees of fault. As with assumption of the risk, contributory negligence was not limited to work place accidents but served to answer for any allegedly negligent conduct.

As with the fellow servant rule, modifications were imposed upon assumption of the risk and contributory negligence by both the courts and legislature, ameliorating their severity. In 1902, Ohio limited both defenses by legislating that if an employee was injured by a defective or non-conforming machine, the employer was strictly liable to the employee for damages.[20] Further, in Ohio trial practice both defenses were further diluted by juries, who often declined to apply the all-or-nothing severity of contributory negligence against arguably careless workers, and were apparently skeptical of the optimistic contractual suppositions underlying the theory behind assumption of the risk.[21]

In 1910 the Norris Act legislated the jurors' biases into the statutory scheme defining employer liability. The bill incorporated and expanded the defective machine or unsafe condition exception to assumption of the risk and revamped the extreme consequences of the contributory negligence doctrine by substituting a rule that allowed the worker to recover where his negligence was "slight" and the employer's "gross in comparison." The new rule of "comparative negligence" allowed the jury or judge to take the employee's relative fault into consideration by reducing the recovery from the employer "in proportion" to the worker's own negligence. Moreover, the Norris Act codified the long standing Ohio trial practice that left issues of negligence, contributory negligence and assumption of the risk to the laymen-jurors' judgment: "All questions of negligence, contributory negligence, and assumption of the risk, shall be for the jury, under the instruction of the court."[22]

* * * * *

Having routed the competition from the Nikopopulos kitchen, it was now incumbent upon Henk to win over the confused and leery Mrs.

Nikopopulos. Not to worry, it's all been arranged with Twist, right down to the timing . . .

The field having been cleared of the enemy Henk addressed himself to Mrs. Nikopopulos with suave loquaciousness.

"Me a partner of Mark Leffingwell—the great lawyer," he began—evidently imagining foreigners understood broken English best—"me got the witnesses—you und'stand? Me got five witnesses"—(Henk spread out the five fingers of his left hand in the shape of the tail of a strutting turkey)—"and me get you fifty thousand dollars"—(bringing the fingers of both hands together five times)—"Yes, fifty thousand dollars."

"He my lawyer," poor Mrs. Nikopopulos shrugged her shoulders, with a wave of her hand in my direction. "Him good man."

"Yes, he, too, Mark Leffingwell's partner," Henk instantly made room for me in the firm. "You'll have three lawyers" (and three fingers went up eloquently)—"Twist, what are you doing here?" And he suddenly turned to the young man minus one hand with whom he had carried on a whispered conversation earlier in the day. Twist had slipped into the room unnoticed by me.

Twist stepped forward and shook hands with Henk as if he had not seen him in years and was just renewing an old acquaintance.

"Dis woman from my country," Twist dropped into the same vernacular. "Her man and me good friends. Too bad, dis woman's man hurt."

"Is she very poor, Twist?"

"Very, very poor. Her man lost his tools in a lawsuit," he recited history well known to me. "And den when he goes to vork gets hurt—too bad."

"Give her this (and Henk handed Twist a twenty dollar bill) and tell her if we don't get fifty thousand dollars, she need not return the money."

Mrs. Nikopopulos shrank from touching the proffered money and looked at me with evident embarrassment.

"Tell her, Twist, how much we got for you when you was hurt," suggested Henk.

Twist spoke voluminously for a moment or two in Mrs. Nikopopulos' native tongue and exhibited the ugly stump of his hand cut off at the wrist and his crooked arm.

The poor woman took the money and then a dialogue ensued between her and Twist.

"She says her man went to work in the morning as strong as the ox and then some lawyers come and tell her man got hurt in the shop. She says there was thirty lawyers here since last night and gave her their cards—"

"Tell her the other lawyers wanted to rob her and she should tear up them cards," counseled Henk . . .

After some more small talk, Henk, with the practiced assistance of the stump-wristed Twist, persuades the diffident Mrs. Nikopopulos that Mark Leffingwell was her best hope. Soon they all leave for the hospital to have Nick "sign up" his case with "Mark's office."

As soon as we were in the automobile—Henk and I in front and Twist and Mrs. Nikopopulos in the rear—Henk whispered to me, "We have got it sewed up all right."

"I thought you said you had it signed up last evening," I remarked.

Henk gave me a side glance, chuckled, and said, "You certainly are a boob—that's the game. I had to get rid of those shysters. Once they find it signed up they drop out. Competition in the personal injury business has been too keen of late . . ."

*   *   *   *   *

If an injured worker was able to make out a *prima facie* case of liability against the employer and survive the gauntlet of employer defenses then, and only then, was it incumbent upon the "trier of fact"—in the state court most often a jury—to determine the worker's damages. Though less often addressed by the reformers, the common law of tort damages was a crucial feature of the doctrinal landscape transformed by the reform scheme of workmen's compensation. The predictable sums injured workers recovered once the compulsory compensation system went into effect supplanted a legal theory of damages that was in practice notoriously fickle and uncertain and dynamic. And quite unlike the rules of liability, the rules of damages in personal injury actions were most often decried as oppressive by employer groups.

The common law's theoretical objective in compensating for negligently inflicted personal injury was to arrive at a verdict (or settlement) sum that would put the injured person in the same position he was in before he was injured, or in the rubric of tort, "make him whole" again. What could be properly included in that attempted restoration of diminished wholeness encompassed elements both certain and easily translated into dollar amounts (such as medical bills and lost wages), along with matters of far less certainty, not necessarily subject to readily calculated pecuniary equivalents. In practice, most of the uncertainty derived from a single factor: the common law's cognizance of the injured worker's "pain and suffering" in the calculus of damages. It was usually a given that a serious injury caused the worker to incur some hospital and medical expenses, along with some loss in wage income during the period of convalescence. These were sums that could be proved at trial and, in the event the employer was held liable, calculated as likely to be included in any damage award. But pain and suffering are not matters given to precise remunerative calculation and their subjectivity —and the law's steadfast refusal to adopt any rigid formula to guide judges or jurors in setting monetary amounts for their fair compensation—proved the occasional scourge of defendant-employers.

An example of the very limited guidance a jury could expect from the court regarding the law of damages in a work injury case is contained in the following "jury charge" given in a railroad accident case in Mahoning County (Youngstown) Ohio, in 1894. The judge presiding over the trial had already instructed the jurors on the liability issues between the injured conductor and his employer railroad. Turning then to the matter of damages, the judge instructed the jury as follows:

> If your verdict is for the defendant, say so in general terms. If for the plaintiff, you should so state, and also incorporate in your verdict the amount which you may find, he is entitled to recover, an amount that would be sufficient to compensate him for the damages actually sustained by him, directly resulting from the negligence of the defendant. This would include the pain which the plaintiff has suffered, and the pain that he will continue to suffer if his injuries are of such character as to cause him pain in the future. His diminished capacity to earn money from the time he received his injuries until the present, and his diminished capacity to earn money in the future, if you find his injuries are of such a character as to diminish his capacity to earn money in the future. And you may also include any expenses actually and necessarily incurred by him in consequence of the injuries received which have been proven in this case. He is entitled, if entitled to recover at all, to be

made whole; more than that would be unjust to the defendant; less
would be unjust to the plaintiff.[23]

The damages for personal injuries properly included: past and probable
future medical expenses; past and probable future (if the injuries resulted in
a continuing or permanent disability) wage losses; past and probable future
incidental or miscellaneous expenses related to the injuries; and most
ethereal but not least, recompense for past and probable future pain. Note
how exasperatingly little guidance was provided to the jurymen in regard to
assessing a dollar equivalent for the injured conductor's pain. Little wonder
employers routinely lamented the sometimes wildly fluctuating verdicts
rendered against them.

No authoritative record exists for determining "typical" recoveries
obtained in the Ohio courts for non-fatal personal injuries, much less work
related injuries, in the period preceding passage of the workmen's
compensation act.[24] The available Ohio sources are mostly anecdotal and
presumably unreliable as it was the remarkable exceptions that provided the
material for the best and most widely circulated "horror stories." However,
there is a record of contested verdicts in some reported appellate cases and
a few trial level opinions. Again, these cases were probably not typical
because they were verdicts considered aberrantly high by defense counsel
and appealed on that basis. Nonetheless, certain clear patterns of judicial
thinking emerge from the courts' decisions.

As a rule, the published opinions involved jury verdicts. The guiding
rule articulated by the reviewing courts was that the jury's verdict would be
allowed to stand unless it clearly appeared to result from "passion and
prejudice" and "shocked sound judgement and a sense of fairness."[25] When
the appellate panels deigned to discuss the specifics of verdicts, their focus
was usually upon the "pecuniary" aspects of the plaintiff's damages. Thus,
with very few exceptions, the courts' opinions would skirt the matter of pain,
suffering and disfigurement,[26] and evaluate a verdict's "reasonableness"
according to the anticipated lost wage and support consequences of an
injury. If an injury incapacitated a person for only a short period of time and
had no long term effect upon the plaintiff's earning capacity, then an award
far in excess of the wage loss might well be overturned on appeal.[27] If, on the
other hand, an injury permanently disabled a person and prevented him from
continuing in a long and promising career, the courts would tolerate
extraordinarily high verdicts.[28] The effect of this judicial tendency was to
tolerate higher awards for those plaintiffs with higher occupational or social
standing.[29] However, the cases defy mathematical predictability. Whereas a

federal court awarded a permanently injured man earning $300 a month $7,500 in his action against a railroad, in the same year another permanently injured man earning only $110 a month was awarded $19,000![30]

One legal treatise of national scope from the period[31] surveyed verdicts obtained for injuries of like kind in an attempt to determine where appellate courts would "draw the line" on jury damage awards. The reported opinions revealed that for injuries resulting in total and permanent disability $30,000 verdicts were "frequently sustained" on appeal. For the loss of sight in one or both eyes $5,000 awards were upheld. For loss of both legs $25,000 would probably survive an appeal, while for "only" one leg, verdicts ranging between $10,000 and $22,500 had been sustained on appeal. For loss of a foot numerous verdicts in the range of $10,000 survived review by appellate courts. Likewise $10,000 seemed safe on appeal for the loss of an arm, although there might be considerable variation between awards depending upon the consequent loss of livelihood following the amputation. For the loss of a hand $10,000 again seemed to set the limit for most state appellate courts. Note that these were not ordinary verdicts but the upper limits to recovery in the reported cases, circa 1901. There could be significant variations depending upon the particular facts of each case. Again, the greatest single determining variable seemed to be the injury's effect upon the continued earning capacity of the plaintiff.

While the pain and suffering of a surviving injured worker was subject to recompense under the common law of negligence, if a worker was killed as the result of a work accident, the measure of damages was limited. Historically, at common law, a dead man could not bring a suit, and there was no right of action that survived in the heirs of the deceased individual. Any cause of action against a wrongdoing or negligent individual (or corporation) expired with the passing of the victim. (It was oft remarked that it was far cheaper to kill a man at common law than to merely injure him.) For obvious reasons, the rule was not without its detractors, and in the middle of the nineteenth century "Wrongful Death" statutes were passed in most state legislatures modifying the common law with a statutory legal action vested in the heirs and dependents of the decedent.

In Ohio, as in most other jurisdictions, the wrongful death statute[32] provided for a diminished measure of damages. The emphasis of the statute was on recovery for the pecuniary damages sustained by the dependent survivors of the deceased victim. There was no provision for the pain and suffering of the lingering, or momentarily-surviving decedent, and no provision for the grief and emotional suffering of the survivors:

> Every such action shall be for the exclusive benefit of the wife, or husband, and children, or if there be neither of them, then of the parents and next of kin of the person whose death shall be so caused (wrongfully) . . . and in every action the jury may give such damages, not exceeding in any case ten thousand dollars, as they may think proportioned to the pecuniary injury resulting from such death, to the persons. . . for whose benefit such action shall be brought . . .[33]

In addition to the $10,000 ceiling, the courts uniformly held that pain and suffering and grief were not compensable as "pecuniary injury."[34] Further, when calculating a decedent's likely prospective earnings, the law required a deduction from the award for what the decedent would have consumed as a member of the household, had he survived. Thus, the common law's aversion to a dead man's suit carried over in these limiting aspects of the statutorily created wrongful death action. The exclusion of the emotional factors from the damage calculations was reflected in the verdicts. Since actions for death were not as valuable as actions for surviving, badly injured workers, the verdicts in "death cases" tended to be lower than might be expected. In 1912, the Ohio Constitution was amended, banishing the statute's $10,000 recovery limitation. But the practical effect was negligible: the statute's "pecuniary" limitation remained intact and continued to keep the verdicts in industrial death cases from approaching the astronomical potential of the very worst injury cases.

Whether the claim was brought by a surviving worker or his surviving dependents for wrongful death, the gist of the damage equation usually reduced to how much the worker earned in wages before the accident. The "make whole" doctrine necessarily focused upon pecuniary equivalents. To the extent that the injury deprived the worker of wages, past, present or future, the damages could be set to a relatively certain formula. And while the common law provided recovery for pain and suffering, those issues were so speculative and subjective that allowance for pain and suffering was more of a "sub-rule"—a discretionary matter within the larger realm of damages—than a primary rule of recovery. Awarding large sums for pain and suffering could serve as a punitive measure for the reviled defendant, or as a bonus for the especially sympathetic plaintiff. Recalling the jury instruction in the Youngstown case—the jury did not have to separate out or account for the pain and suffering from the single verdict amount, but only award one "make whole" sum. And, as will appear later, Cleveland juries did not abuse this latitude against the American Steel and Wire Company.

Rather, they appeared to focus upon the wages and the out of pocket costs in setting damages.

When an injured man came to the common law to recover for his negligently inflicted injuries, the fact finder, whether judge or jury, looked first, not to the injury, nor the disfigurement, nor even the pain and suffering, but to the man and his demonstrated earning capacity before sustaining the injury. This pre-accident income earning ability was the damage doctrine's baseline. From this baseline all the other matters sanctioned for recompense, the pain, and disfigurement, and continuing disability could be added in as factors of the lost earning capacity. In short, the common law looked to the man more than the injury when assessing the damages incurred in industrial accidents. This correlation in part explains the tendency of the common law of negligence to award greater damages to those with greater social status—to the extent elevated status is usually related to higher wage or salary levels.[35]

*   *   *   *   *

But enough of what lawyers say they do, let us again turn from the doctrine of law to the practice of law as we rejoin our attentive *picaro*, "Mr. Lawyer"; his sage teacher, Henk; one-handed Twist; and the bereaved Mrs. Nikopopulos. Finally persuaded to cast her lot with Mark Leffingwell over all the other solicitous ambulance chasers, it was now left for the foursome to connive a visit with the convalescing Nick so that he could "sign up" his case. Getting in to see Nick would prove more problematic than might at first appear. It seems that St. Agnes Hospital[36] was presided over by no less formidable and wary a personage than Mother Superior, who as we shall see, shared a more than passing interest in the increasingly expensive social problem of industrial accidents:

> We soon arrived at St. Agnes Hospital, Henk in the lead.
> With his hat off, his cigarette absent from its wonted place, Henk stood facing the rigid-looking, mask-like face of the Mother Superior with all the solemnity and the humbleness of a devout Catholic at confession. His face had suddenly become the very expression of affliction and distress. He briefly explained to the Mother Superior that he was Nikopopulos' brother, and that the woman back of him was his sister-in-law, and that they wished to see the injured man. The Mother Superior informed him in a

scarcely audible voice that there had been such a run of lawyers after this case that she had given orders that none but the members of his family should be admitted.

"It's terrible, Mother Superior," assented Henk lugubriously and, giving his speech a foreign intonation, wiped an imaginary tear from his eye, "how them lawyers have the heart to bother the poor man, when he is in such great pain. Them lawyers only think of the money." Henk's voice sounded tearful. "But we are the only relatives my brother has got. We want to see if we couldn't take him home and save the hospital expense. If the company doesn't pay nothing he won't be able to pay hospital bills—he's so poor—"

The Mother Superior softened perceptively. She remarked that the hospital was losing thousands on accident cases.

"And who are the other people with you?" she asked with a sweeping glance at the rest of us.

"This (pointing to Twist) is Mrs. Nikopopulos' brother and this (indicating me) is the man of the invalid carriage—he'd like to see if my brother could be moved," was Henk's ready answer.

For a moment I was nonplussed. His boldness, his deception, the whole incident seemed to me so much a stage scene in a farcical play, that I was robbed of speech. I am ashamed to confess that my silence under the circumstances was an unforgivable falsehood; and the only true excuse I can offer is that the whole thing was so brazen that I could not think quickly enough of how I could extricate myself of my equivocal position, and, besides, "the fictional interest" held me spellbound.

The Mother Superior pressed an electric button. A Sister presently appeared and led us to Nikopopulos' ward. We followed in grave silence . . .

*   *   *   *   *

The formal doctrinal rules that governed injury litigation between workers and their employers were not confined to the substantive issues of liability and damages. Although the tort doctrines that sketched the broad outlines of where an injured employee stood in the negligence system (given the particular facts and circumstances of his accident and injuries) were important, they were not the exclusive nor even the most important rules used to evaluate a worker's potential recovery. To understand the reality of the worker-initiated litigation, it is crucial to delve into the procedural law, both formal and informal, that governed the conduct of civil litigation. In short, it is important to understand the dynamic anatomy of a lawsuit. By way of illustration, this discussion will refer to the patterns of practice which emerged in the worker initiated actions brought against the corporate subject of this study, the American Steel and Wire Company.

The worker had first to obtain counsel on a contingent fee basis to pursue his injury claim. The contingent fee arrangement stipulated that if there was no recovery from the employer the lawyer would not get paid. The advantage to the worker was that if his suit was ultimately unsuccessful he would not incur any legal fees. If, however, there was a recovery from the employer the lawyer would take a percentage of the damages as his fee (in Cleveland the usual cut was twenty-five percent of any settlement obtained before trial and thirty-three percent if a matter went to trial).[37]

Before proceeding to seek counsel for an injury claim against the company, the worker had to consider the possible employment consequences following the filing of suit. Although it never surfaces in the court records or testimony concerning the American Steel and Wire Company, employers often brought extra-legal pressures to bear against injured workers to discourage their filing suit or even retaining a attorney to negotiate a settlement. Some companies had written contracts with their workers that required waiving in advance the right to file suit, in the event they sustained an injury on the job. Other concerns required that an injured worker returning to the job after a period of convalescence sign a release before being put back on the payroll.[38]

After being hired, the lawyer, armed with the alleged facts and circumstances of the injury, would ordinarily attempt to settle the case with the employer prior to filing suit. Failing to reach a settlement he would draft what was known as a "Petition" and file it with the court. Filing the petition formally initiated the lawsuit and invoked the court's jurisdiction over the parties. The petition itself was a legalistic narrative identifying the parties; the date, time and circumstances of the accident, including the alleged negligence of the employer; the nature and severity of the injury; and the consequential damages suffered by the injured employee. Always the petition concluded with a clause known as the "Prayer." The prayer requested the sum of money damages the employee claimed as fair compensation for the injuries suffered. Once the petition was filed, the Clerk of Court would have a bailiff effect "service of process" by delivering a copy of the petition, along with a court issued "Summons" to the defendant-employer. In the case of the American Steel and Wire litigation, process was served on the company when the bailiff went to the offices of the company (a few blocks from the courthouse) and attempted to personally deliver the petition and summons to the president of the firm, or, if the president was unavailable (as was usually the case), to a general manager or superintendent, and if the general manager or superintendent was not available, on down the corporate hierarchy until an officer or senior staff of the corporation was "served."

In the event the employer carried liability insurance, it would turn the court papers over to its liability insurance company. If the employer carried insurance, the liability policy would cover the legal defense costs and any settlement amount or court judgment rendered against the employer. In the case of the American Steel and Wire Company, petitions were turned over to the law firm of Squire, Sanders & Dempsey which represented the company in every worker suit filed. The company was "self-insured." As was true of many large companies, it carried no liability insurance and therefore had to pay for its own legal fees and settlement sums or a judgment, in the event that one was rendered, directly out of company funds.

The employer's counsel filed a responsive pleading to the petition called an "Answer." The answer was supposed to identify matters in the petition that the employer did not concede and therefore served to frame the contested issues for trial. For example, if the petition alleged that the defendant was a corporation formed under the laws of the State of New Jersey and doing business in Cleveland, Ohio, the answer of American Steel and Wire would admit that fact and it would not require proof at trial. However, when the petition alleged (as it invariably did) that the company was negligent in exercising control over its manufacturing operations and thereby (somehow) caused the worker's injury, the answer would deny any negligence on the part of the company, and allege contributory negligence on the part of the employee. This response would put the employee to his proof at trial. The answer was always a responsive document and, in the context of work injury litigation, raised the defenses of assumption of the risk, contributory negligence and the fellow servant rule. In the American Steel and Wire litigation, the answers rarely invoked assumption of the risk or the fellow servant rule, but invariably asserted contributory negligence on the part of the employee.

The next stage in the litigation sometimes involved filing motions and counter-motions—usually addressed to relatively minor procedural points intended to inconvenience the other side or to set up an advantageous strategic position for trial. In the American Steel and Wire litigation these preliminary motions were never dispositive of the lawsuit (excepting motions for removal, discussed below). During these preliminary phases there were no confrontations between the worker and the employer. All the petitioning, pleading and motioning were done through the court and primarily engaged the time and attention of the lawyers, not the parties. However, there were procedures for taking the depositions (sworn testimony) of parties and witnesses. Depositions generally involved subpoenaing the relevant witness to the office of the lawyer who wanted to make inquiry. The witness was sworn in by a court stenographer, who would then take shorthand notation of the exchange between the questioning counsel and the answering witness. On the rare occasions when they were used (depositions were costly) it was usually to "preserve" the testimony of crucial witnesses who would be unavailable for trial.

Usually within the second year following the filing of the petition, the matter would be set for trial. At trial, the "burden of proof" or the task of producing sufficient evidence to demonstrate liability fell upon the plaintiff-employee. The worker had to prove his case by a "preponderance" of the evidence. That is, the employee had to produce evidence that was, on balance, fifty-one percent persuasive when considered in combination with the employer's evidence. The employer was not required to prove anything until such time as an employee put on a case sufficient to meet the minimal factual requirements for a claim of negligence. At the conclusion of the plaintiff's case, the employer, who had the opportunity to cross-examine all of the plaintiff's witnesses, was given an opportunity to put on his own witnesses in support of the defense or defenses to the worker's claim. Note that the employer could request that the judge dismiss the worker's action before putting on its own case by contending, in essence, that the employee failed to meet his initial, or *prima facie*, burden of proof.

A trial could be either to a judge alone, in which case the judge would be both the "finder of fact" and the decider of law; or it could be to a jury, in which case the jury would act as the fact finder while the judge would retain the decision-making prerogatives on the procedural and evidentiary law. This often tenuous distinction of, and complex interaction between, "facts" and "law" and the consequently fluid theoretical border dividing the authority between the jury and bench was subject to considerable discretion on the part of the judge hearing the case. The judge had to determine and supervise procedural issues raised during the trial (such as ruling upon the admissibility of disputed evidence) always with the objective of giving the jury legally reliable facts upon which to base a determination as to liability and damages.

Ordinarily, the decision whether to try a case to a judge or a jury rested with the plaintiff-worker but the constitutional right to a jury trial extended to both parties to a lawsuit. If a plaintiff elected to try a case to a judge and the defendant agreed by waiving its right to jury trial, it would be a "bench trial." If a plaintiff chose to try the case to a jury (the more commonly elected alternative) then the defendant had to try its case to a jury. If a plaintiff elected to try his case to a judge but the defendant wanted a jury—then it would be tried to a jury. Ordinarily, if a worker elected to try a case to the bench, the defendant would readily waive its jury right. A bench trial assured the defendant-employer that even if there was going to be a plaintiff's verdict, the damages (a matter of "fact") would be determined by a seasoned legal professional, presumably less inclined to the empathetic excesses juries were supposedly heir to.

If the case was tried to a jury, the trial process would begin with *voir dire* or jury selection, a procedure where the lawyers would direct questions to prospective jurors to flush out any predispositions or biases on the part of individual jurors. To a very large extent, the selection process was an effort by the lawyers to give the potential jurors a preliminary education about what the relevant testimony would be.

During the period under study, the jury would always consist of twelve men because women were not yet electors and not qualified to serve on juries. In their capacity as finders of fact, the jurors decided the credibility of the testimony and evidence submitted by the parties. The question throughout the proceedings was: who produced the required fifty-one percent of the evidence? For example, if a "safety device" was legally required on a piece of machinery involved in the accident, and there was a conflict in the testimony as to whether the safety device was operative at the time—the worker's witnesses claiming that it was not, and the employer's witnesses claiming that it was—it was up to the jury to decide which of the witnesses to believe. As can be readily understood, this power to determine facts-in-issue was crucial to the juries' role and power in litigation and, as will be made clearer below, served to the great disadvantage of American Steel and Wire and corporate defendant-employers, generally.

Once impaneled and sworn, the jury listened to the opening statements of counsel, the worker's lawyer going first, then the employer's lawyer. Following the opening statements the plaintiff presented his "case," the evidence and witnesses, all of whom were subject to cross-examination by the employer's counsel. At the conclusion of the worker's case the employer could move for the judge to "direct a verdict" against the worker.

This matter of directed verdicts was a procedural manifestation of the dicey "facts-law" distinction and one that always lay, at least theoretically, within the discretion of the judge because a ruling on the motion was considered a matter of law and not a matter of fact. A motion for a directed verdict had to rest upon an interpretation of the facts that would lead the judge to believe that the law required that he "direct" the jury to return a verdict in favor of the employer. To the extent that was true, any granting of a motion for a directed verdict impinged upon the domain of the jury and its theoretically exclusive mandate to determine facts. In the federal courts, judges trespassed upon that domain with impunity, while in the state common pleas courts the judges deferred to juries more readily, at least in part because of Ohio's "Scintilla Rule."

The scintilla rule dated back to the Ohio Supreme Court's 1856 holding in the case of *Ellis & Morton v. Ohio Life Ins. & Trust Co.*[39] The *Ellis* appeal concerned a "nonsuit" granted in the trial of a case involving disputed commercial paper. "Nonsuit" was the term of art later supplanted by "directed verdict" and, for the purposes of this discussion, can be considered synonymous. After a general discussion of the constitutional principles involved in the right to jury trial and the approach taken by the courts in other states, the Ohio Supreme Court announced the following rule for all Ohio trial courts to follow when faced with passing upon the thorny facts-law dilemma:

> . . . When all the evidence offered by the plaintiff has been given, and a motion for a non-suit is interposed, *a question of law* is presented, whether the evidence before the jury *tends* to prove all the facts involved in the right of action and put in issue by the pleadings. In deciding this question, no finding of the facts by the court is required, and no weighing of the evidence is permitted. All that the evidence in any degree *tends* to prove, must be received as fully proved; every fact that the evidence, and all reasonable inferences from it, conduces to establish, must be taken as fully established . . .
>
> . . . (A motion for nonsuit) leaves nothing but the question whether, as a matter of law, each fact indispensable to the right of action has been supported by some evidence? If it has, no matter how slight it may have been, the motion must be denied; because it is the right of the party to have the weight and sufficiency of his evidence passed upon by the jury—a right of which, without his consent, the court is incompetent.[40]

This original statement of the Ohio rule, later disparagingly referred to by its opponents[41] as the "scintilla rule" (because a mere scintilla of evidence sufficed to "get a case to the jury") served to favor plaintiffs over defendants and empowered juries to decide matters that, at least in the federal courts and in some states, would be routinely and summarily disposed of by judges. One critic of the rule noted that variations of the plaintiff-favoring doctrine tended to prevail "in many states, more especially in those of the West and South."[42] The scintilla rule was abandoned in Ohio in 1934[43] but defined the terms upon which all contested civil cases, including work injury cases, were decided in Ohio throughout the period examined here.[44]

If the motion for directed verdict was not granted, and in the American Steel and Wire Company experience in the *state* courts it never was, then the defendant-employer had the opportunity to put on its own case. In this instance the plaintiff's attorney had the right to cross-examine the defense witnesses. At the conclusion of the defendant's case, the employer could again renew the motion for a directed verdict upon the same terms and issues as the initial motion.

In the probable event that the court declined to grant the employer's motion, the case would "go to the jury." The worker's attorney was then given an opportunity to make a two-part closing argument to the jury. At this point in time the lawyers were allowed to "argue" or embellish the case, as opposed to simply recounting facts to the jury. Within the lore of the profession, this was the stage of the trial where the very large verdicts were obtained. Freed from the pitiless shackles of fact, a clever and suitably dramatic plaintiff's lawyer could wax eloquent regarding the worker's pathetic, there-but-for-the-grace-of-God-predicament, especially as it contrasted with the defendant's relative comfort and evident good fortune. Once the worker's attorney was done with the first portion of his closing argument, the employer's counsel made his argument to the panel, whereupon the worker's attorney was again allowed one final harangue at the twelve men in the box. This obvious advantage was given to all plaintiffs in civil litigation because the "burden of proof" rested upon the plaintiff.

At the conclusion of counsels' arguments, the judge would then "instruct" the jury as to the law involved in the case. The instructions to the jury were usually oral, but the parties could request that written instructions be provided for the jury to take back into the deliberation room. If, in the course of deliberations there was some confusion, the jury could request that the court clarify the law on any given matter. Instructions of law from the bench to the jury included all the tort doctrines involved, evidentiary matters which the jury was bound to consider when evaluating the testimony of the witnesses (credibility, bias, etc.), and evidence which could be considered in determining damages—in the event the jury decided that the defendant-employer was liable.

Having received instructions on the law, the jury then deliberated on the controversy until all the members arrived at a unanimous verdict for either the plaintiff or the defendant. Once a verdict was returned, the losing party had the opportunity to move to vacate the verdict and request a new trial, usually upon the basis that some procedural error had been committed in the trial of the case. In the American Steel and Wire litigation only one new trial was granted in eighteen years, notwithstanding the company's numerous motions, and that was on the motion of the plaintiff-worker who claimed irregularities at trial when the jury returned a verdict in the worker's favor, but for the paltry sum of $50.

Within the context of work injury litigation, there was a severe practical problem presented to the injured employee. That problem was being able to sufficiently reconstruct the facts and circumstances of the work-accident at trial so as to meet his burden of persuasion. In this regard, the employer stood at a great tactical advantage. The accident occurred, with rare exception, upon the employer's private property, and the employer was in no way obligated to allow the injured worker or, more importantly, his attorney, to come onto the property to examine the machine or scaffolding or whatever contrivance was related to the manufacturing process that injured the worker-client. Further, witnesses to the mishap were almost invariably on the payroll of the defendant-employer and therefore subject to dismissal if they appeared overly cooperative with the injured worker's lawyer.[45]

*   *   *   *   *

Having slipped past the austere Mother Superior with his ingratiating small talk and familial ruse, Henk and entourage are escorted to suffering Nikopopulos' bedside.

We found our victim writhing in pain, scarcely conscious. He was badly injured. I learned that after his release, he moved away from his former dwelling and for want of funds with which to buy new tools and resume his trade, went to work in a tool factory, where he was caught in a wheel and sustained these injuries.

As soon as the Sister left, an "interne" came in. He beamed jovially upon Henk and shook hands with him.

"Hello, Doc," Henk greeted him cordially. "Is it as good as it first appeared to you?" (this in a lowered tone).

"Better," the white-clad young physician spoke through his teeth, while he was pretending to feel the patient's pulse. "I had some job keeping the other lawyers and 'runners' away. What did you tell the Mother Superior?"

"The old gag—I am his brother"; Henk showed all his rotten teeth at once as he laughed.

The physician laughed, too. "You're a bird," he commented.

Henk then introduced me, and I noticed them exchange glances.

In the meanwhile, the grief-stricken wife had settled upon the edge of her husband's bed and was patting his arm tenderly.

"I don't believe he is conscious," the physician murmured. Henk then produced a typewritten sheet and fountain pen while the "interne" stood at the door as if guarding it.

"Ask her if he can write?" Henk inquired of Twist.

She answered in the negative.

Henk then placed the fountain pen in the hand of the unconscious Nikopopulos and, addressing Twist, said, "Tell her when he puts his mark on the paper we'll get her the fifty thousand."

The imprint of a cross having been made through the skillful dexterity of Henk, he placed the typewritten sheet in his inside coat pocket, and the interne stepped forward.

"The usual divvy," murmured Henk.

"I think I ought to get a little more in this case," bargained the physician. "I ran some risk this time. The Mother Superior suspected."

"Mark will make it all right," Henk assured him.

The interne disappeared.

"Now we must go to see the witnesses," Henk turned to me.

"I thought you said you had them."

In answer to my remark, Henk lifted his eyes ceiling ward with a funny grimace on his face and said, "Come along and learn the rest of the game . . ."

*   *   *   *   *

Having reviewed the substantive tort law of employer liability and damages, and the basic procedural rules governing civil litigation and trial practice, it is now necessary to turn to one final aspect of the "rules of the game:" jurisdiction. During the period under consideration, there were two primary forums that could hear work injury cases originating in Cleveland, Ohio. The focus of the discussion so far has been upon the Cuyahoga County Court of Common Pleas, state courts which had the power to hear most of the work accident suits arising in the Cleveland area.[46] But the common pleas court shared its broad jurisdiction with another trial forum, the United States Sixth Circuit Court for the Northern District of Ohio, Eastern Division. Located mere blocks away from the county courthouse, the federal circuit court sat in a jurisprudential world apart from the common pleas court whenever its jurisdiction was successfully invoked over worker injury suits.

To understand the course of the employee litigation against the American Steel and Wire Company, it is crucial to examine the federal court's role in the company's experience under "common law compensation." Over the eighteen year period examined (1898-1915), there was a sympathetic, informal, but very real alliance between the American Steel and Wire Company, its attorneys, Squire, Sanders & Dempsey and the federal judiciary. This alliance of the like-minded allowed the company to use the federal court as a kind of jurisdictional backstop against the onslaught of worker-initiated injury litigation.[47] Unfortunately, discussion of the distinction between the state court system and the federal court system, the extent to which their jurisdictions sometimes overlapped, and how and why this overlapping was significant, necessarily wanders into treacherously complex and esoteric areas of legal theory and practice. However, an understanding of the differences between the two court systems and how the American Steel and Wire Company, along with other large "foreign" concerns, was able to summon the aid of the federal courts against the rising tide of worker litigation will provide considerable assistance in understanding the evolving corporate policy formulation and advocacy that contributed so much to the eventual nationwide adoption of the workmen's compensation reform.[48]

In describing the unique geographic, social, economic, and jurisdictional features of the litigation conducted in the United States Circuit Courts in the Sixth Circuit, then Senior Circuit Judge, William Howard Taft, provided the following sketch for his 1897 contribution to the (Ohio) *Bench and Bar*:

> The Sixth Circuit embraces the four great States of Michigan, Ohio, Kentucky and Tennessee. It reaches from Lake Superior to

Lookout Mountain and embraces within its jurisdiction nearly all the different types of American manhood. Its population is great, and its commercial, farming, manufacturing and mining interests are enormous. Though rich in itself, much of the wealth of the Eastern States is invested within its borders, and this circumstance leads to litigation of great magnitude in its Federal courts by reason of their jurisdiction over controversies between citizens of different States . . .[49]

A goodly portion of what Taft candidly referred to as "the wealth of the Eastern States" was represented in the theretofore unheard of capital aggregation organized under the umbrella of the United States Steel Corporation and its Cleveland-based subsidiary, the American Steel and Wire Company of New Jersey. As Taft pointed out, federal court jurisdiction extended to "controversies between citizens of different states" and while employees injured in the diverse Cleveland facilities of the company were residents, and therefore citizens, of Ohio, the American Steel and Wire Company was considered a "citizen" of New Jersey.[50]

The pre-emptive procedural device used by "foreign" (out-of-state chartered) corporations to get worker suits out of the state common pleas court and into the local federal court was known as "removal."[51] Although not mentioned in the federal Constitution and unknown at common law, removal procedure was provided for in the First Judiciary Act passed by Congress in 1789. Removal jurisdiction thereafter continuously expanded through a succession of federal statutes that culminated, in 1887, in the act of Congress so often invoked by the American Steel and Wire Company.[52] That statute provided that any "foreign" defendant, sued in a state court (in this case the Cuyahoga County Common Pleas Court) could, if sued for more than $2,000, remove the action to the federal court. The removal procedure was only available to "foreign" or out of state resident defendants and required that the prayer of the plaintiff's petition request at least $2,000 in damages.

Initiating the removal procedure in the state court was *pro forma*. All the foreign defendant had to do was file a "Petition for Removal" and post a bond, alleging that the defendant was an out of state resident and that the local plaintiff had requested more than $2,000 in damages. Upon the filing of the $500 bond, the common pleas court automatically lost jurisdiction over the matter,[53] and the case would be transferred to, and decided in, the nearest federal court. As has been pointed out, this rather anomalous jurisdiction worked only in favor of defendants and sometimes led to the federal court hearing cases that it otherwise may have had no "original" jurisdiction to hear. Nonetheless, the procedure was never seriously challenged and was considered quite constitutional during the period under consideration here.[54]

However, just because it was possible to get a case into the federal circuit court doesn't explain why an employer-defendant would want to do so. In part, the answer was that, procedurally, the federal court proved a far more accommodating forum for employer-defendants in a typical work injury suit. The appointed (as opposed to elected) federal judiciary was, as a rule, a more conservative lot than most of their state court brethren. The trial procedures of the federal courts were decidedly more defendant-favorable. With no binding "scintilla rule" judge-directed verdicts in favor of employers were the rule rather than the exception of federal trial practice.[55] Federal jury trials were exceedingly rare in any event, in large measure because of the "puissant"[56] federal judges who guarded their procedural decision making prerogatives jealously. When jury trials did occur, the federal judges not only controlled but, in the Sixth Circuit, actually conducted jury selection in lieu of counsel. When charging the jury before submitting a case to them, the federal judges, unlike their state court counterparts, were allowed to "comment" upon the evidence. Finally, the federal bench took an active and proprietary role in policing the plaintiff's bar in their relations with their worker-clients, especially in reducing the lawyers' percentage share in their contingency fee arrangements[57] thereby discouraging any plaintiff's attorney from long considering an over-zealous prosecution of an injured worker's cause.

Additionally, removal to the federal court added substantial costs to the suit that had to be paid either by the worker or his counsel. Judge Taft acknowledged this problem 1908 when he wrote, "The court officers, the clerk and the marshal, have not failed, especially in the Federal courts, to make the litigation as expensive as possible."[58] A contemporaneous study done comparing litigation costs in the state and federal courts in Cleveland found that at the trial level federal costs were three times as high if a case settled, and almost five times as high for cases that went to trial. Federal appeals, which had to be prosecuted in Cincinnati, Ohio, ran to more than a year's wages for most workers, averaging $574 in the four appeals examined. (See Appendix.) Finally, the delays in federal court cost the plaintiff-workers money, because it put inordinate pressure on the client and lawyer to accept lower settlement offers so as to get matters finally resolved. Non-fatal injury cases took an average of six months longer to work through federal court, and if a worker took his chances and won at trial, an employer's appeal would effectively negate the verdict for years, even if the favorable judgment was eventually upheld.[59]

Moreover, the advantages that devolved to the employer-defendant who could remove a case to federal court were not merely procedural and institutional. Once removed to the federal court the worker usually found that the substantive rules of employer liability changed as well. Simply stated, the federal courts did not consider themselves bound by the common law of the state where the accident occurred. Thus, to the extent each state's decisional law developed different, albeit usually minor, variations in the substantive rules governing negligence actions, those variations, taken together, provided a kind of doctrinal smorgasbord from which the federal bench could pick and choose for the authority to support the desired outcome (usually employer-favorable) in a work injury suit.

The basis for this wide discretion vesting in the federal judiciary was contained in a section of the First Judiciary Act of 1789. The language in question,[60] known as the Rules of Decision Act, later obtained a judicial gloss from the Supreme Court in the pivotal case of *Swift v. Tyson*[61] decided in 1842. Justice Story's opinion in *Swift* effectively licensed the federal bench to ignore the local peculiarities of the state decisional law where an action arose. The practical effects of this doctrinally facile approach to the "rules of decision" was cogently demonstrated and legally reinforced in the Ohio-originated, federal circuit court case of *Baltimore & Ohio Railroad Company v. Baugh*, 149 U.S. 368, (Fed. 1893), decided on appeal by the United States Supreme Court. The *Baugh* case was both an articulation of, and additional constitutional authority for, the federal judiciary's abiding conservatism in determining matters between employers and employees. It, perhaps more than any other single decision from the period, illustrates how the federal courts went about providing legal sanctuary to large, nationally-based corporate concerns during the late nineteenth and early twentieth centuries.

John Baugh was a fireman employed by the Baltimore & Ohio Railroad. On May 4, 1885 he was assigned to a "helper" locomotive engine along with an engineer by the name of Hite. A helper engine temporarily attaches to freight trains, usually to assist the train's own engine get a particularly heavy load up a long or steep grade. On the day in question, in company with, and under the direction and control of, the engineer, one Mr. Hite, Baugh stoked on the helper engine escorting a freight train out of Bellaire, Ohio, up an approximately twenty mile-long grade. As planned, at the top of the grade the helper engine detached from the train to return back to Bellaire. Ordinarily, there were two ways for a helper engine to safely return to its starting point. Upon special instructions from a regional dispatcher it could return to its terminal on track that the dispatcher knew to be clear. The other and more usual method was known as "flagging back." Under this procedure the helper engine would fall in closely behind a regularly scheduled train that had a pre-arranged right of way on the section of track leading back to the helper's destination. The lead, regularly-scheduled train would carry flags signaling the helper's trailing position, thereby alerting any trains awaiting clearance on a siding that the helper engine was following close behind.

On that day in May, Hite, the engineer, in clear violation of B.& O. policies, elected to return to Bellaire without either a dispatcher's clearance or a regularly scheduled train's "flag-back" lead. Apparently, Hite believed that if they came upon any trains coming from the other direction he could (somehow) quickly maneuver his locomotive onto a siding to await the other train's passing before again proceeding on to Bellaire. Hite's ill-conceived stratagem led straight to disaster: the helper engine collided with a regularly scheduled passenger train proceeding in the opposite direction, causing Baugh to sustain severe injuries, including an amputated right arm and paralyzed right leg.

Baugh filed suit against the B.& O. in the Belmont County Court of Common Pleas. By virtue of its incorporation in the state of Maryland and the large amount of damages requested in Baugh's "prayer," the B.& O. obtained removal of the action from the common pleas court to the federal Circuit Court for the Southern District of Ohio.

In the trial to a jury in the federal court, Baugh introduced the written policies of the road which clearly established that Hite, the engineer, was delegated the authority to run the engine in lieu of a conductor (none being present on the helper once it detached to return to Bellaire). Thus, by reason of the engineer's being automatically "promoted" for lack of a conductor, Baugh, a mere fireman, was under Hite's authority and direction. At the conclusion of Baugh's case the road moved for a nonsuit (directed verdict) against the fireman. The motion was overruled. The B.& O. did not put on a case. The circuit judge presiding over the trial instructed the jury that if Hite and Baugh were fellow servants then Baugh could not recover from his employer, inasmuch as Hite's negligence was admitted and the fellow servant rule exempted the B.& O. from liability for injuries sustained as a consequence of a fellow servant's carelessness. However, in conformance with the long established rule of the Ohio courts limiting the scope of the fellow servant defense when the negligence was attributable to a *superior* employee (recall *Little Miami Railroad v. Stevens*, (1856)) the trial judge went on to instruct the jury that if they found that Hite had properly constituted authority over Baugh at the time of the collision, then he was not a fellow servant. In that event, the court said, Hite was an agent of the employing road, and Hite's negligence was the B.& O.'s negligence. The jury returned a verdict in favor of Baugh for $6,750. The B.& O. took the case to the Supreme Court of the United States.

The United States Supreme Court reversed the circuit court and remanded the matter for a new trial. In a wide-ranging discussion of the fellow servant rule and its many variations in the individual states, the Court's majority concluded that it was the job of the federal judiciary to apply the rules of "general law"—a matter of the federal judge's own judgment, "uncontrolled by the decisions of the courts of the several States." Just how a federal judge was to determine the proper "general law" without reference to the forum state's own merely "local" doctrines was then demonstrated in the majority opinion written by Justice Brewer. Before deciding that the instruction to the jury regarding the Ohio exception to the fellow servant rule was in error, Brewer reviewed numerous cases decided by the highest appellate tribunals of Minnesota, Kansas, New York, Massachusetts and Michigan as well as sundry federal decisions (including some of the Supreme Court's own opinions) which Brewer, and hence the majority, felt had been particularly successful in divining the fellow servant rule of "general jurisprudence:"

> . . . all the cases proceed upon the ground of some breach of a positive duty resting upon the master, or upon the idea of superintendence or control of a department. It has ever been affirmed that the employe assumes the ordinary risks incident to service; and, as we have seen, it is as obvious that there is risk from the negligence of one in immediate control as from one simply a co-worker. . .
>
> . . . In other words, an employe carelessly manages an engine, and another employe who happens to be near enough is injured by such carelessness. It would seem, therefore, to be the ordinary case of the injury of one employe through the negligence of another.[62]

Therefore, the B.& O.'s own regulations notwithstanding, Baugh's plight was merely "the ordinary case" of one employee injuring another employee. Note that the opinion employs a doctrinal one-two punch, pairing the fellow servant rule with a follow up jab of assumption of the risk. Artfully combined, the two defenses provide a kind of endless onion of syllogistic reason upon reason to deny recovery to the luckless co-worker "who happens to be near" the resulting accident.

The *Baugh* case served to enshrine the broad discretion of the federal bench to pick and chose from the bountiful common law smorgasbord of the several states in support of their individual conclusions of exactly what "general," as opposed to merely "local," law controlled any given fact pattern. But far more remarkable than the longstanding efficacy of the rule re-affirmed by the majority opinion in *Baugh,* was the starkly contrasted and scathingly blunt dissenting opinion penned by Justice Stephen J. Field.

Field begins his dissent by reviewing the procedural history of the case (the majority opinion neglected to mention that Baugh originally brought his suit in state court). He then goes on to ridicule the "legal ether" proposed in the majority opinion by suggesting that "general law" was nothing more or less than the thinly disguised personal preferences of the individual federal judges:

> . . . I cannot assent to the doctrine that there is an atmosphere of general law floating about all the States, not belonging to any of them, and of which the Federal judges are the especial possessors and guardians, to be applied by them to control judicial decisions of the state courts whenever they are in conflict with what those judges consider ought to be the law . . .[63]

> I am aware that what has been called the general law of the country—which is often little less than what the judge advancing the doctrine thinks at the time should be the general law on a particular subject—has been advanced in judicial opinions of this court to control the conflicting law of a State. I admit that learned judges have fallen into the habit of repeating this doctrine as a convenient mode of brushing aside the law of a State in conflict with their views. And I confess that, moved and governed by the authority of the great names of those judges, I have, myself, in many instances, unhesitatingly and confidently, but I think now erroneously, repeated the same doctrine . . .[64]

*Mea culpa*s dispensed with, Justice Field turns to the anomalous circumstance of a "foreign" corporation prevailing upon rules quite different from those provided by the law of the state where the action arose.

Having already noted the initial filing of the action in Ohio's own Belmont County Court of Common Pleas, Field continued:

> . . . This court thus assumes the right to disregard what the judicial

authorities of that State declare to be its law, and to enforce upon the State some other conclusion as law which it has never accepted as such, but always repudiated. The fireman, who was so dreadfully injured by the collision caused by the negligence of the conductor of the engine (Hite) that his right arm had to be amputated from the shoulder and his right leg was rendered useless, could obtain some remedy from the company by the law of Ohio as declared by its courts, but this court decides, in effect, that that law, thus declared, shall not be treated as its law, and that the case shall be governed by some other law which denies all remedy to him. Had the case remained in the state court, where the action was commenced, the plaintiff would have had the benefit of the law of Ohio. The defendant asked to have the action removed, and obtained the removal to a Federal court because it is a corporation of Maryland, and thereby a citizen of that State by a fiction adopted by this court that members of a corporation are presumed to be citizens of the State where the corporation was created, a presumption which, in many cases, is contrary to the fact, but against which no averment or evidence is held admissible for the purpose of defeating the jurisdiction of the Federal court . . . Thus in this case a foreign corporation not a citizen of the State of Ohio, where the cause of action arose, is considered a citizen of another state by a fiction, and then, by what the court terms general law of the country . . . is given immunity from liability in cases not accorded to a citizen of that State under like circumstances. Many will doubt the wisdom of a system which permits such a vast difference in the administration of justice for injures like those in this case, between the courts of the State and the courts of the United States.[65]

Justice Field's dissent notwithstanding, the *Baugh* decision controlled work injury litigation in the federal courts throughout the period of policy formulation leading up to the workmen's compensation reform. As we shall see from the study of the American Steel and Wire Company's experience, the *Baugh* decision established the distinctly *federal* rules of the game.

Notes

1. Testimony of John Sykes, representing the American Society of Carpenters and Joiners, before the Ohio Employers' Liability Commission sitting in Cleveland, Ohio, November 2, 1910. Employers' Liability Commission of Ohio, *Report to the Legislature* (Columbus: F.J. Heer, 1910), Vol. II, 223.

2. Ibid., Eastman, 188. Eastman sat on the Employers' Liability Commission of New York.

3. Ibid., 220.

4. The phrase appears in a piece written by one of the reform's most articulate and avid promoters: E. H. Downey, "The Present Status of Workmen's Compensation in the United States", *American Economic Review*, March 1922, 129.

5. *Tort* is French for "wrong," from the Latin *tortus* or "twisted." "A civil wrong for which the remedy is a common law action for unliquidated damages, and which is not exclusively the breach of a contract or the breach of a trust or other merely equitable obligation." John William Salmond, *Law of Torts* (London: Sweet & Maxwell, 5th Ed., 1920), 7.

6. The stark contrasts between the federal and state forums will become clearer in subsequent chapters. For now, it will suffice to suggest that Mr. Sykes' son would have probably fared far better had his case been litigated in the state common pleas court, instead of the federal circuit court where it was "thrown out" because of the fellow servant rule.

7. See Appendix.

8. See Note 4.

9. Most scholars identify the Massachusetts case of *Brown v. Kendall*, 6 Cush. 292, (Mass. 1850) as the seminal articulation of the abandonment of trespass in favor of a fault-based negligence theory of tort recovery, but see Horwitz, Ibid., 90.

10. Ibid., Friedman, 468.

11. *Prosser and Keeton on the Law of Torts*, W. Page Keeton, Ed. (St. Paul: West Publishing Co., 5th Ed., 1984), Section 28, 160, 161.

12.   The first judicial pronouncement of the fellow servant rule is contained in the English case *Priestly v. Fowler*, 3 M.&W. 1, 150 Eng. Rep. 1030 (1837).

13.   Justice Lemuel Shaw is generally given the credit (or blame) for establishing the American variant of the English rule in the decision he authored on behalf of the Massachusetts Supreme Court in *Farwell v. Boston & Worcester Railway*, exonerating the railway for injuries Farwell sustained in an employee-caused accident, 4 Metc. 49, (Mass. 1849). Shaw also penned the early classic negligence case *Brown v. Kendall.*

14.   *Little Miami R. Co. v. John Stevens,* 20 Ohio St. 416, (1856).

15.   Railroads were veritable hotbeds of legal and corporate experimentation in the pre-compensation responses to work injuries. For an example of railroad path-breaking see: Walter Licht, *Working for the Railroad: The Organization of Work in the Nineteenth Century* (Princeton: Princeton University Press, 1983); in the Canadian context see: Paul Craven, "Law and Railway Accidents, 1850-80" presented before the Canadian Law in History Conference, Ottawa, June, 1987.

16.   *Superior officer and fellow servant defined,* 87 Ohio Laws 150.

17.   101 Ohio Laws 195.

18.   The classic application of the defense is to a spectator injured at a baseball game. If a foul ball struck an inattentive or slow-to-react fan, he or she was usually deemed to have assumed the risk of injury by electing to attend the game—where foul balls are to be expected.

19.   Consider the "Third Amended Petition" of Egnac Komorowski concerning the circumstances of the horrific burns he sustained in a boiler explosion at American Steel and Wire:

> . . . that after the repairs were made on (the) boiler . . . it was discovered that (the) mud drum continued to leak; that Plaintiff called this to the attention of his foreman . . . whose orders under his said employment he was required to obey, and that (the) foreman informed this Plaintiff that it was all right and assured him that there was no danger from the leaking of the mud drum, and then and there ordered and directed him to fire said boiler, and that Plaintiff, relying upon said assurance, continued in said service and performed said labor as directed . . .

The company settled with Komorowski for $6,200, the highest settlement (of record) in the 18 years of worker litigation against the Steel Corporation subsidiary. *Egnac Komorowski vs. American Steel and Wire Company*, United States Circuit Court for the Northern District of Ohio, Case No. 7318 (1907).

20. *Act to make employers liable in damages for injuries caused by negligence in the inspection and repair of machinery, etc.*, 95 Ohio Laws 114.

21. The ameliorating role of juries in worker injury actions will be treated at length in Chapter IV.

22. 101 Ohio Laws 195. As will appear below, the statute's language simply codified longstanding Ohio trial practice. Ohio juries were traditionally given very broad discretion in deciding the liability and damage issues in negligence actions.

23. *Robert Bycraft v. Lake Shore & Michigan Southern Railway Co.*, 8 Ohio N.P. 588 (1894), 594.

24. The Ohio Employers' Liability Commission did sponsor a thorough statistical study of *death* cases in Cuyahoga County between 1905 and 1910, and a more cursive and muddled study of non-fatal injuries. See Appendix. As will appear below, these "wrongful death" cases were typically less "valuable" precisely because of the exclusion of pain and suffering from the compensable elements of damages.

25. *Mansfield Railway v. Barr*, 2 Ohio App. 367, (1914); *McWeeny v. Standard Boiler & Plate Co.*, 210 F. 507, (1914).

26. Two unusual cases that attempted to distinguish between pecuniary damages and suffering damages were: *Lake Shore & M. S. R. Co. v. Topliff*, 6 O.C.D. 23, (Ohio 1895); and a federal court opinion written by Judge Taft, *Olmstead v. Distilling and Cattle Feeding Co.*, 9 Ohio F. Dec. 288, (1895). Interestingly, both cases, the former from a state appellate court and the latter a federal "trial" level decision, agreed that "pain and suffering" awards amounting to approximately 1/3 of the plaintiff's pecuniary damages were appropriate, although neither court actually endorsed a mathematical formula for such determinations.

27. *Interurban Ry. & Terminal Co. v. Beirman*, 21 O.C.D. 663, (Ohio 1910); *Greve v. Cincinnati Traction Co.*, 27 Ohio Dec. 625, (1913).

28. A verdict for $40,000 was upheld in 1916 for a 43 year old, permanently disabled man who, prior to the accident, had been earning $15,000 per year. *Wallis v. Moore*, 26 Ohio Dec. 250, (1916).

29. Thus, a man earning approximately $35 per month was held entitled to recover $2,950 for injuries which prevented him from continuing in his trade: *Street Ry. Co. v. Rohner*, 6 O.C.D. 706, (1895); whereas a

permanently disabled "first class engineer" earning $110 per month was deemed entitled to a verdict of $19,000: Ibid., *Lake Shore v. Topliff.*

30. *Lowry v. Mt. Adams & Eden Park Incline Plane R. Co.*, 68 F. 827, (Fed. 1895); Ibid., *Lake Shore v. Topliff.*

31.   Archibald R. Watson, *Damages for Personal Injuries* (Charlottesville: The Mitchie Company, 1901).

32. The Ohio wrongful death statute was passed in 1851.

33. 91 Ohio Laws 408. The original Ohio wrongful death statute set a damage limit of $5,000.

34. *Steel v. Kurtz*, 28 Ohio St. 191, (1876); *Hall's Adm'x. v. Crain*, 2 Dec. Repr. 453, (Ohio 1860).

35. The Illinois Employers' Liability Commission did a study of fatal accidents and concluded that average recovery amounts varied with the decedent's occupation:

Skilled trainmen	$1,000
Steelworkers	$874
Railroad laborers	$617
Skilled building tradesmen	$348
Unclassified workmen	$311
Skilled electric railway employees	$310
Miscellaneous trades	$292
Packing house employees	$232
Mine workers	$155
General laborers	$154
Electrical railway laborers	$75
Teamsters	$0
Building laborers	$0

Reprinted in OELC, *Report*, Vol I, xxxi.

36. "St. Agnes Hospital" was a thinly disguised reference to Cleveland's own St. Alexis Hospital located adjacent to the heavy industries of the city's Flats (or as Brudno refers to them in *The Jugglers* "the Dumps"). St. Alexis, like St. Agnes, was a Catholic charity hospital and had special arrangements with many of the large employers in the area to provide acute-care to their work-injured employees. Over time, St. Alexis developed a reputation for its special expertise in industrial medicine.

37. OELC, *Report*, Vol. I, xli.

38.	There was a curious dearth of testimony before the Ohio Employers' Liability Commission regarding these aspects of employee injury suits against their employers. Whether and to what extent these tactics were used against employees was probably a matter of each employer's own policies, and likely, they were not freely discussed with investigators. See Edward A. Purcell, Jr., *Litigation and Inequality: Federal Diversity Jurisdiction in Industrial America, 1870-1958* (New York: Oxford University Press, 1992), 38,39.

39.	*Ellis & Morton v. Ohio Life Ins. & Trust Co.*, 4 Ohio St. 628, (1856).

40.	Ibid., 635. The emphasis is the court's.

41.	The rule's detractors were legion and powerful. Judge William Howard Taft took pains to distinguish the Ohio rule from the federal practice when he sat on the U.S. Sixth Circuit Court of Appeals, in *Ewing v. Goode*, 78 F. 442, (Fed. 1897). But there were many in the state, as well as federal, judiciary who fought against the rule's acceptance. *Quay v. Quay*, 4 Nisi Prius N.S. 529, (Ohio 1906).

42.	Address of George Alger to the New Jersey State Bar Association, June 13, 1914. 10 Ohio Law Bulletin, 375.

43.	*Hamden Lodge v. Ohio Fuel Gas Co.*, 127 Ohio St. 469, (1934).

44.	As Alger noted, how the judge-jury line was drawn followed a regional pattern. Judges were not allowed to comment on evidence to the jury in most of the American states up until 1913. The states that preserved that prerogative for the bench were: Vermont, New Hampshire, Connecticut, Rhode Island, New York, New Jersey, Pennsylvania, Minnesota and Wisconsin. The federal courts also preserved that common law power for judges. Kenneth A. Krasity, "The Role of the Judge in Jury Trials: The Elimination of Judicial Evaluation of Fact in American State Courts from 1795 to 1913", 62 *University of Detroit Law Review* 595, 595.

45.	Crystal Eastman noted the tactical problems workers encountered trying to prove their cases:

> . . . The burden of proof, as we have seen, rests upon the plaintiff. He can do nothing without witnesses, and his only witnesses in the majority of cases are his foreman and his fellow workmen, employes of the same company. It stands to reason that they will not as a rule testify freely against their employer. It would take a large-minded employer to retain in his service a man who had deliberately and knowingly spoken against his interests. And even though it is true that in some large concerns an employe who thus

testified would not actually be discharged, nevertheless the fear of
dismissal would be likely to keep his mouth shut.

Ibid., Eastman, 187.

46. In Ohio, Justice of the Peace courts also had power to hear worker
injury claims, but their jurisdiction was limited to claims under $250. Thus,
up until 1910, when they were replaced by the Cleveland Municipal Court,
the J.P. courts could, and sometimes did, hear minor injury claims. However,
for all but relatively trifling injuries the court of general jurisdiction was the
Common Pleas Court of Cuyahoga County.

47. In his history of the federal courts and corporate diversity litigation,
Purcell argues that while the federal courts provided undeniable and
sometimes overwhelming advantages to corporate litigants, the favorable
conditions for large national corporations in the federal forum didn't
necessarily devolve from shared "social attitudes and values" between the
corporate interests and the federal judiciary. Purcell posits a more complex
tangle of legal and extra-legal factors that contributed to the business
corporation's advantages over individuals in the national courts. This
"balance of inequality" was part of what he terms a "social litigation
system," that favored large business enterprises both within and without the
legal system. Purcell, Ibid., 8.

48. The many advantages for national corporations litigating under
diversity jurisdiction in the federal courts are discussed at length by Purcell,
Ibid. Purcell's work identifies the many and expensive practical burdens
visited upon claimants who found their cases removed to federal court, in
addition to the corporation-favoring "federal common law" concocted by the
federal judiciary from the whole cloth of multiple, and sometimes
contradictory, state court precedents.

49. *Bench and Bar of Ohio*, ed. George Irving Reed (Chicago: The
Century Publishing & Engraving Company, 1897), Vol. II, 21.

50. Gates' initially consolidated firm was the American Steel & Wire
Company of Illinois, having been incorporated under the legal stewardship
of his Chicago-based corporate counsel, Elbert H. Gary. In 1899 the
company's charter was filed in New Jersey. The final, Morgan-financed trust
likewise chose New Jersey because its incorporation fees were much lower
than other potential incorporation states; its corporation statute was longstanding (1846) and stable; its corporate taxes were low; it allowed
corporations to write their own powers into their charters, almost without
limitation; and it had very favorable shareholder and director liability laws.
Ibid., Wilgus, 68-73.

51. The discussion that follows is, in the interest of brevity and clarity, focused on removal jurisdiction. Precedent conditions to that extraordinary procedure becoming available were that federal "diversity jurisdiction" exist as a result of a "foreign" defendant, in this instance a foreign *corporate* defendant, being named as a party in a state court proceeding. The "diversity" then, arose because the other party was a resident of a different state.

52. Act of March 3, 1887, 24 Stat. 552, corrected by Act of August 13, 1888, 25 Stat. 433.

53. If there was a dispute concerning the facts alleged in the Petition for Removal the issue would be resolved in the *federal* court.

54. Charles Allen Wright, *Law of Federal Courts* (St. Paul: West Publishing Co, 3rd Ed., 1976). Then Supreme Court Justice William Howard Taft, advocating in support of retaining federal diversity jurisdiction, again had occasion to voice concern for the "wealth of the Eastern States" when he wrote:

> . . . no single element in our governmental system has done so much to secure capital for the legitimate development of enterprises throughout the West and South as the existence of federal courts there with jurisdiction to hear diverse citizenship cases."

William Howard Taft, "Possible and Needed Reform in the Administration of Justice in the Federal Courts," 47 A.B.A. Rep. 250, (1922), 258-259. Compare the regionalism of Taft's observation with the remarks of George Alger to the New Jersey State Bar Association concerning the jury-empowering scintilla rule, notes 41 and 43, above.

55. This federal aversion to empowering juries and the Ohio-sanctioned "scintilla rule" was discussed at length by Judge Taft in the work injury case of *Vany v. R.B.F. Peirce*, 8 Ohio Dec. 691, (Fed. 1898); and a medical malpractice case, *Ewing v. Goode*, 7 Ohio Dec. 574, (Fed. 1897).

56. The description is Professor Wright's:

> A federal judge is a very puissant figure . . . He retains the powers that judges had at common law, including notably the power to comment on the evidence, though one of the results of Jacksonian democracy was to deny such powers to judges in most states. He is appointed for life, and need not justify his record to an electorate at regular intervals. In many respects he is given power unknown at

common law, because one of the principal ideas embodied in the rules that it is wise to leave many details of procedure to the informed discretion of the judge, acting in the particular case rather than regulating such details by rigid provisions.

Ibid., Wright, 482.

57. In the federal court all settlements and judgments were paid into the court Clerk who then distributed the proceeds to the worker and his lawyer pursuant to the terms dictated by the judge's signed order. This procedure was not followed in the common pleas court.

58. William Howard Taft, "The Delays of the Law," 18 *Yale Law Journal* 28 (1908), 35.

59. Purcell notes that removal to federal court invoked social and professional, as well as legal, norms and biases against the injured worker: "By the last quarter of the nineteenth century . . . the legal profession itself was dividing into elite and non-elite tiers, with the former servicing the corporations and the latter the individual middle-, lower middle, and working class litigants. 'The ordinary lawyer prefers to sue in a State court, when he has a choice, on account of his greater familiarity with the practice there. . . Many American lawyers have never brought an action in a federal court.'" Ibid., Purcell, 54, quoting Simon E. Baldwin, *The American Judiciary* (New York, 1905), 140-41.

60. ". . . the laws of the several states, except where the constitution, treaties, or statutes of the United States shall otherwise require or provide, shall be regarded as the rules of decision in trials at common law in the courts of the United States in cases where they apply.", 1 Stat. 92.

61. *Swift v. Tyson*, 41 U.S. 1, (Fed. 1842).

62. Ibid., 389, 390.

63. Ibid., 399.

64. Ibid., 401.

65. Ibid., 400-401.

I I I

Plaintives

"Well?" Kracha said.

The man looked up. "Is this where Mrs. Dobrejcak lives?

"Yes. What do you want?"

"Who are you?"

"Her father."

The man murmured something under his breath. Then he told Kracha what he had been sent to say, and after a while he went away.

Kracha had sunk down on his knees beside the window. Now, chilled, he raised his head heavily. The night was quiet, the street empty. The air was thick with smoke and fog; a little way in either direction street and houses faded into nothingness. It was silent and motionless, sharp in the throat, something that came with the night and would be gone with sunrise, as though lack of people in the street gave it opportunity to gather, just as in the morning people moving about would stir it and make it disappear.

Kracha got slowly to his feet, dust on the window sill dry against the palms of his hands. He lowered the window most of the way; then he went out of the room and across the landing to Mary's.

She was asleep. She had left the lamp burning low, no doubt because Agnes might awaken during the night, and the dim light threw shadows across the walls, the bed. Kracha looked down at his daughter. She was lying on her side, her lashes shadowy against her cheeks, her hair loose around her face. The lamplight found dull gleams in it.

> He let out his breath in a shuddering sigh, wondering why God had chosen him to do this dreadful thing to her. Then he put out his hand to touch her shoulder, to wake her and tell her that Mike was dead.[1]

The prospects for the workmen's compensation reform were accelerated and greatly enhanced by the shift in American turn-of-the-century immigration patterns from the formerly predominant "old," northern and western European groups to the "new," central, eastern and southern European groups.[2] Moreover, it was in large measure because of this work force transformation that the compensation reform amounted to a major (and largely unacknowledged) constitutional reordering of the American political economy that effectively demoted the American industrial worker from the theoretical status of co-equal with his employer to a courts-disenfranchised, legal dependent of his employer. To put it in different, but arguably "truer" if more discomforting terms, workmen's compensation was the legal acknowledgment and institutionalization of a new American proletariat class.

Of course, the past is never quite as neat and simple as any single historical construct. But as this case study will confirm, there *was* something different about these "new" immigrants: they were more "agrarian," more Catholic, somehow more "foreign" and less "American" than their old immigrant predecessors. Subjective though all these perceptions were, they were not without factual basis and were, in any event, real enough as perceptions. More importantly, these notions served to define very concrete ways of thinking about this swarm of newcomers to the American mills and factories.

The perceptions concerning these new immigrants sometimes emerged in unlikely ways and unlikely places. Take for example an exchange (in November of 1910) at the Cleveland hearings between Commissioner Winans and C.E. Mauer, a representative of the coal operators of eastern Ohio. Winans, one of the labor representatives on the Ohio Employers' Liability Commission, asks Mauer pointed questions about the realities of co-existence between workmen on the shop floor:

> Mr. Winans: . . . Here is a careless workman . . . who is a foreigner, over which the employe who is careful has no control. I want to say to you that 90 per cent of the employers today in the State of Ohio, if you were to object to working with these foreigners, who know little of the English language, would say, "I will take care of myself, you look after yourself."

Mr. Mauer: I think that is hardly fair. The foreign workman is a necessity in this country. We cannot get rid of the fact that the foreign workman is a necessity. The foreign labor is necessary for [a] certain class of labor. Why? Because the American workmen stand above that class of labor. We have got to have them, and we have got to handle them like children and take care of them like children.[3]

To the extent these new immigrants flocked to the American steel industry to man (and "child") the labor force, risking the extreme hazards involved in iron and steel manufacture, they were the principal objects of the steel industry's in-house policy formulations addressing the inter-related corporate problems of industrial safety and work injury litigation. The policies that were ultimately formulated by the Steel Corporation, (embodied in the American Steel and Wire Company's Accident Relief Plan) reflected the overwhelming numerical reality of these industrial migrants whose foreshortened, almost-American lives and limbs hung together in the social and equitable balance against the purely economic interests and frankly "nativist" sympathies of their employers. Crucial to this historical formulation is the following fact: The Steel Corporation's solution emerged as the American solution to the work injury dilemma. Thus, what appears at first blush as mere historical happenstance—the changing demographics of the steel-working labor force—became in social and legal fact a delimiting factor in the workmen's compensation legislative schemes that stand to this day, we are told, as legal and moral monuments to enlightened, Progressive American social policy.

So it is appropriate to consider these objects of corporate policy making—as subjects—who provided not only the labor to drive the mills, but served as the actuarial fodder for the Steel Corporation's finance officers to design a working, in-house, injury compensation plan. This chapter will examine the shift from the steel industry's "old" to "new" immigrant work force, some accident patterns in the many hazards of steel making generally, and finally, will turn to the specific traumatic and toxic perils common to the manufacture of the commodity American Steel and Wire monopolized, steel wire.

* * * * *

. . . True, the employer may protect himself by making it the bounden duty of the employe to report all defective and unsafe conditions, but the carrying out of this protective feature will be found impracticable, I might say impossible, particularly in industries employing men of mixed nationalities, the majority of them wholly unable to speak or understand the English language.[4]

*   *   *   *   *

The labor force transformation in the steel industry between 1890 and 1915 both reflected and exaggerated national immigration trends. As the steel industry expanded, doubling its manpower requirements between 1890 and 1900, the need for unskilled and semi-skilled workers increased exponentially. In its voluminous 1911 investigation the Senate-appointed Immigration Commission concluded that at least part of the "immigration problem"[5] resulted from this rapid growth in the manpower needs of the American steel industry. The influx of eastern and southern Europeans to the iron and steel works caused, in the words of the Commission's report, massive "racial displacements" within the steel working labor force.

> Prior to 1880 the iron and steel workers were exclusively of native stock or of races from Great Britain or northern Europe. During the early eighties a small number of eastern and southern Europeans entered the industry in Pennsylvania and the East. They gradually increased in numbers until 1890, after which year the employment of this class of immigrants became rapid and extensive. During the decade 1890 to 1900 the employment of the older immigrants from Great Britain and northern Europe also rapidly declined, as compared with former periods.[6]

Indeed, the transformation of the work force was profound and thoroughgoing. The Commission found that by 1910, 81.8% of the national steel working labor pool had been in the United States less than 10 years. The vast majority of these new arrivals were eastern and southern Europeans.[7]

The newcomers were most often forced to abandon their European homelands by the emerging discontinuity between local agricultural, land-based economies and burgeoning local populations. The resulting scarcity of land eventually left little to inherit among surviving children and drove the available farm prices far beyond the means of most young men. Often reduced to a choice between landless penury or migration, those who could raise the cost of passage (or had a relative send it from America) often chose to brave the New World where ready, unskilled and relatively high-paying industrial employment beckoned. Crucial to this migratory dynamic, and what distinguished these new arrivals from many of their emigre predecessors, was their resolve to return to their ancestral homes with savings earned in the American factories. The common dream was to use the savings to buy land for farming. Thus, for these displaced peasants and farmers, the American experience often started as a mere interlude, an adventure to secure a stake hold—less often was it their intention to stay in the very strange world across the Atlantic. And, in fact, many did return to their homelands: from 1908 to 1910 forty-four new immigrants left the United States for every hundred that arrived, well over half a million returning to Europe in the three year period. But overall, far more stayed than returned.[8]

Their common agrarian background was charted by the Senate Immigration Commission which sought (seemingly obsessively) characteristics that served to distinguish the newer "races" from their old immigrant counterparts. Whereas the older groups often brought acquired

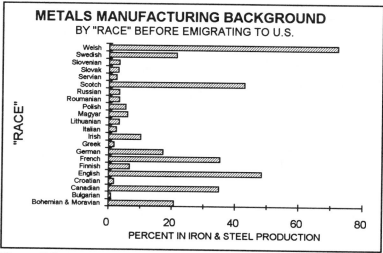

Figure 2 Source: *Immigrants in Industries*, 41.

iron and steel making skills with them to the new world, the new east and south Europeans were rarely employed in iron or steel production prior to coming to the American mills. Generalizing, the vast majority of the new immigrants worked on farms and had little or no experience with urban or industrial life, much less steel making. The Immigration Commission's study tracked this vast occupational gulf between the two groups, Figure 2.

As worker migrants they were twice removed from their new, industrial, often urban environs. Non-English speaking and predominantly Catholic, they lived and worked in a world apart from the English speaking native, Irish, English and German workers who preceded them to the mills. Their diverse languages and cultures relegated them to separate communities in the steel towns (local "Hunky Hollows" were a mill town commonplace) and in the plants they tended to congregate in separate departments and work crews where their co-linguist foremen could act as translators, go-betweens and arbiters with the English speaking managers.[9] Without exception the new immigrant groups were relegated to the bottom of the steel working hierarchy. They worked in the menial, low paying, "de-skilled" positions that were fast supplanting the older, craft-based occupations in iron and steel manufacture.[10]

The jobs they took were the dirtiest, hottest and typically, the most dangerous. In short, they would do the work that was scorned by the native born and old immigrant workers. ". . . only Hunkies work on those jobs," (in

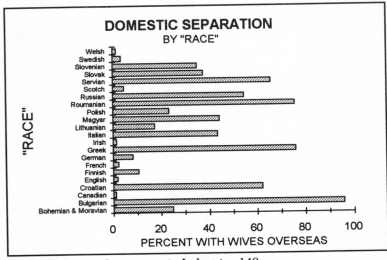

Figure 3 Source: *Immigrants in Industries*, 148.

the blast furnace) an investigator was told, "they're too damn dirty and too damn hot for a 'white' man."[11] The discrimination followed the immigrants in their new careers and played itself out over the entire promotional ladder of the industry.[12] A visiting Hungarian churchman, upon touring a Pittsburgh steel facility, lamented: "Wherever the heat is most insupportable, the flames most scorching, the smoke and soot most choking, there we are certain to find compatriots bent and wasted with toil."[13] The wages paid for these unskilled positions were predictably lower than for the more skilled positions held by the north and western Europeans and native born workers.[14]

Consistent with their status as industrial migrants, the newcomers lacked strong, local family ties, often working in the mills for years at a time without the benefit and support of their wives and children. In the sample surveyed by the Immigration Commission, patterns of domestic separation predominated in most of the new immigrant groups, see Figure 3. The "boarding boss" system accommodated these aggregations of married and single bachelors. When a wife was present in a household, the couple could open the home to countrymen who would then share in the domestic expenses by contributing some portion of their wages for room and board. The system worked surprisingly well given the cramped accommodations that were the rule. Here, the steel industry's infamous twelve hour day, seven day week, provided some relief—keeping the healthy boarders either working or sleeping, with little time to hang about the house, aggravating the boarding boss' wife in the already over-close quarters.

The grueling 84 hour week actually served the aspirations of those men who still planned to return to their villages in Europe. With so much work, there was little inclination, and even less energy or time, to spend the mill's hard won wages on entertainments or carousing. So long as there was work, the dream to return home as a propertied citizen held. "A good job, save money, work all time, go home, sleep, no spend."[15] But long periods of unemployment haunted the aspiring land owners, and the endemic boom-bust cyclical nature of the steel industry depleted many a savings account. Even steady and long standing work was no guarantee of a triumphant return to the homeland.

Sickness and work injuries ravaged savings too, especially without a family to nurse a man through a convalescence and provide for the bare household amenities required during a spell of disability. The single man or "married bachelor" could usually stay on at the boarding boss' home but could ill afford the cost. Without an income from the plant to offset the room, board and medical bills, too often dreams, as well as bodies, lay broken by mill mishaps and misfortune.[16]

*   *   *   *   *

We attempt to exclude foreigners who have come to this country and left their wives and families in the old country. We do not think that we should be obliged to send to any foreign country any large amount of money.[17]

*   *   *   *   *

Recalling the brain-damaged Felix Letmenski, and the problems his counsel encountered in federal court trying to prove exactly how the accident at his wire drawing machine actually happened,[18] let us return to our lately dumbstruck young advocate as he takes further instruction from Henk, runner *extraordinaire*, in the business of "getting witnesses in one's *mitt*," notwithstanding leery and uncooperative employers:

From the hospital Henk drove to The American Tool Company and on the way stopped to pick up a legless Slavish fellow. The tool manufacturing plant spread over many acres and was constructed in a u-shape. The enclosure was filled with a noise of whirring wheels, and the screeching of saws and the chuckling and snorting of engines.

Henk drove his car close to the office door and jumped out in a hasty manner as if every second meant life and death. I hurried after him. The Slavish fellow, whom he called Vlasek, limped along after us.

Henk approached one of the men in the office hastily, and asked to see an employee by the name of Vladislav Kolokolchick.

"We don't permit anyone to see the men at work," the office man in shirt sleeve responded, without looking up from his work.

"But this is most urgent, Mr.—most urgent," Henk spoke impressively, with a touch of pathos in his voice (while he was speaking he produced a leather cigar case from his vest pocket, stuck one cigar in his own mouth and held the case before the man inside the partition)—"Have a smoke."

The man took the cigar and as he was about to place it in his vest pocket, Henk struck a match, handing the light to the man in the office.

"Thanks. Can't smoke—against orders"; and he smiled rather good naturedly.

Henk leaned against the office railing, standing on one leg and crossing the other, and said in a confidential tone, "I am sorry for these Slovaks. This fellow Kolokolchick had saved and saved until he accumulated enough to buy a steamship ticket for his wife and kids, and now when they come across, the immigration authority would not let them land because one of the kids has a sore eye or something. The authorities demand a bond that the family won't become a public charge."

The man inside the railing raised a pair of sympathetic eyes. Henk instantly waxed eloquent.

"Fortunately," he added, "We have made a collection and will furnish the bond and we want him to start for New York immediately. Can't you help us out?" drawing at his cigar and leaning against the railing Henk looked beseechingly at the man in the shirt sleeves.

Without replying the man touched a button.

"Fetch Vlad Kolokolchick," he ordered.

"Thanks, ever so much," Henk spoke politely.

"Since that Greek—what's his name—Nikopopulos—was hurt the other day, about a dozen ambulance chasers have been here to bother us," explained the man somewhat apologetically, "So I have refused admittance to everybody."

"We won't intrude upon you here," Henk said, as he noticed the approach of a tall, sandy haired man, in an undershirt and sooty trousers, following the boy who had been ordered to fetch Kolokolchick; and thanking the man once more, we walked outside.

Now Vlasek was the interpreter. Henk had told him to tell Kolokolchick to come along with us and explain all about the accident.

"He say he can't lose a days wages," Vlasek interpreted.

Henk fished out a five dollar bill from his pocket and pushed it into Kolokolchick's hand.

"Tell him to come along with us and he'll get plenty of money," said the magnanimous Henk.

The Slovak's sooty face brightened. He crumpled the money

in his fist and nodded his head.

After some explanations from Vlasek, Kolokolchick went back into the factory, but soon returned, buttoning his shirt and pulling his coat on. Several workmen around the plant starred enviously at Kolokolchick as he got into the automobile.

* * * * *

There are several things which may occur to endanger the wire drawer. If the wire does not uncoil freely the reel may be dragged forward and crush him against the frame of the machine . . .[19]

Plaintiff further says that at times...the spindle would be subjected to vibrations and jerks, while the wire was being wrapped around . . .

. . . suddenly and without warning and while he was near said spindle the metal pin jerked loose, causing (the) spindle to burst through the iron door of the metal frame in which it was enclosed, and to strike plaintiff on the inner side of his right forearm lacerating and penetrating the flesh thereof at a point about three inches below the elbow and so severely injuring the right forearm that it has ever since been partially disabled and will forever remain so.

Petition, *Felix Krulikowski vs. American Steel and Wire Co.*, Case No. 134,103, Cuyahoga County Common Pleas Court
Date of Injury: July 20, 1912.

* * * * *

When William Hard's feature article about the South Chicago Works of the Illinois Steel Company, "Making Steel and Killing Men" appeared in *Everybody's Magazine* in November of 1907[20] it reached a large reading public and set off a fire storm of adverse publicity for Illinois Steel's parent firm, the United States Steel Corporation. Casualty managers for the subsidiary companies of the Steel Trust had begun meeting to discuss common safety concerns the year before. Five months following Hard's muckraking piece, Judge Elbert H. Gary, now President and Chairman of the Board of the Steel Corporation, chose one of these informal meetings of the casualty managers to announce the formation of the new, Corporation-sanctioned Committee of Safety.[21] Soon after the launch of what came to be known as the "Safety Movement," the federal Bureau of Labor Statistics and other investigators gained access to, and cooperation from, the steel industry in the effort to examine and compile records on mill accidents. Thereafter, what had been only local, uncoordinated and sporadic efforts to obtain reliable data on work injuries slowly evolved into a national and methodologically consistent approach to recording and analyzing accident information and statistics.[22]

One of the most exhaustive, long-term safety studies of any industry was conducted by the Department of Labor's Bureau of Labor Statistics and published in 1922 as "Causes and Prevention of Accidents in the Iron and Steel Industry, 1910-1919."[23] Another detailed, though earlier and less systematic study was included as the final volume in the massive *Labor Conditions in the Iron and Steel Industry.*[24] This report, *Accidents and Accident Prevention*, was a precursor to the 1922 study and just began to address some of standardization issues in the statistical gathering process that hampered uniform national data accumulation. A third study conducted by the Labor Department's Bureau of Labor Statistics, *The Safety Movement In the Iron and Steel Industry, 1907 to 1917,*[25] acted as a kind of bridge study between the 1913 and 1922 efforts. Subjected to the intensive analysis and extended, decade-long perspective provided by these early federal studies, very distinct patterns emerged in the statistical profile of steel mill accidents.

Of all the factors contributing to accidents, worker inexperience headed the list. Perhaps more than any other "worker factor" (excluding perhaps simple carelessness) a man's lack of job experience reliably predicted his liability to sustain a serious injury. At one large steel plant the job experience of injured workers was compared to their accident frequency rates[26] over a 5 month period. The results appear in Table 1, below. Plainly, a "green man" labored in harm's way at a steel mill.

Related to the matter of inexperience was another striking pattern in the steel industry accident rates: non-English speaking workers suffered accident frequency rates 2.3 times greater than native born workers and an accident

JOB EXPERIENCE AND ACCIDENT FREQUENCY RATES	
Period on the Job	Frequency Rate
6 Months and Less	37.1
6 Months to 1 Year	34.8
1 Year to 3 Years	28.9
3 Years to 5 Years	14.1
5 Years to 10 Years	6.6
10 Years to 15 Years	2.8
Over 15 Years	0

Source: *Causes and Prevention*, 167.

Table 1

over severity rate[27] 1.4 times that of the native born group. The Labor Bureau investigators deduced that the language deficiency undoubtedly contributed to the higher rates, especially when non-English speaking workers labored along side, or under the supervision of English speakers, but also speculated that the inexperience of the non-English speaking workers was a major aggravating factor.[28] In a same-plant study where the English/non-English accident rates were compared over an eight year period (1906-1913), another interesting, albeit predictable and discouraging, trend emerged. Whereas the native born and English-speaking, foreign born workers showed a definite improvement in both their frequency and severity rates over time, the higher rates among the non-English speakers proved relatively intractable, the much lauded, industry-wide Safety Movement's best efforts notwithstanding.

Nightfall was a killer-maimer. Industry wide, night time accident rates were always higher—even though the lower production levels and reduced work force for the night turns might have otherwise lowered injury rates. In large measure the problem was simply inadequate lighting, although the researchers suspected other factors that proved beyond statistical verification. Fatigue of the night shift workers was suggested as an aggravating factor (from lack of refreshing sleep during the warm daylight hours) but not conclusively proven. Investigators also suspected that a tendency for men to drink more heavily on the night turns contributed to higher accident rates, but again, conclusive verification was lacking. In only one plant could the investigators find a consistently enforced disciplinary policy against drinking on, or before going to, the job and even those records proved inconclusive.[29]

Investigators also looked for higher rates during certain times of day to try to verify what had been observed in other industries concerning a predictable "wave pattern" in plant frequency rates: the wave started low at the beginning of the shift, rose until midmorning, tapered down to noon, then rose again to mid-afternoon, and fell toward quitting time. The cause of this pattern was thought to be worker fatigue. However, no such clear pattern emerged in the steel industry figures because, the researchers speculated, other accident factors unique to the steel mills were so much stronger as to mask fatigue's significance in the accident "equation." Other factors examined were whether a worker's age or conjugal condition had any effect upon accident rates. Neither inquiry yielded anything conclusive.[30]

Soon after establishing the Committee of Safety, the Steel Corporation began compiling corporation-wide facts and figures involving mill accidents, both for in-house publication and distribution to sympathetic magazines. The Corporations's Bureau of Safety, Sanitation & Welfare began publishing charts and tables demonstrating the progress being made in the Corporation-wide safety initiative. Nearly always though, the publicists felt compelled to include an analysis of the first cause of nearly all industrial accidents, the workers themselves:

> Nearly one-half, or 44.78% of these accidents were attributed to "hand labor," and one third of those were due to falling material. The conditions under which these accidents occur are almost wholly within the control of the workmen and are largely due to their carelessness or thoughtlessness . . . In carefully analyzing the causes of any 100 accidents it will be found that at least 90 of them might have been prevented if a little more care had been exercised.[31]

Sometimes the charts and tables were irreconcilably inconsistent and contradictory. The contradictions might have resulted from the intended (and untutored) public audience for the safety data, and the assumption that no one would question the impressive array of facts and figures. The glaring deficiencies among and between the statistical categories (apparently "eyes" and "burns" *caused* 12% of all steel mill mishaps) might have been the result of the studied confusion of the publicists, rather than the ineptitude of

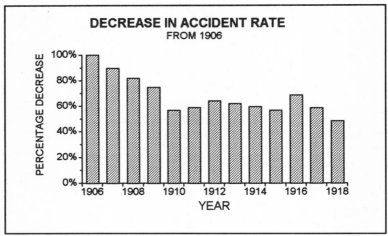

Figure 4   Source: U.S.S. Corp., Bureau of Safety, Sanitation & Welfare

the data gathering casualty managers.

According to the industry's count, the accident rates did improve once the Safety Movement got underway. Figure 4 used the 1906 accident rate Steel Corporation-wide as a starting point, and then measured successful rate reductions for the years following as decreases from that baseline. Although, these were private figures, compiled and shared for private purposes, the federal Bureau of Labor Statistics own work confirmed remarkable improvements in both the frequency and severity rates once the concerted, industry-wide safety effort began in 1906.[32]

*   *   *   *   *

> *. . . a loop may spring over the top of the reel and catch his arm or foot, so that if the block is not stopped promptly the loop will tighten and lacerate . . .*[33]

Plaintiff says that. . . a portion of the #5 wire . . . came off the reel . . . Plaintiff thereupon . . . endeavored to stop the revolving block which is done by means of pressing the operator's foot upon a lever but . . . before he could do so the wire . . . caught in a loop around plaintiff's right leg throwing plaintiff to the floor and dragging him towards said #6 die. Before, however, plaintiff's body reached said die a fellow workman stopped the revolving block and extricated plaintiff . . .

Petition, *August Klawezynski vs. American Steel and Wire Co.*, Case No. 69559, Cuyahoga County Common Pleas Court Date of Injury: September 29, 1899.

* * * * *

Steel making is actually many discrete processes which combine to produce raw steel in the form of ingots, slabs and bars or, in some instances, "finished" steel products such as plate, sheets, tubing, rails, rods or wire. Raw materials, essentially coal, iron ore and limestone, must be mined or quarried and transported in bulk to the steel making facility. The coal is converted to "coke" (a more efficient fuel) and is then loaded into a blast furnace along with large quantities of iron ore and limestone. The furnace heats the mixture to between 1,500 and 2,000 degrees Fahrenheit and, after a period of about four hours of "cooking," relatively pure, molten pig iron is drawn out of the furnace along with the floating impurities, now separated out of the ore, an orange-yellow, sulfurish, lava-like byproduct called slag.

The slag is skimmed off the molten iron, and the iron is transported to a Bessemer converter or open hearth facility to add oxygen and carbon, changing it into the stronger, more malleable alloy known as steel. After the transformation into steel, the molten metal is poured into large molds which are set out to cool into ingot, slab or bar shapes. If the customer's order was for a finished steel product such as rail or rods, the cooling, but still red hot, ingots would be sent on to "hot rolling" mills where they would be rolled into a rail or rod form. If the customer's order required, the "hot rolled" rods, now cooled, could be further fabricated into wire, by a "cold working" process known as wire drawing. The American Steel and Wire Company specialized in, indeed monopolized, wire fabrication.

The Cleveland properties of American Steel and Wire included riverside shipping docks (for unloading the iron ore and limestone brought by freighter from around the Great Lakes); railroad facilities—the Newburgh and South Shore Railway Company (for moving raw materials to, molten iron and steel between, and finished products from the scattered plant facilities); storage yards; five blast furnaces; four open hearth furnaces; several Bessemer converters; four rolling mills (for rolling ingots of steel into plates, bars and rail); three rod mills; and four wire drawing mills.[34] Needless to say, throughout the course of time studied here, work accidents happened at all of the company's Cleveland plant facilities during every phase of the steel making and finishing process. However, the emphasis for the remainder of this chapter will be upon only one phase of the steel finishing process, the making of wire products.

*   *   *   *   *

. . . or even cut off the member . . .[35]

That . . . while plaintiff was engaged in drawing wire, the wire leading from the reel . . . to the wire drawing machine became kinked, which necessitated stopping the blocks through which the wire was being drawn, in order to prevent damage to . . . the machinery . . . and to prevent the breaking of the wire . . . That in order to stop (the) machinery, it was necessary for the plaintiff to put his foot on a treadle located on the floor beside the frame to which the block was attached . . . and while so doing his right leg became entangled in the kink or loop of wire, which tightened round his right leg below the knee with such force that it resulted in instantly cutting off his right leg several inches below the knee.

Petition, *Leon Nawrocki vs. American Steel and Wire Co.*, Case No. 79,884, Cuyahoga County Common Pleas Court Date of Injury: June 18, 1902

*   *   *   *   *

With the more malleable metals—gold, silver and bronze—wire making dates back to biblical times.[36] Exodus, Chapter 39, describes working gold into threads by beating the metal into very thin plates, then cutting strips from the plates into threads suitable for weaving into fabric. The hammering of the metal tended to harden the metals and the final "wire" produced was generally limited to use as jewelry, or in clothing and decorative arts.

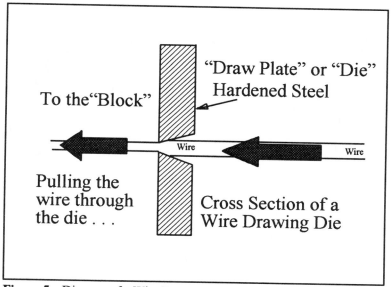

Figure 5   Diagram of a Wire Drawing Die

The earliest known references to actual wire "drawing" are found in monastic manuscripts that describe the building trades used to erect and decorate medieval churches and cathedrals. One Theophilus, a monk, circa uncertain,[37] described the wire drawing process quite precisely: "Mix two parts of tin with one of lead, hammer out the ingot long and slender and draw it through the holes of a wire drawing plate." Apparently, wire drawing was a fairly common process during the period in which Theophilus lived and wrote because he often casually alluded to the procedure in his multi-volume work on the decorative arts.[38] Probably the earliest machine-drawn wire was produced in Germany in the 14th or 15th century. The industry turned up in France in the 16th century and finally crossed the Channel to England when a mill, driven by water power, started up in Holywell, under authority granted by Queen Elizabeth.[39]

In simple terms, drawing wire is akin to forcing clay through a funnel to get a tube-shaped strand out the narrow end. However, because of the tensile physical property of steel, the same "narrowing" can be achieved, not by pushing, but by pulling or "drawing" the strand of wire through the funnel shape. A cross section of the basic physical process is diagramed above in Figure 5. The shaded area represents a cross section view of a plate of hardened steel with a funnel shaped hole drilled in it. This is the "die" or "draw plate." The force applied to the process comes from pulling the wire from the narrow side of the draw plate. The diagram exaggerates the reduction of the wire diameter for the purpose of illustrating the basic principle of the process.

As a rule, each pass through a die would narrow the diameter of the wire by five to ten percent. Typically, the process of cold drawing wire would begin with a 1/4 inch diameter steel rod. By drawing the rod through a succession of smaller and smaller gauge dies, the rod could be reduced in diameter (and simultaneously very greatly increased in length) until, if required, it was no thicker than a human hair. The applications for steel wire were innumerable and ever expanding.[40]

The wire drawer's job was considered semi-skilled and consisted of "threading" the die for each reduction pass and, once the mechanism was engaged, monitoring the unwinding of the thicker wire as it was drawn off its reel towards the funnel-shaped die. The wire was pulled through the die or draw plate by a revolving reel or "block" turning on the opposite side of the die. If the wire kinked, broke or became entangled, it was the wire drawer's job to cut the power to the block, untangle the wire and résumé the operation. As a practical matter, the job required standing in close proximity to the unreeling wire, where most of the snags occurred, so that problems could be spotted and addressed before the irregularity in the wire reached the die. If a snag in the wire traveled all the way to the die then the wire might break, damage the die, or, at a minimum, create a malformation in the "squeezed" wire—weakening the strand and rendering it useless.

*   *   *   *   *

. . . *or the wire may break and the flying end put out an eye* . . .[41]

. . . and while so working upon and operating said block . . . the wire broke between the die and the block and the block failed to stop . . . by reason of the defective and worn condition of said block and clutch . . . and said wire . . . which had broken . . . was thrust upward with great force and rapidity against and into plaintiff's right eye . . . causing him great and excruciating pain from which he was confined to his home for a period of sixteen weeks . . . and has permanently lost the sight of his right eye . . . and the sight of his left eye has materially weakened . . . by reason of said injury has been deprived of his ability to follow his trade of wire drawing . . .

Petition, *Frank Domualski vs. American Steel and Wire Co.*, Case No. 101871, Cuyahoga County Common Pleas Court Date of Injury: January 5, 1907.

* * * * *

The greatest hazard for wire drawers was entanglement in the moving wire. With the thicker gauges, the wire moved comparatively slowly through the draw plate, affording the wire drawer sufficient time to respond to problems and avoid ensnarement in an errant loop in the strand. However, after the wire had been passed through numerous reducing dies, the speed with which it unreeled off the spool and sped through the draw plate increased dramatically. To illustrate, as a length of wire was drawn down from a diameter of 1/5 of an inch to 1/20 of an inch (that amount of reduction would require 7 to 9 passes through successively smaller gauge dies), the speeds at which it would travel past the workman and through the die would increase from 250 feet per minute to 600 feet per minute (10 feet per second!).[42] The peril was manifest and the toll in limb, and sometimes life, was dreadful.

Statistically, what distinguished the wire drawers' lot from other steel workers was the rate of "permanent" as opposed to "temporary" injuries they sustained from entanglement. While a worker in the blast furnace department was far more liable to sustain a fatal injury on the job (7.1 deaths per 10,000,000 hours of exposure versus .08 deaths for the same exposure for the wire men), wire drawers were the more likely to suffer a permanent injury, furnace-related deaths notwithstanding. Considering only non-fatal permanent injuries, wire drawers suffered a frequency rate almost 3 times greater than their hot-metal working brethren on the furnaces (20.5 permanent injuries per 10,000,000 wire drawer hours vs. 7.5 for the blast furnace workers).[43] Fingers were the most common casualties (7.6 lost per

10,000,000 man hours of exposure); followed by "all other"[44] permanent injuries (7.2); loss of an eye (3.4); thumbs (1); any two toes or a great toe (tied at .3); three fingers (.2); while loss of an arm, hand, leg, foot or two fingers all tied at a frequency rate of .1.[45]

Over time, safety devices were incorporated into the wire drawing process to help prevent and ameliorate the dire consequences of the frequent ensnarements. The most common and theoretically effective device, called a "stop," was a shaft that protruded through the floor between the unreeling spool of wire and the die. The shaft was connected to a clutch for the revolving block pulling the wire through the draw plate. When pushed or pulled toward the draw plate the stop would disconnect the power to the pulling block halting the progress of the wire toward the draw plate. At the top of the shaft was an eye or loop giving the stop an appearance much like a giant sewing needle. If a snag (or, for example, say, an arm) was caught in the wire before it traveled through the eye of the stop, then the snag in the wire (or arm) would cause the stop to be pulled forward disconnecting the machine's power and saving the strand from a defect and/or the ensnared worker from losing his arm. These "stops" were common in the newer facilities but, according to investigators, not many of the older mills had been retrofitted with the safety appliance even as late as 1919.[46]

But according to company representatives even where the stops had been installed, managers had tremendous problems persuading the workers to use them. Sometimes the levers were too sensitive and might stop the block even when there was no real problem with the strand. This "falsing" effect shut down the wire mill and required the worker to slowly reengage the clutch for the block to résumé production. Too often, over time, the temptation to disconnect or bypass the stop overwhelmed the careless or indifferent worker.[47]

* * * * *

Plaintiff further says that on the 24th and 25th of January, 1906, he was instructed . . . to put a composition represented as soap powder on the dies through which . . . the wire proceeds; that after the wire had passed through a die or dies covered with said substances, it was covered or immersed in lime acids and various chemical substances, the nature and properties and effects of which were not explained to plaintiff and of which he then was and still is ignorant; that after said wire . . . was so covered or immersed with . . . powder, lime, acids and other chemical substances, plaintiff was ordered, required and directed to handle said wire in various ways with his hands; that while so handling said wire . . . his hands were severely burned and his eyes inflamed and injured by some dangerous, poisonous, injurious, and harmful property or substance in said ingredients, acids or chemicals, which were upon said wire . . .

Petition, *Burnett H. Jones vs. American Steel and Wire Co.*, Case No. 91573, Cuyahoga County Common Pleas Court. Date of Injury: January 24th and 25th, 1906.

* * * * *

As awful and commonplace as the ensnarement injuries were, the amputations and other traumatic injuries caused by the wire drawing process pale to relative numerical insignificance when compared to the toxic hazards that were a constant and deadly, though less sensational and mostly unacknowledged, threat to the wire drawers' health. Considered in isolation, wire drawing does not require much in the way of noxious chemical agents to accomplish the actual drawing down of wire diameter from one size gauge to the next smaller. But before the wire could be drawn through a die, it had to be cleaned to remove excess "scale," irregularities and rust on the surface of the wire. If the scale wasn't removed before drawing, the final length of wire would contain imperfections making it weaker and less valuable. Essentially, the rust and scale would be "squeezed" into the metal. As the drawing down continued on the strand, the imperfections would become more and more exaggerated, eventually rendering the length completely useless. To prevent this, the wire was cleaned before it was drawn by immersing it in an acid bath, a process known as "pickling."

In the United States, the most common pickling solution was sulfuric acid.[48] So as to increase the efficiency of the sulfuric acid solution, the vats or "baths" were kept heated well above room temperature. This heating caused the vats to constantly emit steam vapors which carried the sulfuric acid (and other impurities) into the air around and adjacent to the pickling operations. As a practical matter, pickling operations were conducted in areas immediately adjacent to the wire drawing mills to cut down on materials handling and the length of time the cleaned metal was exposed to the air and oxidation the pickling was intended to counteract. As might be guessed, the airborne sulfuric acid had severely deleterious effects upon the health of those continuously breathing its vapors.[49]

Aside from the caustic sulfuric acid, the steam from the pickling vats contained numerous poisonous byproducts, including arsenic (found as an impurity in both the acid solutions and the treated metals) and its derivative compounds such as arsine gas. Arsine gas (AsH_2) is a colorless, garlic-smelling vapor emitted by the chemical interactions in the pickling baths. Acute poisoning, though rare in an industrial setting, is often fatal. The effects of acute poisoning were well understood during this period, as verified by a 1914 state-wide survey of industrial health.[50] Among arsine's various sustained, low dose, chronic health effects upon exposed workers are: "tiredness, pallor, breathlessness on exertion and palpitations."[51]

In 1915, the Ohio State Board of Health, published findings of its state-wide survey on industrial hazards and occupational diseases.[52] The Hayhurst study was prepared at the direction of the Ohio General Assembly and sought to examine all of the major manufacturing industries in the state. The results of the survey were organized not only by industry, but by occupation and industrial process. In this way the staff investigators were able to focus upon verifiable tendencies within occupational sub-groups to contract diseases caused by exposure to chemical agents and industrial processes. Among the many occupations and industrial operations examined in the Hayhurst study was metal "pickling."

Dr. Hayhurst, then Director of the State Board's Division of Occupational Diseases, and his staff investigated sixteen separate manufacturing establishments in twelve Ohio cities that contained on-going pickling operations. The industries involved included iron and steel fabrication, automobile manufacturing, foundries, sign and advertising novelty concerns, machine shops, tinning and galvanizing operations and, of course, wire mills. In the factories visited, there was an estimated total of 180 workers directly involved in pickling operations.

The Board of Health investigators found that most of the pickling operations were conducted in work areas that were damp and either badly ventilated or very drafty. This increased the risk of cold drafts due to the very "humid and steamy atmosphere" in and around the pickling operations. Six places were badly lighted (presumably during the day) and, in practically all the investigated establishments, the hours were very long, with additional night shifts the rule in some plants. The report repeatedly emphasized that pickling work was "very sloppy and steamy."

As to the specific effects of the sulfuric acid fumes:

> The liability to poisoning lay in the effects of the acid fumes and in one or two instances, alkali vapors,[53] . . . While sulfuric acid is itself not volatile, steam particles easily carry it. The same may be said of the alkali solutions. The effects of such poisonings are local upon the nose, throat and digestion, and especially upon the teeth; as the fumes also incite coughing, they are very predisposing to lung disease . . . Our investigators found a considerable number of workers with very bad teeth, as well as pyorrhea, the effects, unquestionably, of the small but constant amount of acid vapors which they breathe.[54]

The all-pervading and corrosive fumes notwithstanding, the investigators found that only a few of the concerns had installed any form of ventilating device for their pickling operations. In the sixteen factories visited, only three had efficient ventilating appliances, while two plants had hoods that seemed "fairly efficient" and one concern "bad." The remaining ten pickling departments had no ventilation devices at all.

At one pickling operation suspected by the investigators to be particularly unhealthful (the local city Tuberculosis Department reported a case of consumption as originating from the plant's pickling room), the employer assured the investigators that, "the men get fat on it." But the employer's sanguine boast belied the picklers' ages as estimated by the State Board's staff. Of the 180 pickling workers employed at the sixteen plants visited, 163 were between 20 and 40 years old; 14 were between 40 and 50; while, in the estimation of the investigating staff, only 3 picklers were over 50 years old.[55]

* * * * *

. . . I say we are responsible if we are negligent, no matter how ignorant the workman, whether Polish, Bohemian, or what, we are absolutely responsible.[56]

* * * * *

In addition to the associated process of pickling, wire drawing mills were often located adjacent to galvanizing operations. Galvanizing is a process that coats iron and steel with a thin layer of zinc. The zinc coating resists rust and helps preserve the wire (often employed in fencing) from the weathering process. As was true of wire drawing, galvanizing requires a clean surface on the metal before being coated with zinc. Therefore, most galvanizing departments had pickling operations that preceded the actual zinc coating process. The State Board staff noted that, as a rule, galvanizing workers were subject to the same toxic hazards associated with pickling.[57]

After being cleaned in the acid bath, the wire was run through a chemical that prepared the strand for immersion in the molten zinc vats. This agent, a substance called "sal ammoniac" (NH_4Cl, ammonium chloride) acts as a "flux," helping the zinc to adhere to the steel.[58] Then the wire would be run through a vat of molten zinc. The zinc baths were heated to a temperature between 850 and 900 degrees (Fahrenheit), and emitted numerous gases and fumes into the areas adjacent to the galvanizing operations. Lead and zinc chloride ($ZnCl_2$) were added to the zinc bath to enhance the coating process.[59]

Galvanizers were subject to the chronic health effects of the many fumy agents and byproducts from the zinc coating process. Zinc chloride is a skin irritant and, when ingested in powdered form, causes ulcers of the esophagus, stomach and septum.[60] Zinc oxide, a by-product of the vaporous molten zinc baths, is another skin irritant,[61] and causes what is variously known as "zinc chills," "zinc fume fever," "brass founder's ague," "smelter shakes" or "metal fume fever." This strange and apparently temporary malady follows a very distinctive, well documented, but little understood course.

The exposed worker is usually struck ill after leaving work, experiencing a sudden chill accompanied by dryness of the mouth and throat, a cough, a tightening of the chest and nausea. Often a fever occurs, but temperatures rarely exceed 103 degrees. After the chill ceases, the victim breaks out in a profuse sweat and, usually, feels well enough to return to work the next day. It is more common in cold weather. Workers appear to build an immunity to the disorder. Once having suffered an attack, a worker will not usually have another onset of the "chills" unless removed from the daily influence of the metal oxide, as by a long holiday or vacation, in which event the immunity is lost. The literature seems unanimous that repeated bouts of the zinc fume fever do not cause chronic ill health effects.[62] However, one writer has suggested that ingestion of zinc oxide may cause irritation and even "erosion" of the stomach because of the formation of zinc chloride from the interaction of the zinc oxide with the hydrochloric acid of the stomach's gastric fluids.[63]

The Ohio State Board of Health also investigated galvanizing operations in its statewide survey. In this instance, the staff investigated 14 factories in 11 cities, accounting for a total of 724 workers. The report noted that the vast majority of galvanizing was done in the rolling mills of the iron and steel industry. Of the 14 galvanizing operations surveyed, only 7 had ventilating hoods to draw off the noxious fumes rising from the zinc baths, and of the 7 establishments that had hoods, only 3 worked to any considerable effect. In the other 7 plants there were no ventilating appliances at all. Galvanizing work was characterized by long hours, hurrying piece-work, "monotonous application," constant standing and loud noises.

As for chronic health hazards to galvanizing workers:

> The chief hazard in the process is poisoning, which may be due to zinc fumes. . . lead (a small amount of which is usually added to the zinc bath); to sal ammoniac . . . and to the fumes of the pickling processes, if located nearby. . . The risk of slow poisoning was considered negligible in 1 place, fairly so in 7 more, but considerable in the remaining 6. The forms of poisoning which may be present are; "zinc chills," chronic lead poisoning (except to the person that handles the lead this risk is only nominal), catarrhal trouble, due to the sal ammoniac fumes, and carious teeth as well as pyorrhea as noted among the "picklers."
>
> . . . There were not many complaints made by the workmen (few could speak English), but these consisted of the irritating effects of the fumes, as well as of "metal chills." The investigators reported specific occupational complaints as follows: 3 with burns, 2 who mentioned "zinc chills" and 1 in whom the breathing of the fumes had produced chronic bronchitis. In addition, skin irritations and ulcers were brought to notice.[64]

As was done in the case of the picklers, the investigators conducted an estimated galvanizing worker census. Of the 724 wage earners observed in all the plants, 661 were between 20 and 40 years old, 57 were between 40 and 45; while only 6 were over 45 years old.[65]

*　*　*　*　*

Plaintiff says that in the course of his employment by Defendants, Defendants carelessly and negligently assigned him without warning to certain dangerous duties to wit; oiling the wheels of certain ladles and that he was compelled to remain continuously at or near the place where the contents of said ladles was deposited. That said ladles contained waste material known as slag from which a dangerous gas or acid arises; that in the performance of his duties, he was continually compelled to inhale the fumes of said gas or acid; that as a result of inhaling said gas or acid, Plaintiff was first affected during the month of July 1902 by cramps and stomach trouble. That he at that time notified said Defendants of his condition but was assured that his position was not dangerous, that he continued in the employ of said Defendants until September 11th of 1903 when he was compelled to retire owing to a partial paralysis of the lower limbs, partial paralysis of the right shoulder and stomach trouble caused by his continued inhalation of said gas or acid.

Petition, *Winslow J. Shaw vs. American Steel and Wire Co.*, Case No. 85048 Cuyahoga County Common Pleas Court
Date of Injury: July 1902 through September 1903

* * * * *

The common law was just beginning to address the injuries caused by chronic worker exposures to noxious industrial agents. Winslow Shaw's suit was transferred to the federal Circuit Court where it was dismissed by the judge, without opinion, prior to going to trial. The common law negligence action employed in work injury suits evolved from the old trespass actions, which implied that a traumatic event had occurred causing the plaintiff's injury. Shaw's lawyer was pushing the boundaries of the existing common law further than they had been pushed before. Further probably, than they were going to be pushed for some time to come, but the *idea* of using a negligence action to remedy preventable industrial disease was clearly articulated by Shaw's counsel and, presumably, other workers' attorneys.

The Ohio State Board of Health's investigation suggests that it wasn't so much ignorance of industrial disease that hampered regulation of toxic chemical agents, as an apparent disinclination to regulate the industries that relied upon the agents. Some clues to understanding this reluctance are contained in the State Board's report. When investigating pickling operations the State Board staff noticed "largely ignorant foreigners" labored in 6 of the 16 factories. When they visited galvanizing operations they didn't get many health complaints from the workers, but allowed as that was probably because "few could speak English." When they visited two wire drawing mills the staff noticed that the majority of laborers were foreigners, "mostly non-English speaking."[66]

When the Ohio workmen's compensation reform was finally enacted, it faithfully mimicked the common law's failure to compensate for the sickness and disability that followed chronic exposure to toxic work place environments. Although Ohio's constitutional provision enabling the passage of the compensation reform contained language that specifically authorized legislative recompense for industrial disease,[67] the Ohio House and Senate declined to include "disease" in the list of compensable injuries.[68] As was then true of the flawed tort theories, the compensation reform scheme provided no avenue for the chronically poisoned worker to pursue against his employer. But, unlike the evolving law of negligence,[69] workmen's compensation would prove a structurally resistant and intractable system with few incentives to adapt to, and compensate for, the growing number of noxious chemical agents being introduced into the industrial work place. Disability, early retirement, and one supposes, premature death, provided its own quieting solution for these men.

* * * * *

Having absconded from the offices of the American Tool Company with the crucial, if reluctant, witness to Nikopopulos' accident, Henk, in company with his hobbling translator, a legless "Slavish fellow" named Vlasek, and our increasingly incredulous hero, proceed to "Mark's" office—by way of a saloon. The initially reticent witness (a *very* new immigrant as yet wholly untutored in the finer points of negligence) will require some remedial instruction in the peculiar majesty of the American common law, and the congenial atmosphere of a saloon proves the best setting for Henk to reconvene his continuing seminar on yet another facet of "the rules of the game."

On the way to Leffingwell's office, Henk put questions to
Vlasek, and he in turn clothed them into Kolokolchick's
vernacular.

"He say he had his face turned when the Greek got hurt,"
Vlasek interpreted.

"Tell him it makes no difference;" Henk now slowed down his
machine and turned upon Vlasek significantly.

"He mustn't tell that. All he has got to tell is that the machine
on which he and the Greek worked did not work right—you
unde'stand?—That something was broke—and that he had told that
to the foreman, but the foreman ordered him to go on and
work—you unde'stand?"

Vlasek evidently understood. For at this point he talked to
Kolokolchick a long while, and made many gestures, during which
at first Kolokolchick seemed to make objections but finally
scratched the back of his head, and murmured, "*Tak—tak* (so),"
and seemed to agree with Vlasek.

"He says he thinks that's so," at last Vlasek imparted to Henk.

"Tell him a witness in court mustn't say `I think'. He must say
`I know'—you unde'stand? If he says I think, the judge mightn't
believe him, and he gets no money and the Greek gets no money."

Some more small talk between Vlasek an Kolokolchick.

"He says the lawyer must tell him what to tell the judge,"
explained Vlasek.

"That's right—that's the stuff," cried Henk triumphantly.

By the time we reached Leffingwell's office, Henk and
Kolokolchick had become fast friends. On the way, Henk had
stopped at a saloon to get a drink, but I remained in the automobile.
And judging from Kolokolchick's loquaciousness on his emerging
from the saloon, with one of Henk's cigars between his teeth, he
must have had an abundance to drink.

As soon as we got back into the office, Henk took
Kolokolchick into Leffingwell's private room, where he dictated a
"statement" covering a few pages, at the bottom of the last of which
Kolokolchick affixed his scrawl. He was then told to wait for
"Mark," which Vladislav Kolokolchick, heavy of tongue, with
drooping head and arms, did, leisurely reclining in a large armchair
and drawing at one of Henk's cigars.

About noon Mark arrived, with an expensive looking brief-
case under his arm, radiant with smiles, followed by his assistant,

a cripple on crutches, the plaintiff in a case then on trial, and a friend of the cripple.

"Well, Henk, my boy," Mark said jovially, "How is the poor unfortunate Greek getting along?"

While addressing Henk, Mark leaned over his desk and put his little nose to the American Beauty's on the table, with an expression on his face as if the fragrance of the flowers almost overwhelmed him, and then settled in to a soft cushioned chair.

"The fellow is in bad shape—very bad shape," reported Henk. Then turning to Kolokolchick, who had dozed off in the meanwhile, he shook him by the arm and said, "This is Mr. Vladislav Kolokolchick, who was at work with Nikopopulos at the time the accident happened. Here is his statement."

Mark winked to Henk, who was standing at attention, with his chest thrust forward, his hat cocked on one side, the aperture in the left corner of his mouth showing the missing tooth rather conspicuously. While Mark's eyes were scanning the "statement" Henk's eyes rested studiously upon Mark's face. "Vadislav will get us two more witnesses," added Henk. "Poor, poor Nikopopulos" (he pronounced it "Poo-er—poo-er"), sighed Mark, shaking his head compassionately. "And the poor unfortunate man has a wife and six little children—what a terrible catastrophe, what a cruel fate!"

Then, turning to Vlasek, he added, "Tell your friend, Kolokolchick, that he can help the poor, unfortunate Nikopopulos very, very much, and I'll see that he is well taken care of."

Vlasek conveyed Mark's words to Kolokolchick, who nodded his head drowsily and murmured, "*Tak—tak*."

After Kolokolchick and Vlasek had departed Mark said to Henk, " You must get at least one English speaking witness."

"Leave it to me," Henk responded reassuringly.

Notes

1. Thomas Bell, *Out of This Furnace* (Pittsburgh: University of Pittsburgh Press, 1941).

2. For the purposes of this chapter, the "old" immigrant group includes the English, Irish, Welsh, Scots, Germans and Swedes; the "new" immigrants include those of Polish, Croatian, Greek, Italian, Lithuanian, Hungarian, Rumanian, Russian, Serbian, Slovak, and Slovenian descent.

3. Ibid., OELC, *Report*, Vol. II, 159.

4. Ibid., OELC, *Report*, Vol. II, 159.

5. Immigration Commission, *Immigrants In Industries, Iron and Steel Manufacturing*, Senate Document No. 633 (Washington D.C.: Government Printing Office, 1911), 4.

6. Ibid., 21.

7. Ibid., 27.

8. Ibid., Brody, 105.

9. John Bodnar, *Immigration and Industrialization: Ethnicity In An American Mill Town, 1870-1940* (Pittsburgh: University of Pittsburgh Press, 1977). Bodnar portrays what he calls a "turn inward" within the new immigrant communities that formed in Steelton, Pennsylvania. This separateness from the larger community tended to delay assimilation and participation in the local power structure only recently occupied by the old immigrant groups.

10. Ibid., Brody, Chapters I, II and III. As Brody tells the tale, the craft skills were driven out of the industry by both the shift in emphasis from iron to steel and by the unrelenting drive for economy in the American steel industry. As the industry became increasingly mechanized, the slots for skilled labor diminished while the need for unskilled labor grew along with the yearly increases in American steel production.

11. Charles R. Walker, *Steel: The Diary of a Furnace Worker* (Boston: Atlantic Monthly Press, 1922).

12. Thomas Bell's (Belejcak) naturalistic novel, *Out of This Furnace* charted the not-so-fictional careers of his father and uncles in the Braddock works of Bethlehem Steel. Hiring patterns appear in the interior monologue of Bell's central protagonist, the doomed "Mike" Dobrejcak,

Of the two thousand or so men working in the mill a good half were Slovaks or other non-English speaking foreigners, and of that half not one had a skilled job. Departmental heads did their own hiring, and, whether American, English or Irish, tended to favor their own kind.

13. Ibid., Brody, 99.

14. Ibid., Immigration Commission, Vol. I, 50.

15. Ibid., Walker, 28.

16. Ibid., Brody, 101.

17. Stephen Tener of the American Steel and Wire Company, explaining the firm's new in-house compensation plan, before the Ohio Employers' Liability Commission. Ibid., OELC, *Report*, Vol. II, 128.

18. See page 1, above. As Crystal Eastman put it:

. . . Many cases are conducted honestly. But the contingent fee lawyer who hastily visits an injured man in order to urge him on to litigation, is well matched by the claim agent who hastily visits him in order to urge him to a settlement. The plaintiff's attorney who "manufactures" a witness to fit his case, is no worse than the defendant's attorney who bribes a witness to disappear. The employers' liability law is an encouragement to dishonesty, and both sides play the game.

Ibid., Eastman, 195.

19. David S. Beyer, "Safety Provisions in the United States Steel Corporation," *The Survey*, 24 (May 1910): 205-38, 222. Beyer was the Chief Safety Inspector for United States Steel.

20. William Hard, "Making Steel and Killing Men," *Everybody's Magazine* XVII, no. 5 (November 1907): 579-91.

21. Ibid., Brody, 159, 165.

22. Agreement on methods for gathering and compiling information was slow in coming. Matters as apparently simple and straightforward as what kind of occurrence would qualify as a recordable "accident" still hadn't been universally accepted, even as late as 1922. Many states and some industries continued to use different definitions rendering comparisons and aggregations of statistics impossible. The Bureau of Labor Statistics and the International Association of Industrial Accident Boards and Commissions both pushed for uniform standards, but never completely succeeded in

getting all the public and private systems to tabulate data consistently.

23. Lucian W. Chaney, *Causes and Prevention of Accidents in the Iron and Steel Industry, 1910-1919*, Bulletin No. 298 (Washington D.C.: Bureau of Labor Statistics, June, 1922).

24. United States. Congress. Senate., *Accidents and Accident Prevention*, Conditions of Employment in the Iron and Steel Industry, 4 vols., vol. IV (Washington D.C.: Government Printing Office, 1913).

25. U.S. Bureau of Labor Statistics, *The Safety Movement in the Iron and Steel Industry, 1907-1917*, Bulletin No. 234 (Washington D.C.: Government Printing Office, 1918).

26. "Frequency Rate" was ultimately standardized to mean the number of accidents occurring within a given worker group, occupation, department, mill or industry, per 1,000,000 man hours of labor.

27. Ultimately, the statisticians found they needed another yardstick to measure the true costs of industrial accidents. "Accident Severity Rate" was developed to analyze, not how often accidents occurred in a particular occupation, but how serious and disabling those accidents tended to be. A system of disability "time equivalents" was agreed upon for certain injuries. For example, a fatal accident was considered equivalent to 6000 days of lost work time, while the loss of an arm equaled 4000 lost work days. Thus, while the machine building industry reflected a nearly identical frequency rate as steel making (approximately 39 accidents per 1,000,000 man hours) the severity rate for the steel industry was 7 days lost per 1000 man hours, while machine shops averaged only 1.8 days lost per 1000 hours of exposure. The scale of time equivalents used for death and dismemberment injuries was developed by the Committee on Statistics of the International Association of Industrial Accident Boards and Commissions.

28. Ibid., Chaney, 9, 176-78.

29. Ibid., 178-184.

30. Ibid., 9,10.

31. Bureau of Safety, Sanitation & Welfare, "The Safety Provisions of the United States Steel Corporation," Bulletin No. 7 (New York: United States Steel Corporation, December, 1918), 14.

32. Ibid., Chaney, 284.

33. Ibid., Beyer, 222.

34. Ibid., Hogan, Vol. I, 264.

35. Ibid., Beyer.

36. J. Bucknall Smith, *A Treatise Upon Wire, Its Manufacture And Uses* (New York: John Wiley & Sons, 1891); Alastair Thomas Adam, *Wire-Drawing and the Cold Working of Steel* (London: H. F. & G. Witherby, 1936).

37. Adam, 13. Adam refers to Theophilus as either Saxon or German and as living "somewhere about A.D. 700-1000."

38. Ibid., 14.

39. Ibid., Smith, 2.

40. Fencing in the Great Plains for livestock production was the most immediate and well known demand for barbed wire. Telegraph wire was also an ever expanding market. Less obvious uses extended from production of nails, pins and needles to strings for musical instruments. Heavy applications like cable for suspension bridges, elevators, replacement of rope in the maritime industry were sources of great and dependable demand along with smaller more specialized markets such as special alloy wire for making watch springs, etc.

41. Ibid., Beyer.

42. Ibid., Adam, 45.

43. Ibid., Chaney, 13, 144, 258. These figures were compiled from the industry experience between 1915 and 1919. Blast furnaces were notorious for "slips" which occurred without warning and caused horrific, inferno-like explosions that typically resulted in multiple fatalities. However, even counting the fatal blast furnace accidents, wire drawing was still, far and away, the most disabling occupation in the industry.

44. Although Chaney's report doesn't define "all other" it probably referred to non-amputation injuries that were severe enough to damage the affected body part beyond rehabilitation. For example, see the allegation concerning the gouging injury to Felix Krulikowski's right forearm.

45. Ibid., 144.

46. Ibid., 258.

47. As was stated by David S. Beyer, the Chief Safety Inspector for the American Steel and Wire Company:

> In all of our mills some form of wire stop has been put in. A number of different applications of it were assembled on one drawing and prints sent to each plant. It is simple and effective, the only objections to it being the amount of floor space it occupies and the second's time it takes to place the wire through the lever. It may save an arm, an eye or even a life--and yet some of the workmen

have broken them off, others have refused to use them, and after a campaign of several years along this line, one never goes into a mill without seeing some places where the operators carry the wire past the safety lever without using it.

Ibid., Beyer, 222-23.

48. Ibid., Adams, 30.

49. A more recent text cataloguing commonly encountered industrial chemical agents and their effects upon worker health states:

Sulfuric acid exposure causes irritation of the mucous membranes, including the eye, but principally the respiratory tract epithelium. The mist also causes etching of the dental enamel followed by erosion of the enamel and dentine with loss of tooth substance. Central and lateral incisors are mainly affected. Breathing high concentrations of sulfuric acid causes tickling in the nose and throat, sneezing, and coughing. At lower levels sulfuric acid causes a reflex increase in respiratory rate and diminution of depth, with reflex bronchoconstriction resulting in increased pulmonary air flow resistance. A single overexposure can lead to laryngeal, tracheobronchial, and pulmonary edema. Repeated excessive exposures over long periods have resulted in bronchitic symptoms, and rhinorrhea (runny nose), lacrimation (watery eyes), and epistaxis (bloody nose). Long exposures are claimed to result in conjunctivitis (inflammation under the eyelids), frequent respiratory infections, emphysema and digestive disturbances.

Ibid., Key, 438.

50. E.R. Hayhurst, *Industrial health hazards and Occupational Diseases in Ohio* (Columbus: Ohio State Board of Health, 1915), 152. See also: Jewett V. Reed and A.K. Harcourt, *The Essentials of Occupational Diseases* (Springfield: Charles C. Thomas, 1941), 11.

51. Marcus M. Key, et al., ed, *Occupational Diseases, A Guide to Their Recognition* (Washington D.C.: U.S. Department of Health, Education and Welfare, 1977).

52. E.R. Hayhurst, *Industrial Health-Hazards and Occupational Diseases in Ohio* (Columbus: Ohio State Board of Health, 1915). Hayhurst went on to become a respected and nationally known figure in industrial hygiene.

53. Often strong alkali solutions were used to arrest the acid's corrosive effect upon the treated metal once the desired cleaning was accomplished.

54. Ibid., 154.

55. Ibid., 154. The informal census results were not further remarked upon in the report.

56. Mr. C. E. Adams, President of the Cleveland Hardware Company, October 31, 1910. Ibid., OELC, *Report*, Vol. II, 137-38.

57. Ibid., Hayhurst, 156.

58. Sal ammoniac has the pharmacological property of an expectorant and was actually prescribed as a medication for that purpose. Predictably, galvanizers often suffered from "catarrh" (inflammation of the mucus membranes of the nose and throat).

59. Ibid., Hayhurst, 155, 156; Adam, 138.

60. Ibid., Reed and Harcourt, 99; Key, 406-408.

61. Causing a form of dermatitis called "oxide pox." Ibid., Key, 409.

62. Ibid., Reed and Harcourt, 99; Key, 409. But see note 61.

63. *The Cyclopedia of Medicine, Surgery, Specialties* (Philadelphia: F. A. Davis Company, 1969), 132-422.

64. Ibid., Hayhurst, 156.

65. The results of the census were again recited without comment. One medical text has observed that zinc smelters, "rarely live beyond forty five, and die, some of a pneumococcic or gastrointestinal disturbances, others of a peculiar nervous affection which commences with burning superficial pains, exalted sensibility, and reflex activity in the legs, and afterward puts on still more clearly the features of myelitis." *The Cyclopedia of Medicine, Surgery, Specialties*, Vol XIV, pg. 1039.

66. They also noted that most of the workers were under 40 years of age. The investigators determined that wire drawers were subject to poisoning hazards to the extent that they worked adjacent to galvanizing and pickling operations. Ibid., Hayhurst, 316.

67. Section 35, Article II, Ohio Constitution (1912).

68. The issue was repeatedly litigated, but the consistent interpretation of the courts—denying recovery to diseased workers because of the absence of "occupational disease" in the statutory language—held well past the era examined here: *Industrial Commission v. Brown*, 92 Ohio St. 309, (1915); *Industrial Commission v. McManigal*, 11 Ohio App. 384, (1919); *Industrial Commission v. Cross*, 104 Ohio St. 561, (1922).

69. It will be argued at length in Chapter VI of this study that workmen's compensation didn't reform the common law of employers' liability so much as arrest it by legislating in place the scope of injuries and extent of recoverable damages recognized under negligence theory in the American courts, circa 1910. Thought of in this way, the compensation reform negated a redeeming characteristic of common law tort theory and practice, its adaptability, its fluid and dynamic vitality.

I V

Juries Inviolate

Jury lawlessness is the great corrective of law in its actual administration. The will of the State at large imposed upon a reluctant community, the will of a majority imposed upon a vigorous and determined minority, find the same obstacle in the local jury that formerly confronted kings and ministers.

Roscoe Pound

. . . we must say that in our opinion the jury system for fixing responsibility of industrial accidents is nothing more than the greatest monumental farce in existence. The general run of jurors are without question very often men extremely illiterate. Men who are chosen simply because they have nothing else to do or because they have a political pull, or are placed on the jury this year because they have served several years in the past, and many of them, as soon as they are paid their dues, will pass around the corner to the first saloon and spend most of them in short order. However, bear in mind that we are not condemning all men on the juries, because many of them are intelligent law-abiding citizens in every sense of the word, but the great majority, in our opinion, is the reverse.

J. P. Brophy, Vice Pres. and
Gen'l Supt., Cleveland
Automatic Machine Co. (1910)

The right of trial by jury shall be inviolate . . .

Constitution of Ohio (1912)
Article I, Section 5

Perhaps no other single feature of American self government engenders such praise in theory—and such condemnation in practice—as the jury. Certainly, no other single feature of the system that preceded workmen's compensation proved as controversial and divisive in the employers' liability reform debate as the power of juries to decide the issues of liability and damages between injured workmen and their employers. No other single feature of the litigation system so clearly and vividly distinguished the "employer view" from the "workmen's view" than the two starkly contrasted perceptions about juries and their assigned role as "finders-of-fact" in the worker suits against employers.

Employers claimed with near ritualistic cant that juries were, understandably, sympathetic to the maimed workman, but generally disinclined to protect the legitimate property rights of employers. Moreover, the jurors' natural bias in favor of the worker was especially pronounced if the employer-defendant was an impersonal and anonymous corporation. According to the employer view, the judges, professionals who were more detached from the injured plaintiff, could be fair to employers but too often left the case determination to the wide discretion of juries. Workers and worker organizations, on the other hand, testified *ad nauseam* that while juries were usually fair in their determinations, too often judges autocratically assumed control over trials, denying the jury an opportunity to reach a verdict on the facts by directing a verdict in favor of the employer.

Both in their testimony around the state and in their written responses to the Ohio Employer's Liability Commission questionnaire, employers of labor consistently and sometimes bitterly complained that juries tended to identify with injured workers while ignoring the just and legitimate concerns of employers. Of the employers who submitted written responses to the Commission's question on juries[1], 28 claimed they were unfair to employers while 1 claimed they were fair. Of the employee responses, 55 reported that they were in favor of juries, but opposed to judge determinations of work injury cases; 21 reported they were opposed to both judges and juries as a system for resolving disputes; while only 7 employee groups reported satisfaction with the judge and jury system. None of the worker groups proposed banning juries, leaving the field entirely to the judiciary. The ground of most acute dissension in the pre-compensation debate was the role of the jury in hearing and deciding worker injury suits.

This chapter will examine the jury system in the Cleveland-area common pleas court (Cuyahoga County) during and just past the pre-compensation era, beginning with a Cleveland jury scandal in 1897 and ending with a 1921 foundation-sponsored study[2] of the still problematic jury system.[3] Between those dates we will look at the jury experiences of the American Steel and Wire Company, and a local Civic League investigation of jury practices conducted in tandem with the Bar Association in 1915. What emerges from these sources is a story rich in both ambiguity and irony. At once corrupt and equitable, common pleas court juries administered a common law compensation system that effectively held the American Steel and Wire Company to a strict liability standard fully a decade and one half before Ohio's compulsory workmen's compensation act was passed. Further, and more curiously, notwithstanding the bias implied by that strict liability standard and the evident "deep pockets" of the local Steel Trust subsidiary, the damages juries awarded to injured workers under this compensation regimen were not particularly generous to injured workers.

The problematic urban jury was dragged to the forefront of public affairs in 1897 by a courthouse scandal that came to be known in Cleveland as the "Jury Bribery Cases." The sordid details of the imbroglio, and the local bar's fractious response to the embarrassing and divisive mess, provide an appropriate starting point for looking at the role and dynamics of the jury system that dominated the Cleveland-area state courts during the pre-compensation era.

* * * * *

It promised to be an extraordinary afternoon for the Cleveland legal community, with standing room only in the Circuit Appellate Court chambers for an emergency meeting of the Cleveland Bar Association. The gathering was called at Common pleas Judge Walter C. Ong's request in reference to certain recently notorious "jury bribery cases." Both the *Cleveland Leader* and the *Cleveland Plain Dealer* news accounts of the meeting included reference to a "rather warm discussion" that ensued concerning the manner in which Judge Ong had handled the thorny problem presented to him in chambers one Monday morning in November of 1897.

As one supporter of the Judge remarked to a reporter, "Judge Ong has been practically charged with aiding and abetting the bribing of jurors. That is the plain meaning of the rumors that have been flying about." However, taking as accurate the various newspaper accounts along with the "official" version of the bribery attempt presented to the assembled members by one of the involved lawyers, Judge Ong was not involved in the bribing of jurors, but did consent to play a pro-active role in exposing the corruption. His choice not to inform the plaintiff's lawyer about the developing scandal tweaked a raw and divisive nerve in the already bifurcating Cleveland legal community. In short, what was causing the furor wasn't what Ong did, but how he did it. The plaintiffs' bar had the corporate bar on the defensive and the corporate lawyer-controlled Bar Association was embarrassed into calling the meeting to clear the air and provide an official forum to vindicate Judge Ong and the manner in which he had routed out the corruption.

The bribe attempt occurred during the trial of a personal injury action between James Reardon and the Lake Shore & Michigan Southern Railway Company. According to his petition,[4] Reardon was employed as a fireman for the United Salt Company of Cleveland. United Salt's plant was located adjacent to railroad tracks owned by the defendant railroad. On the afternoon of November 22, 1895, he left his home for work and while crossing the tracks in front of United Salt's plant gate was knocked down by a line of "suddenly moving" railroad cars. He was taken to the St. Clair Street Hospital where it was found necessary to amputate his right leg below the knee. Reardon claimed the line of railroad cars was standing still at the time he began crossing the track. The road defended on the theory that Reardon was trespassing at the time he was injured inasmuch as there was no legally sufficient right of way over the tracks at the gate to United Salt Company's facility. It was conceded by the railroad, however, that notwithstanding the absence of a formal, recorded right of way, United Salt's workers were required to (and routinely did) cross over the tracks to get to United Salt's plant entrance.

Reardon's suit was filed in the common pleas court and set for trial in the September term of 1897. Plaintiff's counsel was Martin A. Foran, a former school teacher, veteran of the Civil War, and cooper by trade who was at one time elected to the presidency of the Coopers' International Union. Having read the law "more or less" he was later admitted to the bar (1874), elected Cleveland City Prosecutor and, in 1882, began serving the first of three consecutive terms as a Democratic Representative to Congress.[5] Counsel on behalf of the road was "Judge" Moses R. Dickey. The honorific "Judge" related to two terms Dickey served on the common pleas bench in Richland County, Ohio (Mansfield). He emigrated to Cleveland as the result of "business inducements" in 1882. Like Foran, Dickey was a veteran of "the rebellion" and a man of wide and varied experience. However, Dickey was no trade unionist, but a late nineteenth century prototype of "the corporate lawyer." He was, upon arriving in Cleveland and up until 1890, a senior partner with two of the founders of Squire, Sanders & Dempsey, (soon-to-be counsel for the yet-to-be-formed American Steel and Wire Company).[6]

According to Dickey, who presented his written narrative of the events to the Bar Association assemblage, he was working one Saturday morning at his office while the trial of *Reardon vs. Lake Shore & Michigan Southern* was in adjournment. It was anticipated that the jury would receive the case to begin their deliberations the following Monday afternoon. Judge Dickey received a telephone call from a Mr. Jerome of the Legal Department of the Lake Shore & Michigan Southern Railway Company. Responding to Jerome's urgent request for a personal interview, Dickey went to the road's offices where Jerome told him that a Mr. Harry Silberman had proposed obtaining a favorable verdict for the railroad in the Reardon case in exchange for the payment of money to certain unnamed jurors. Apparently Jerome did not refuse the proposition out of hand, but contacted Dickey as soon as Silberman left. After discussing the situation with Dickey, they decided to present the problem to the judge hearing the matter, Walter C. Ong, the following Monday morning before the opening of court. According to Dickey, they wanted to get Ong's permission to set a trap to ensnare Silberman and the corrupt juror or jurors. According to newspaper reports, it was at this time that Jerome instructed private detectives (it is never made clear whether they were actually road employees) to shadow the aspiring bagman, Silberman.[7]

Judge Ong was elected to the Cuyahoga County common pleas bench in 1894. Born in rural Jefferson County, Ohio, he attended Richmond College where he conducted studies in classics. He read the law under an attorney in Steubenville, Ohio and then attended the University of Michigan's "Law Department" where he obtained a Bachelor of Laws in 1874. He was admitted to the Ohio bar that same year and practiced in Steubenville before emigrating to Cleveland in 1882. He was a Republican "with convictions on the subject of finance and coinage" and had, before assuming the bench, practiced law and served as a Cleveland city councilman.[8]

As planned, before the opening of court Monday morning, Dickey and Jerome obtained a private audience with Judge Ong. After Dickey and Jerome briefed Ong on the weekend's developments, there ensued a discussion of who the probable corrupt juror was, but all agreed there was insufficient proof to accuse anyone of wrongdoing. According to Dickey's statement to the Bar Association, the three men discussed two other instances from that term of court where "there were strong indications and circumstantial evidence looking in the direction that jurors had been bribed." Dickey urged Judge Ong to "let the matter develop" so as to secure enough proof to pursue the culpable parties. By Dickey's recounting, the conversation was as follows:

> Thereupon Judge Ong said, "I see no reason why I should interfere
> with this trial or jurors taking bribes if any of them desire so to do."
> and then asked by saying, "Judge Dickey you have a world of
> experience on the Bench and at the Bar and I would rather rely on
> your judgment than my own." I said to him in reply that in my
> opinion it was not only his right, but his duty to permit this matter
> to develop and the parties, if possible, convicted and punished for
> their corruption. That it was a duty he owed as Judge to the public
> to purify, if possible, the channels and foundations of justice.[9]

Judge Ong agreed. And so began their short, sensational and unhappy
adventure "to purify foundations and channels."

What was remarkable about the 'in camera' Monday morning
conference, and what caused the ensuing maelstrom within the legal
community, was that it was *ex parte*. Reardon's attorney, Foran, who was in
no way implicated in this nascent plot, was excluded from the discussions
regarding what to do about Silberman's solicitation and continued to try the
case that Monday morning and afternoon wholly ignorant that the trial would
likely prove a nullity. In keeping with what was now a farce, the case was
submitted to the jury that afternoon, but they adjourned their deliberations
until the next day. Whether by oversight or by design, Foran was not
informed of the weekend's developments until after the sensational Monday
evening arrest of Silberman and the culpable juror, one Max Rosenblatt.

It seems that upon returning to his office following the morning
conference with Messrs. Ong and Dickey, Jerome instructed a detective to
pose as a representative of the railroad, and inform Silberman that a bribe
would be paid at the Kennard House, a large downtown hotel, where they
should meet that evening with the interested juror. Unknown to Silberman
or Rosenblatt, the detectives had set up the appointed parlor of the Kennard
House so that a stenographer was secreted behind a sideling bed, while
double doors leading into an adjoining room concealed two other detectives
who could also hear any conversation in the meeting room. According to
newspaper reports,[10] prior to the $300 bribe being paid, there was some
conversation about other bribes having been paid that term of court along
with the names of the allegedly involved attorneys.[11] Upon payment of the
bribe, the detectives from the adjoining room burst in, arrested the pair and
took them to the criminal court where they were charged that same evening.

It was undoubtedly an unusual hearing before Judge Ong on the Tuesday morning following Silberman and Rosenblatt's sensational arrest, when Foran first learned of the affair. Apparently, Foran was confident of how the trial had gone. He suggested that the deliberations continue with the remaining 11 jurors, but Dickey objected and Judge Ong declared a mistrial. Presumably, Foran's remarks at the hearing that morning were simply more than a good plaintiffs' attorney could resist: "I want it stated here in open court," he protested, "that it was Lake Shore money that was used with these two men."

Now, more than a month following the arrests, the legal community was meeting to air the matter. Some in attendance were clearly concerned with upholding Ong's good name. Others apparently viewed the meeting as an opportunity to embarrass both Ong and the corporate bar. The proceedings were noisy and clamorous but ultimately, anticlimactic. After reading his statement of the particulars of the incident to the assembled members of the Bar Association, Dickey offered a resolution worded so as to express the membership's warm approval of Judge Ong's role in the matter. The response to Dickey's resolution was not unanimous and a small but shrill group led by Judge Ingersoll complained loud, and some in attendance thought over-long, that the Bar Association had no proper business passing resolutions endorsing judges for merely "doing their duty." The meeting soon degenerated into an exchange of pompous speeches, resolutions and counter-resolutions and parliamentary maneuvers to bring the competing resolutions to a vote. Ingersoll, a brother judge on the common pleas bench, evidenced considerable personal enmity toward Judge Ong, who was conspicuously absent from the meeting.

> Judge Ingersoll said that since the association had declared that it had jurisdiction to take action, he was in favor of making a thorough investigation. He thought that there might be much to be investigated, declaring that no judge had the right to tempt a juror into accepting a bribe.[12]

Ingersoll seemed to delight in the parliamentary thrust and parry preventing the members, most of whom supported Ong, from getting an acceptable resolution to a vote. Finally, a watered-down version of Dickey's glowing and effusive resolution of endorsement was submitted to a vote. The new resolution rather weakly declared that based upon the uncontradicted version of events submitted to the members in attendance (by Dickey), the Association endorsed Judge Ong's actions and stated that there appeared to be no basis upon which to refer the matter to committee for further investigation. The resolution passed overwhelmingly. When Judge Ingersoll called for a count of the "yeas" and "nays" he was resoundingly and unceremoniously hooted down.[13]

Foran put the best face on it when he spoke to reporters at the meeting, being careful to commend Judge Ong's heroic and dogged pursuit of the courthouse corruption. But Foran apparently couldn't resist the opportunity to take another shot at the corporate bar. He told reporters he "regretted that it had developed to the advantage of the side taken by Mr. Dickey:"

> We were permitted to go on trying the case, although the other side knew that it would be a nullity. It is not the first time that a corporation has introduced corruption into a case that I was trying. I am satisfied that such work has been carried on for years in this Court. Such things must be stopped, and therefore, I for one heartily approve of the course which Judge Ong took.[14]

Foran was quoted by a rival newspaper on the very same subject as follows:

> I was the attorney on the other side but was left entirely in the dark until the arrests were made. Aside from this I have nothing to complain of. In fact, I am glad that these men were arrested. I am satisfied that this bribing of jurors has been going on for years and I know positively that I have tried many cases against corporations where the corporations managed to get into the jury boxes.[15]

And what happened to Silberman and Rosenblatt? Upon their arrest, the newspapers picked up the case and played it for all it was worth—and then some. Silberman, a junk dealer, and Rosenblatt, a blacksmith, were brothers-in-law. There was suspicion of another juror, but it was apparently without foundation in fact, or at least, proof. Silberman, who was savvy enough not to talk to reporters directly, managed to leak his improbable version of the events to the press through friends who attended his initial court appearances after his arrest. Silberman claimed that one Detective Joy approached him on the Monday morning of the arrests to borrow $400. Silberman claimed to know Joy was a railroad man and "supposed him to be a high official of the road." So he loaned him $300 (he didn't have $400) and arranged for Joy to repay the loan that evening at the Kennard House.

The details of the railroad's "sting" operation were followed in great and vivid detail in front page stories in the competing daily papers. At one point, a private detective involved in the operation received a letter offering him $2,000 if he arranged it so that an unnamed witness would not testify against Silberman, "who is a fine man."[16] No charges were brought. Their cases were pushed through the preliminary criminal case procedures in record time. Arrested on November 22, 1897 they were charged, arraigned, indicted, released from contempt proceedings by Judge Ong and set for trial on December 8, 1897. Vernon H. Burke (Rosenblatt's soon-to-be-disbarred attorney—for an unrelated matter) in a desperate and transparent ploy to buy time, filed an "affidavit of prejudice" against the judge hearing the case. The prosecutor was asked by an incredulous Burke, why, given all the other defendants languishing in jail awaiting trial for more serious offenses, Rosenblatt, who was free on bond, was being rushed into trial.[17] It was no use; the case was assigned to a new judge and reset for trial on December 13, 1897.

Things could have gone much worse for the pair of enterprising in-laws. Much to the surprise and chagrin of the prosecutor, jury bribery was only a misdemeanor offense, punishable by a maximum term of 90 days in jail and a fine of $500. The penal statute in question was not much used. The last prosecution for the offense in Cuyahoga County was in 1876, some 21 years before. On December 13th they both pleaded guilty as charged. On December 16th, each was sentenced to pay a fine of $500 and to be held at the workhouse until the fines were paid.

And what of Reardon's cause? As Foran complained, the first trial (which took some two weeks to present to the jury) was a "nullity." The case was immediately retried, and on December 8, 1897, the jury returned a verdict in favor of Reardon for the sum of $7,000. The next day the road filed a motion for a new trial charging various errors including that the jury's verdict in favor of Reardon "was against the law of the land." Judge Ong didn't rule on the motion until *after* the Bar Association meeting called on December 28, 1897. On January 6, 1898, Ong granted the railroad's motion for a new trial. The record is thereafter silent until April 4, 1898, when the final entry on the docket indicates that the matter was "Settled without record, at defendant's costs."

* * * * *

Motoring their way along the twisted, gloomy streets that followed the winding river through the grimy industrial-residential valley, through ". . . The Dumps, the factory district, with dingy, smoke-coated, dilapidated frame houses everywhere," Henk grew uncharacteristically quiet. Reviving as they approached their destination to "sign-up" a case, a recent industrial mishap (the Nikopopulos matter), Henk swelled with pride imagining what his boss, the charismatic Mark Leffingwell, would do at the trial pleading to "the twelve bone-heads in the jury box."

"This here case we are going to get signed up is a beauty!—a leg broken off above the knee, a three-inch gash across the forehead, three broken ribs, injured spine—that's a pippin!" He tossed his head and clacked his tongue with inexpressible delight. "Say, what Mark won't do to this here defendant!"

"I can already see the cripple wheeled into the court room, Mark's eyes rolling from the invalid chair to the faces of them jurors, and then back to the invalid chair. And the fireworks start. `I object! I object!' them corporation lawyers holler (and he imitated the voice of the imaginary objector); and Mark, as smooth and as oily as a well greased axle, looks up smilingly at them mad lawyers, and says, (now imitating Leffingwell's voice). `Do you object to have this honorable body of your peers—these twelve just gentlemen in the jury box—do you object to have them know the truth as to how this pathetic figure in the invalid chair—this cripple, who once could walk as firmly, and perhaps as arrogantly, as any of you little brothers of the rich—(rolling his eyes in the direction of them corporation lawyers)—how this poor man who used to embrace his wife every morning, with his six little kiddies clinging to his limbs, as he would leave for the shop to earn his livelihood by the sweat of his brow—do you object to have the facts known about this remnant of the man he once was, who now glances longingly—nay, yearningly—at you and me, who move about freely—and this poor man unable to move without the support of crutches, without the aid of an invalid chair—well make your objection! I won't press this point.' And Mark sits down with a loud sigh, his face as clouded as an April sky, and the twelve bone-heads in the jury box, pull their red bandannas to wipe the rolling tears away and wipe their noses. Some sight that, I'll tell you."

*   *   *   *   *

Is the court and jury system for fixing the responsibility for industrial accidents, now existing in the State, satisfactory in its operation?"

I respectfully submit that no person familiar with conditions, could possibly answer this question in the affirmative.

It will probably not be disputed, that many verdicts are affected by a sympathetic attachment between the jurors and the plaintiff, by reason of the latter's injury and his poverty, as against the more fortunate defendant. This is all natural and human, but it is not exactly justice. In preparing a case for trial, the all important question seems to be, is there evidence of a character that will take it to the jury?[18]

When Stephen W. Tener,[19] Manager of the Accident Department for American Steel and Wire appeared before the Ohio Employers' Liability Commission he read his testimony into the record from a prepared text. He left little to chance before the Commission, as was consistent with the Accident Department's approach to its corporate function of risk management and loss control. As Tener makes clear, that function often reduced to keeping cases away from juries. Tener had two major points to make before the Commission. The first was to advocate, as a delegated agent on behalf of the single largest employer in Cleveland, if not Ohio, for passage of a state-wide workmen's compensation law. The second was to tout to the Commission, and whomever else was present at the Commission's Cleveland hearings, his company's in-house, injury compensation scheme, The Voluntary Accident Relief Plan, which Tener immodestly declared to be "nothing more or less than a voluntary Workmen's Compensation Act."[20]

The American Steel and Wire Company's compensation plan provided an operative model for the Ohio statutory scheme that legislated a statewide compulsory compensation in 1914. By its terms, the Voluntary Accident Relief Plan paid an injured employee a fixed percentage of his wages for a fixed period of time following the injury, without reference to the common law rules which, at least in theory, fixed or frustrated recovery in litigation against the company. By the Plan's terms, if the employee was injured while in the service of the company he was entitled to "relief." But, as was true with the Compensation Act eventually passed by the Ohio legislature, there was a catch. As provided in the company Plan:

13. No relief will be paid to any employee or his family if suit is

brought against the company. In no case whatsoever will the company deal with an attorney or with anyone except the injured man or some member of his family in the matter of relief to be paid under this plan, because it is part of the plan that the whole amount paid shall be received by the employee and his family.[21]

The company's patent aversion to lawyers and the litigation they engendered was born of experience, and bears closer examination here.

Table 2, "A.S.&W. Co. Work Injury Trial Outcomes" is a compilation of all the verdicts rendered in the litigation brought against the company by injured employees in the Common Pleas Court of Cuyahoga County and the United States Sixth Circuit Court for the Northern District of Ohio from the company's inception in 1898 to the passage of Ohio's mandatory workmen's compensation act in 1914. Table 2 only presents those cases that actually went to trial. It does not include cases filed against the company in state or federal court that were settled before trial. While settled cases were the rule, (84 settled for the 43 that were tried) the majority of settled cases did not leave a public record of the amounts paid to the injured worker in exchange for dropping his suit.

Table 2 lists the year the worker's suit was filed (not necessarily the year of injury); the worker's job at the company to the extent it appears in the pleadings; a summary of the injuries sustained; the court where the litigation was resolved (sometimes different from where it was initiated given the company's predilection to "remove" actions from state court to federal court); whether the verdict was rendered by a judge or a jury; the amount of the verdict ($0 is a verdict in favor of the company); and finally whether the trial outcome was the result of a "directed verdict," where the judge took the power of deciding a case away from the jury by "directing" them to return a verdict in favor of the company. Even allowing for the statistical infirmities incident to such a small sample, the cases included in Table 2 provide some insight concerning the prevailing patterns in the cases filed against the company in the Cleveland area.

Perhaps the most striking and utterly consistent finding demonstrated in Table 2 is that during the eighteen years of litigation covered by the table, a jury *never* sent an injured worker home from his day(s) in court empty-handed. The only case where a jury verdict in favor of a plaintiff was so small as to count for a defeat, (Case No. 32) was still, at least technically, a verdict in favor of the plaintiff worker. The worker recoveries from juries in the state common pleas court ranged from a low of $50 to a high of $1800 with an average recovery, over the period, of $487. Two points of context

No.	Year	Worker Occupation	Court	Decided By	Recovery
		AMERICAN STEEL AND WIRE COMPANY WORK INJURIES—TRIAL OUTCOMES 1898-1915			
1	1900	Wire Drawer	Federal	Judge/DV	$0
2	1900	Laborer	Federal	Judge/DV	$0
3	1900	Electrician	Federal	Judge/DV	$0
4	1901	Laborer	Federal	Judge/DV	$0
5	1901	Laborer	State	Jury	$150
6	1901	—	Federal	Judge	$500
7	1901	Laborer	State	Judge	$800
8	1902	Pipefitter Helper	State	Jury	$400
9	1902	—	Federal	Judge	$600
10	1902	Wire Drawer	State	Judge	$700
11	1902	Nail Machine Helper	State	Judge	$150
12	1902	Hooker, rod mill	State	Judge	$125
13	1902	Scale Messenger	State	Judge	$350
14	1903	Laborer	State	Jury	$1,800
15	1903	Hooker, rod mill	State	Judge	$2,000
16	1903	Hooker, rod mill	Federal	Judge/DV	$0
17	1903	Ladle car oiler	Federal	Judge/DV	$0
18	1904	Machinist	State	Jury	$500
19	1904	Laborer	State	Jury	$350
20	1904	Nail Machine Helper	State	Jury	$400
21	1904	Switchman	State	Jury	$250
22	1906	Laborer	State	Jury	$175
23	1906	Roller, wire mill	Federal	Judge/DV	$0
24	1906	Laborer	State	Jury	$175
25	1906	Laborer	State	Jury	$275
26	1906	Laborer	State	Jury	$105
27	1906	Hooker, rod mill	State	Jury	$100
28	1906	Laborer	State	Jury	$1,600
29	1906	Hooker, rod mill	State	Jury	$250
30	1906	Switchman	State	Jury	$1,200
31	1907	Scrap man	State	Jury	$100
32	1907	Helper, nail mill	State	Jury	$50
33	1907	Laborer, rod mill	Federal	Judge	$3,000
34	1907	Laborer	Federal	Judge	$1,060
35	1908	Laborer	State	Jury	$300

Table 2

AMERICAN STEEL AND WIRE COMPANY WORK INJURIES—TRIAL OUTCOMES 1898-1915					
36	1908	Helper, nail mill	State	Jury	$100
37	1909	Loader	State	Jury	$250
38	1910	Laborer, rod mill	State	Jury	$250
39	1910	Laborer	State	Judge	$900
40	1913	Laborer	State	Jury	$200
41	1913	Laborer	State	Jury	$1,200
42	1914	Electrician Helper	State	Jury	$1,500
43	1914	—	Federal	Jury	$3,000

Source: Court Files, Common Pleas, Probate & U.S. Circuit Courts, Cleveland, Ohio.

Table 2 (Cont.)

should be borne in mind when considering that average sum. First, coming off the deflationary economy of the 1890s, $500 was, depending upon the skill level of the worker and the general economic conditions governing the continuity of his employment (full employment over more than a couple of years was rare), about one year's wages in the steel industry. Second, a number of the jury verdicts, especially at the low end of the spectrum, were for the maximum amount the jury could award, i.e. the "prayer" amount stated in the petition filed with the court. Thus, the jury verdicts in 18 of the 24 cases they decided in state court (75%) were for the maximum amount it was in their power to grant. Case Nos. 5, 8, 14, 19, 20, 21, 24, 25, 28, 29, 30, 31, 35, 36, 37, 38, 41, and 42 gave the worker a judgment against the company for the exact sum the worker requested.

Another remarkable pattern demonstrated in Table 2 is that, in federal court, a jury was not allowed to decide a case until 1914; and when that jury was given the rare opportunity to decide liability and damages in a federal proceeding the verdict was for $3,000. Historically, the appointed, as opposed to elected, federal judiciary has zealously guarded its prerogative to decide cases "on the law" thereby depriving the jury of the opportunity to decide cases "on the facts." The table reveals that during the pre-compensation period the only time workers lost their cases at trial against the company was in federal court when, after presenting their evidence to a jury, the judge would take the case away from the jury on the basis that, "as a matter of law," the worker failed to meet one of the sundry technical constraints of the federally-divined, "general" employer liability law. See

Table 2, Case Nos. 1, 2, 3, 4, 16, 17 and 23. Plainly, the trinity of employer defenses was, as a practical matter, only available to American Steel and Wire in federal court.[22]

In the state common pleas court, with its elected judiciary and the "scintilla rule," an altogether different set of circumstances prevailed. The difference was not simply a matter of the two jurisdictions having substantively different rules of negligence. While the federal court applied the employer defenses more stringently than they would have been applied in the state courts, the Ohio *appellate* cases still upheld some version of all the loathed employer defenses. But, more importantly, Cleveland juries would not recognize those defenses. Moreover, Table 2 also suggests that not only were juries more favorably disposed to workers than was technically allowed by the harsh rules of employer liability, but that the common pleas bench was, as a rule, far more sympathetic to injured workers than the common law supposedly tolerated, at least when the behemoth Steel Trust was the defendant named in the suit. This trial-level judicial pattern is demonstrated in Table 2. Case Nos. 7, 10, 11, 12, 13, 15, and 39. Here again, an injured employee of American Steel and Wire never lost his case.

No.	Year	Worker Occupation	Court	Decided By	Recovery
\multicolumn{6}{|c|}{**AMERICAN STEEL AND WIRE COMPANY WORK INJURIES—SETTLEMENT RECOVERIES 1898-1915**}					
1	1899	Laborer	Federal	Settled	$63
2	1899	Laborer	Federal	Settled	$69
3	1905	Machinist	Federal	Settled	$750
4	1906	Wire Drawer	Federal	Settled	$2,200
5	1906	Laborer	State	Settled	$200
6	1907	Wire Drawer	Federal	Settled	$400
7	1907	Laborer	Federal	Settled	$6,200
8	1907	Carpenter	State	Settled	$150
9	1908	—	Federal	Settled	$1,400
10	1909	—	Federal	Settled	$850
11	1911	—	Federal	Settled	$450
12	1912	Laborer	State	Settled	$400

Source: Court Files, Common Pleas, Probate & U.S. Circuit Courts, Cleveland, Ohio.

Table 3

The above discussion of the common pleas judges raises one final issue relevant to understanding what Table 2 does, and does not, mean. If the juries were a powerful factor in the local courts who tended to impose a standard of "strict liability" against American Steel and Wire—the orthodox common law notwithstanding—their power to enforce such "lawlessness" against the company derived from the common pleas bench permitting them to do so. While the discretion vested in the state court judges to grant directed verdicts was limited by the "scintilla rule," there remained in the judges a wide latitude to grant motions for new trial *after* the jury returned its verdict (as was done by Judge Ong in the Reardon case). But not once in eighteen years did the judges in the common pleas court direct a verdict in favor of the company or grant the company's (numerous) post-trial motions to vacate a jury's verdict.

Table 3 catalogues the cases filed by injured workers against the company that were settled before trial and left a public record of the sums paid to the workers in exchange for dropping their suit. One significant point is suggested (the sample is far too small for more than a "suggestion," N=12) by the settlement figures. It appears that when the company did settle a case, it was on relatively generous terms. Finally, Table 4 indicates that in the 12 cases where the settlement amount is known, the average recovery in both courts (even correcting for the apparently aberrant Case No. 7) was $687 exactly $200 more than the average common pleas jury award of $487. What

A.S.&W. Co., Overall Recovery Averages					
Court	Jury	Judge	Trial J&J	Settlm't	All
State	$487	$718	$539	$250	$557
Federal	$3,000	$469	$689	$874	$609
Combined	$587	$566	$578	$687	$599

Source: Court Files, Common Pleas, Probate & U.S. Circuit Courts, Cleveland, Ohio.

Table 4

is most striking about Table 4 is how consistent the overall recovery amounts were for the litigation over the period. Judge or jury, federal or state court, or settlement in either, the recovery averages are remarkably consistent. However, this consistency should not be confused with recovery *rates* which were very distinct as between the federal and state forums. The consistency here relates only to what amount was recovered, *when it was recovered*, not whether it would be recovered.

Tables 2 and 3 also demonstrate that the company's ability to remove the serious cases (prayers exceeding $2,000) to federal court provided it with an opportunity to manage the worker litigation in such a way as to avoid large verdicts during the eighteen years of "common law compensation" imposed in the state courts. In effect, the trifling cases were left in the state courts and the serious injuries were resolved in federal court. Table 3 establishes that the company was willing to pay for settlements to avoid trials. The highest recovery of record in the eighteen year period was a settlement (Case No. 7, Table 3). Moreover, given the size of the plant facilities in the Cleveland area (employing at least 5,000 men) and the well known hazards of steel making generally—and wire drawing in particular—it is clear that the cases that reached the courts were only a very small sample of the total injury cases that could have been filed.[23] The Voluntary Accident Relief Plan was years in the making, not born full blown in May of 1910. Managing litigation was a concept well understood from years of experience by this large employer. Accidents were an actuarial certainty, and the company learned how to minimize both the risk and cost those accidents engendered.

* * * * *

In January of 1916, the Civic League of Cleveland, a local good government organization, released its report on investigations into the jury system of the Cuyahoga County Common Pleas Court.[24] The League's report followed fast upon the heels of the Cleveland Bar Association's own investigation into the jury system conducted in 1914. The Bar Association's report was not published, but its contents and the research supporting its findings were made available to the Civic League, which in turn supplemented the information gathered through the Bar Association's efforts. In adding to the Bar Association's work, the League produced the most detailed and explicit analysis of how the jury system—long accused of being corrupt—actually worked.

The Civic League's investigation began with the premise that trial by jury was a hallowed institution of American government, abolition of which was unthinkable, but:

On the other hand, the opinion is gaining ground in many quarters that this venerable institution in our system of jurisprudence is no longer adapted to the times. A Judge of the Cincinnati Superior Court, handing down a decision, said recently: 'An experience of three years on the bench has perceptibly diminished our reverence for that sacred institution, the jury.'[25]

For anyone unfamiliar with the workings of the Cuyahoga County Common Pleas Court, or for those who might have remained skeptical of the long standing, and usually unsubstantiated, rumors of the jury's corrupt demise within the county, the League's report proved a sobering and disheartening revelation.

At the outset, the Civic League noted that there was a vast gulf between the state laws governing the selection, summoning and supervision of jurors and how those ends were, in practice, accomplished in Cuyahoga County. In regard to the generalized need for reform, the League stood upon common ground with the Bar Association. However, unlike the elite lawyers who concluded that the laws governing juries were obsolete and in need of amendment and revision, the League concluded that the statutes on the books were quite adequate. Rather, it was the men who administered the jury laws who were in need of reform:

In our opinion, the essential fault is not with the law, although it has some defects, but with the administration of the law. The law is adequate to secure satisfactory jurors, and the reason for the unsatisfactory conditions which were permitted to develop can, we believe, be traced almost entirely to the failure on the part of those administering the law to observe its letter and spirit.[26]

The officials the League held most accountable for the corrupt administration of the jury system were the Jury Commissioners, who were appointed annually by the judges of the common pleas court.

Between 1905 and 1912 the Ohio statute required the appointment of four commissioners in Cuyahoga County, two from each political party. In 1913 the number was changed to two commissioners, but the mandated requirement of balance between the political parties remained. The salaries of the commissioners were more honorary than real. Prior to the legislative changes passed in 1913 (which raised the annual stipend to $300—$5 per day, up to 60 days per annum), the most a commissioner could earn in his official capacity was $30 per year. It was the jury commissioners' job to select, summon and supervise the citizens who would perform jury duty during their terms. The statute required that each commissioner subscribe to an oath prior to beginning his term that, "he will consent to the selection of no person as juror," whom the commissioner believes "to be unfit for that position or likely to render a partial verdict in any cause in which he may be called as a juror."

The statutorily prescribed mechanism for the selection of jurors operated in three basic steps. First, the jury commissioners were to cull the county elector lists so as to choose an adequate number of names to meet the requirements of the next term of court. This initial selection process was left largely to the commissioners' discretion except that the jurors were to be selected from the several wards and townships in approximate proportion to the respective populations of those political subdivisions to the county's total population. Having prepared this long list (comprising over 1,000 names a year) of "discrete and judicious persons" the statute next required that each name on the list be entered on separate slips of paper "uniform in size, quality and color." The commissioners were charged to then deposit these slips of paper into a jury wheel, there to be drawn in a random fashion in the presence of the sheriff and county clerk. Once in the wheel, approximately half the slips would be drawn out to meet the court's annual requirement for jurors. The law provided numerous safeguards to protect the integrity of the drawing process. The wheel was to be locked between use and, before any drawing, the statute required that the wheel be turned several times until the slips were thoroughly mixed. Finally, the statute provided for the commissioners to have the sheriff summon the electors whose names were drawn, to report to the court to serve a two to three week term as a juror.

The first juncture where the system broke down in actual administration was in the compilation of names to go into the jury wheel. The Civic League reformers conducted an investigation of all the names certified to be placed into the jury wheel in the ten years leading up to their report. What they found regarding the randomness of this initial selection process undercut the statute's protection entirely, even assuming that the balance of the law was being administered properly. Of the eleven thousand odd names placed into the Cuyahoga County jury wheel in the period between 1905 and 1915, 6,696 names had been selected for inclusion once; 330 citizens had been included twice; 215 citizens had made it to the wheel three times in the ten year period; 198 individuals had been inserted on four occasions in the decade; 143 electors were five times included; 96 names had been inserted six times for jury service; 61 individuals had been selected no less than seven times in the ten year period; 25 eligible voters were selected eight times; 31

individuals had been selected for inclusion nine years of the ten studied; and exactly 12 citizens (an ironic sum) had been honored for inclusion for ten out of the ten years examined. The Civic League observed:

> Three hundred and sixty-eight names appeared a total of 2,317 times in the period of ten years, or an average of six times each . . .
>
>   Cuyahoga County has had a voting population of at least 90,000 throughout the ten years' period. Assuming, as a low estimate, that one-third of the voters are qualified for jury service, then there would have been not less than 30,000 names from which to select the 11,000 names which went into the jury wheel during the ten years. Only one-third of the available material would have been called upon and no names would have gone into the wheel more than once. Yet, we find 1,120 names appearing more than once, and 368 of them appear more than six times each.[27]

Obviously, the selection of jurors in Cuyahoga County was not a random process.

The jury statute stipulated that the commissioners were forbidden to seek or receive suggestions from any source regarding the identification of potential jurors. The statute further stipulated that all other citizens were forbidden to interfere with the commissioners' exclusive task of selecting and summoning the jury venire[28] for each court session. Nonetheless, interviews with former commissioners revealed an altogether different selection process prevailed in Cuyahoga County.

What the League found was that often the "repeaters" in the jury wheel had requested, sometimes even in writing, that they be allowed to serve over and over again as jurors. In addition to direct solicitation on the part of aspiring jurors, it was the long established practice on the part of political leaders from both parties, including courtroom bailiffs and other minor court functionaries, county and municipal officials and even common pleas judges, to provide the commissioners with lists of names of persons who wanted to perform jury service. Often included on these lists were men "out of employment," "hangers on at the Courthouse" and men who preferred an occupation that "neither required great mental effort nor physical exertion." One of the former commissioners had admitted to writing "judges and friends" in order to request suitable names for inclusion in the jury wheel. Often enough, the Judges were only too happy to suggest individuals for service. The same commissioner (unnamed in the report) indicated that "political leaders" would sometimes furnish long lists of names. County and city employees, especially those whose services to the body politic were required on an only seasonal basis, were often given jury service during the winter months. In the words of the Civic League, the task of the jury commissioners:

> . . . degenerated into the indifferent and irresponsible process of accepting the list of names of those who each year were suggested to them by interested persons, and of adding enough additional names to meet the order of the court . . . Once or twice during the period, when the commissioners were being criticized because of the poor quality of jurors, a few names of prominent citizens were placed in the wheel, but they were seldom, if ever, drawn from the wheel.[29]

While the League succeeded in discovering how the repeaters got into the jury wheel over and over again, they met with no success in determining how those individuals were "randomly" drawn from the wheel with such extraordinary regularity. In the decade examined by the Report (1905-1915), 5,489 slips were drawn from the wheel, averaging about 550 per year. When

JURORS DRAWN TO SERVE, CUYAHOGA COUNTY, 1905-1915		
Number of Names That Were Drawn	The Number Of Times Drawn	Number of Resulting "Juror Terms"
1804	Once	1804
409	2 Times	818
322	3 Times	966
216	4 Times	864
64	5 Times	320
43	6 Times	258
42	7 Times	294
21	8 Times	168
1	9 Times	9
1	10 Times	10
Total 2,923		Total 5,511

Source: Civic League, "Report of Investigations . . ."

Table 5

the League's investigators broke down the names drawn from the wheel to examine for "repeaters" they discovered the full and startling extent of the corruption underlying the jury selection process. Table 5 breaks out the jury repeaters on the common pleas venire between 1905 and 1915. Some elementary calculations demonstrate to what extent a small group of the county's electors dominated the jury rolls. Of the 5511 juror/terms only 1804 were filled by "one timers," or approximately 33% of the total juror/terms. The remaining two-thirds of the juror/terms for the decade were filled by "repeaters." Or stated another way, between 1905 and 1915, 1,119 "seasoned jurors," approximately one-third of the total summoned for duty, filled two-thirds of the available juror seats. As was dryly remarked in the League's Report:

> Only one of two conclusions is possible. Either the mathematical law of averages falls down entirely when applied to jury drawing, or else there has been tampering with the jury wheel for the purpose of extracting names wanted by some one for jury service. It is reasonable to assume the latter conclusion is the proper one.[30]

Although the Civic League chose to de-emphasize the issue, certainly a prime motivation for some to repeatedly serve as jurors was the generous per diem allowance paid for jury service. Since the turn of the century, by statute, jurors were granted $2.00 a day for their time. During this period, a day laborer could look forward to receiving anywhere from $1.00 to $1.50 a day in wages while a skilled mechanic would make anywhere from $2.00 to $4.50 a day. Thus, jury service paid a competitive wage.

Moreover, as we have seen, there were ways for an "enterprising" juror to supplement the per diem allowance. The League acknowledged many unsubstantiated stories and rumors, especially as involved the "professional jurors" and their readiness to accept financial inducements to decide cases in favor of the party paying the incentive. Their report summarized the many opportunities for corruption:

> The net result of this negligence in the selection of names for the jury wheel . . . has been the development of a body of professional jurors. Some of whom have been good men, but many of whom have had no other object in performing service than the petty $2.00 a day per diem wage, or the larger amounts which might come from litigants in other ways. This latter group has

contaminated the whole system, and has caused suspicion to be reflected on all jurors alike. Criticisms and complaints against the quality of juries by practicing attorneys; the presence of claim agents, attorneys and detectives about the jury room; the intimate knowledge which some attorneys seem to have of every juror; the large number of manifestly unfair verdicts and numerous other complaints culminated last summer in the offer of one of these professional jurors to accept a bribe from an able and reputable member of the bar.[31]

But the opportunities for corruption were hardly limited to a few enterprising professional jurors. The League discovered a relatively minor court functionary, the jury bailiff, was vested with very broad discretion in determining which jurors would be sent to a courtroom to hear any given case. The jury bailiff had absolute freedom in selecting whom he wished to send up to a courtroom as a venire panel from which the final twelve man jury would be selected. There was no random, or even structured, system for making up that initial group of the jury venire. No alphabetical method, no method of numbers, or birth dates, rather the jury bailiff was allowed to roam over the list "at will." Of course this wide discretion allowed the jury bailiff, having prior notice of a particular case being set to begin trial, to select those jurors whom experience had taught would be inclined to favor one side over the other. Thus, an attorney preparing to select a petite jury to hear his case might look up to survey the venire and find not a single juror favorably disposed to the class or group to which his client belonged. The League discovered that this wide discretion to "pack" a panel for an interested lawyer or litigant formerly rested with the jury commissioners, but as a result of the Cleveland Bar Association's investigation a year and one half previously, that discretionary function was given to the jury bailiff. These shifting but persistent patterns of maintaining avenues for broad administrative discretion (and corruption) will again appear in the Cleveland Foundation's *Survey* of the criminal courts conducted seven years later.

The League called for initiating procedures that might prevent juries from behaving improperly during their deliberations. One of the greatest abuses documented by the Report was "quotient verdicts." During this period, civil lawsuits were tried to twelve jurors and their verdicts, whether for the plaintiff or the defendant, had to be unanimous. As the Report explained, a quotient verdict was reached by each juror writing on a slip of paper the amount of damages he thinks ought to be awarded. Those sums were then added and divided by twelve and the resulting quotient determined the verdict returned by the jury.[32] Acknowledging that jury deliberations would (and should) never be open to inspection, the League proposed that the only way to stem the quotient verdict abuse was to raise the "standard of the jurors" through proper administration of the existing law.

The Civic League called for other reforms. The report expressed approval for the reforms already instituted following the Bar Association's investigation. The League noted that in the court term prior to their investigation, seven of the thirteen common pleas judges (a revealingly close margin) had signed an order reforming the initial selection process of jurors by requiring that the jury commissioners abandon the list of names traditionally provided to compile the pool of electors deposited into the jury wheel. Safeguards had apparently been effected to assure the propriety of the name drawing from the jury wheel itself (the League found few repeaters in the most recent drawing). Whereas the jury commissioners were formerly allowed to select the venires sent to the courtrooms for a trial, that particular abuse had now apparently been corrected—only to reemerge in the office of the jury bailiff.

Finally, the League, evidencing considerable prescience, fully anticipated the resistance reforms would meet from the judiciary and suggested the need to reorient the thinking that pervaded the entire courthouse:

> The Judges, bailiffs, party leaders and those seeking appointment for jury service must first be made to see that jury service is not a method of reward for party service, a means of livelihood, or a remedy for non-employment, but an important judicial service, involving the whole issue of the protection of personal and property rights—a service which must be performed, not for the $2.00 per diem, but as a public duty.[33]

* * * * *

We rejoin our heroic young lawyer almost a year later. He is working late one night at the Leffingwell's office, immersed in the law books, checking a point of procedure for "Mark." It is the nearing the eve of trial for the badly maimed Nikopopulos against his former employer, the American Tool Company. Stillwell can hear the witness coaching going on in the adjoining room with Leffingwell, his assistants, the assorted witnesses and three interpreters "one Greek, one Slovak, one Croatian" all assembled "to make the Master's meaning clear . . ."

When the witnesses left, Leffingwell remained alone with Henk. The door between his private office and the library was only slightly open, but owing to the stillness of the night every word reached my ears in spite of their lowered voices.

"It's fixed. Tim (he was the Jury Commissioner, who assigned jurors to the different court rooms) handed me this list. The case will go either to Judge Snellenbogen's Room or to Cahill's—"

"I don't want Cahill for this case," Leffingwell's voice growing contemplative. "That Irishman will joke too much about Kolokolchick and Mrs. Nikopopulos and take away all the pathos of this case. Besides, I don't believe he likes me. The other day he nearly killed the Vraczek case by making a facetious remark just as I was in the midst of picturing the scene of desolation when his family was notified of the accident."

"I'll see Tim before Court opens," replied Henk, "and he'll steer the case into Snellenbogen's—"

Their plans, however, evidently miscarried. The Nikopopulos case was sent to the room of a "dangerous Judge" (a dangerous Judge was one who did not yield to "influence"), and as a result, several jurors of uncertain learning had slipped in. Consternation struck Leffingwell's camp. Mark summoned his aides to his private office after the first day's Court session. Mark was not blaming Henk for the slip—the suave, smiling Leffingwell never blamed anyone—but he urged him to "get busy."

"I am not asleep, Mark" (everybody addressed Leffingwell by his first name), replied the resourceful Henk. "Number two lives on Holygrail Avenue, and I have arranged with Dan Taggert to pay him a visit this evening—and trust Dan for getting results."

"How about number seven (referring to another doubtful juror)?"

"He hangs out at Weinkeller's. Weinkeller will take care of him. You can always count on Bob to deliver the goods."

"Number eight is safe, so is nine and ten and four and three," Leffingwell was evidently scanning the list in his hand," but I am not so sure about eleven."

"He is all right—a *landsmann* of Tony's—Tony met him as he left the court room."

* * * * *

Lawyers tell the story of a long fight between counsel for the great
public service corporations and the personal injury attorneys, in
which the jury system was debauched by campaigns for the
allegiance of enough jurors to insure victory at the ensuing trials.
In those days, the jury commissioners made up lists of jurors from
names submitted by various persons, so that it was a relatively easy
matter for an influential corporation or a tort lawyer in large
practice to secure picked men on the jury lists. Then in some
mysterious manner, the names were drawn from the wheel.[34]

In 1921, seven years after work injury suits were banished from the
courts, another group of reform minded men had occasion to publish the
results of their investigations into the administration of the jury system of
Cleveland, Ohio.[35] This report, only a chapter in a more substantial
undertaking to survey nearly all of the administrative, professional, economic
and social aspects of the common pleas and municipal criminal[36] courts of
Cleveland, paused to reexamine the same worrisome juries detailed eight
years previously by the anxious Bar Association and righteous Civic League.
In many respects the Cleveland Foundation-sponsored *Criminal Justice In
Cleveland* was a mere echo, albeit a highly resonant one, of the earlier
investigations. The same overriding concern with the lowered "tone" of the
typical Cleveland jury served as the organizing focus in this study.
    Even though the Cleveland Foundation's survey followed the
compensation reform by half a decade, it is of interest for two reasons. First,
it went deeper in its investigation of the "jury problem" by cataloguing and
then analyzing the actual social composition of a typical Cleveland jury
venire. That effort provides us with a crude statistical sketch of the
occupational and residential affiliations of 380 serving jurors from the
Court's Spring Term of 1921. The statistical portrait that is drawn half a
decade following reform of the previously "loaded" jury lists helps to explain
why employers felt so thoroughly disadvantaged when worker suits were
tried before their "peers." Second, this study's reform perspective of the
urban jury problem represented the more cynical, xenophobic and anti-
democratic extreme of the jury reform spectrum. The thin, pre-War veneer
of democratic tolerance for the consequences of including all qualified
electors in the pool of potential jurors had grown thinner still in this post-
War, post-Red Scare, post-May Day riots period of obsessive
"Americanization." Succinctly put, the juries in Cuyahoga County
reflected—quite to a fault—a fair cross-section of the area's varied, ethnic,

recent-immigrant "industrial" population. According to this more cynical view, it was the very democratic nature of the urban jury that tended to undermine its continuing civic and jurisprudential utility. What troubled the elite lawyer-reformers was not just that the jury selection process was saddled, even still, with patronage and corruption—rather, it was the system's institutional predilection, even when honestly administered, to garner the stuff of a "great unassimilated industrial population"[37] into the court's jury pool. This was the less benign view of the urban jury—corrupt and inept—not so much by design, as by default.

Many of the by now familiar problems associated with patronage and corruption, so seemingly endemic to the county's jury administration, reemerged here. In essence, the reformer's refrain remained the same: better men, administering a better law, would lead to better juries, and, we are led to assume, more satisfaction with the courts. As to the administrative personnel, the survey noted that the jury bailiff was still vested with a disquietingly broad discretion in selecting among the idle jurors to compose a venire to hear any given case. And although the formerly traditional jury lists composed by solicitation and suggestion at the outset of the selection and summoning process were no longer in use, the pernicious phenomenon of "repeaters" persisted, the Bar Association's and Civic League's combined efforts and lamentations notwithstanding.

The resilience of the old forms of doing business at the courthouse was brazenly reaffirmed during the term of court in session even while the Foundation-funded lawyer-reformers were scurrying thither and yon at the court house gathering information and statistics for their investigation on juries:

> The winter of 1920-21 coincided with the greatest unemployment since 1914. It is to be assumed that in general, when a factory reduces its force, the least competent workers are laid off first. The action of the presiding judge of the January term, 1921, in permitting jurors to serve an additional two weeks if they desired, and longer on permission of the court, gives some gauge for ascertaining the number of men who preferred $2 a day on the jury to unemployment. During that term 77 jurors elected to serve more than the regular two weeks.[38]

Here again, the repeaters skewed the composition of the available panels for petit juries. The 77 men "out of employment," a mere 6.4% of the summoned venire for the January term of court, ended up serving 20% of the term's "juror/days." As the investigators put it:

> A few of these repeaters may have been retired men who enjoy the
> experience, but, on the whole, they consisted of men who were
> tiding over a period of unemployment by attempting to perform one
> of the most difficult tasks of democratic government at $2 per
> day.[39]

But the Foundation survey exposed more than the court's predictable
resistance to the reformer's agenda. Rather, it was in cataloguing and
counting the jurors summoned to serve during the Spring of 1921 that the
Foundation survey made its greatest contribution to understanding the totality
of the "jury problem."

The chapter on juries argued throughout that if juries were going to
improve, it was going to come about by improving the social composition of
the panels. Over and over the report decried the reluctance of men (and the
more recently franchised women) of substance to serve jury duty:

> The failure of the jury system, however, has a deeper cause than
> any schematic defect. In Cleveland, as in many other large cities,
> most citizens of means or intelligence avoid service. This
> avoidance has become traditional, so that it is a kind of mild
> disgrace for a so called "respectable citizen" to allow himself to be
> caught for jury service—like being swindled, for instance.[40]

Tracing the effects of this default on the part of the citizens of "means or
intelligence" the investigators statistically analyzed the aggregation,
selection, summoning and excusing of jurors during the January term of
court in 1921.

The Foundation discovered that because of the traditional aversion
towards jury duty harbored by citizens of means or intelligence, the typical
juror tended to reside in the poorer wards and districts containing the
"colored," "shifting white" and "foreign" populations. To demonstrate the
mechanisms behind this dangerously skewed culling process, the
investigators kept records at the crucial stages of selecting and summoning
jurors, along with the excuses offered by "drawn" jurors for failing to serve.
Then they put the numbers into a table intended to contrast the poorer, inner-
city wards' contribution to the final jury venire as against the more
prosperous suburban participation. For the poorer districts the investigators

ELECTORS SELECTED, QUALIFIED, DRAWN & SERVED CUYAHOGA COUNTY COMMON PLEAS COURT, SPRING TERM 1921					
Resident Status	Residential District	Letters Sent	Total Qualified	Total Drawn	Total Served
"Colored, Shifting White & Foreign"	Ward 11	255	74	41	29
	Ward 14	145	58	21	19
"Recognized Prosperous Suburbs"	East Cleve.	166	69	38	25
	Lakewood	310	118	39	26
	Cleve. Hts.	226	27	27	18
	Shaker Hts.	37	5	1	1
Cuyahoga	County	10,448	3,968	1,532	1,010

Source: *Criminal Justice in Cleveland*

Table 6

chose Ward 11 ("Colored and Shifting White") and Ward 14 ("Foreign—Poles, other Slavs, and Greeks")[41] For samples of citizens of a better sort, the investigators selected East Cleveland,[42] Lakewood, Cleveland Heights and Shaker Heights. Table 6 is a chart breaking down their findings for the January Term of 1921.

The number of "Letters Sent" is a rough approximation of the proportion (county wide) of electors residing in the given residential district. Thus, Lakewood was the most populous district examined, with 310 "Letters Sent," while fledgling Shaker Heights, with only 37 "Letters Sent," was the smallest and newest community included in the survey's comparison. What the study revealed was already well understood by those familiar with the jury selection process. Eligible electors in the suburbs, who generally wished to avoid service, had more reasons for not serving and more "pull" to escape service even where no colorable excuse was offered when they were summoned. The result, as demonstrated by Table 7 was that the suburbs contributed a significantly lower percentage of its summoned electors to the county's jury pool, while the poorer, blacker, more Catholic and recent residents of the inner city wards contributed a proportionately greater number of electors to the pool.

Ratio of Jurors Summoned to Jurors Serving by Residential District, Spring 1921			
Residential District	Jurors Summoned	Jurors Serving	Percent of Summoned To Serving
Ward 11	255	29	11.4%
Ward 14	145	19	13.1%
East Cleveland	166	25	15%
Lakewood	310	26	8.4%
Cleveland Hts.	236	18	7.6%
Shaker Hts.	37	1	2.7%
Wards 11 & 14	400	48	12%
Suburbs	749	70	9.3%
County Wide	10,448	1,010	9.7%

Source: *Criminal Justice in Cleveland*

Table 7

Even including the aberrantly high figures for East Cleveland[43] (with a 15% "chosen to called" showing) in the suburban figures, Table 7 demonstrates that overall, the inner city wards contributed nearly one third more of their summoned eligible electors (12%) to the jury venire than the more prosperous suburbs (9.34%). This tendency of the ostensibly reformed, and presumably honestly administered, jury selection process to over-represent the lower social strata while simultaneously under-representing the higher social orders, exacerbated what the reformers perceived to be the underlying problem.

While the residential analysis of a term's venire provided insight as to how the system "discriminated" against citizens of substance, the Foundation also sought to analyze the social composition of the typical jury by breaking down the venire into occupational categories. To that end, the investigators took a 4 week sampling (between April 18, and May 18, 1921) of the serving jurors' vocations. The list of self-reported occupations comprised, as the survey noted, "probably . . . the most optimistic appraisal which a man may place upon his own capacities." Table 8 is the list compiled during the four week sampling period, broken down into rough occupational "Classes"

Table 8: Juror Occupations, By Class

Class 1 Executive	3.2%
Office manager	1
Department manager	2
Telephone night mgr.	1
Route manager	1
Sales manager	2
President	1
Superintendent	4
Total	12

Class 2 Technical & Artistic	2.6%
Draftsman	1
Electrical engineer	1
Civil engineer	3
Chemist	1
Transportation expert	1
Artist	2
Designer	1
Total	10

Class 3 Contractors	1.6%
Teaming contractor	2
Electrical contractor	1
Building contractor	2
Auto livery	1
Total	6

Class 4 Agents	1.6%
Insurance agent	2
Real estate agent	4
Total	6

Class 5 Clerical	17.9%
Bookkeeper	5
Stenographer	5
Cashier	2
Accountant	3
Collector	1
Teller	1
Claim agent	1
Saleslady	1
Salesman	24
Clerk	20
Telephone Operator	2
Agent	2
Secretary	1
Total	68

Class Merchants & Tradesmen	5.8%
Merchant	5
Grocer	7
Butcher	2
Grocery store mgr.	1
Meat dealer	1
Laundryman	1
Baker	4
Barber	1
Total	22

Class 7 Saloon Keeper	.8%
Saloon Keeper	1
Hotel-keeper	1
Poolroom proprietor	1

Class 8 Domestic	11.1%
At home	38
Nurse	4
Total	42

Class 9 Farmer	2.3%
Farmer	8

Class 10 Service Employees	5.9%
Chauffeur	4
Footman	1
Janitor	1
Gardener	3
Watchman	5
Guard	1
Cook	1
Porter	2
Elevator Operator	1
Furnace man	1
Total	20

Class 11 Skilled Workers	7.9%
Painter	6
Carpenter	16
Electrician	3
Decorator	1
Plumber	2
Mason	1
Enameler	1
Total	30

Class 12 Needle-workers	1.8%
Furrier	2
Tailor	3
Bushel man	2
Total	7

Class 13 Special Workers	4.2%
Chairmaker	1
Tentmaker	1
Potter	1
Printer	6
Windowmaker	1
Shade finisher	1
Artificial limb maker	1
Asbestos worker	1
Movie operator	1
Cigar manufacturer	1
Grease maker	1
Total	16

Class 14 Foreman	1.3%
Shop foreman	1
Dock foreman	1
Foreman auto worker	1
Turn boss	1
Track foreman	1
Total	5

Class 15 Inspectors	2.9%
Stock-keeper	3
Machine & tool insp.	13
Total	16

Class 16 Engineers & Conductors	7.1%
Railroad switchman	5
Streetcar conductor	5
Engineer	5
Fireman	3
Stationary engineer	4
Brakeman	1
Streetcar yardman	1
Railroad signal block operator	1
Telegraph lineman	1
Railroad man	1
Total	27

Class 17 Metal workers, repairers, laborers and allied occupations	22.4%
Machine hands	2
Steel worker	4
Pipefitter	1
Pattern manufacturer	1
Iron chipper	1
Welder	1
Assembler	2
Iron worker	3
Temperer	1
Cable splicer	1
Sheetmetal worker	2
Electrical worker	1
Boilermaker	1
Boilertube welder	1
Rod mill worker	1
Tool grinder	2
Coremaker	1
Machine operator	1
Car builder	1
Machine hand	1
Molder	2
Solderer tinware	1
Auto body builder	1
Elevator erector	1
Machinist	18
Auto mechanic	2
Car repairman	1
Die & toolmaker	4
Blacksmith	1
Millwright	3
Galley man	1
Teamster	4
Stonecutter	1
Woodworker	1
Toolmaker	1
Truck driver	4
Laborers	10
Total	85

Class 18 Sailor	.2%
Sailor	1

Class 19 Retired	.2%
Retiree	1

by the investigators. Consideration of the listing, even with all its problematic categorical vagueness, provides the reader with a rough statistical portrait of the elite reformers' collective bogey men, the jury of their peers. Or, to draw it another way, consider Figure 6.

Figure 6 illustrates the occupational categories, as broken down into "Classes" by the Foundation investigators, listed in reverse order of prevalence in the melting pot-jury venire for Cleveland, Ohio, circa 1921. Six years following the institution of jury reforms (and workmen's compensation), the typical juror, the most likely to actually sit on any given panel to decide matters of liability and damages, was a member of the city's largest and lowest class, a "metal worker, repairer or laborer." Even six

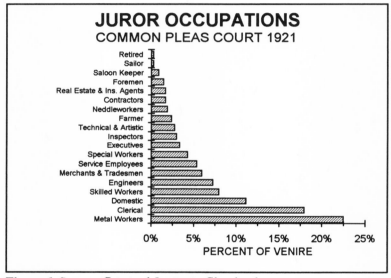

Figure 6 Source: *Criminal Justice in Cleveland*

years after dispensing with the patronage lists, the whole jury system, from initial random selection through to the final empaneling of individual petit jurors, favored placing those of menial abilities in a position to decide contested matters that often affected their social and economic betters.

A simple counter-factual exercise serves to illustrate at least one important operative dynamic that drove the large-employer engine of compensation reform from the previous decade. The counter-factual indulgence required is to assume that workmen's compensation had not been put into effect in Ohio in 1914. Now, submit a work injury case to the statistical jury portrayed in Table 9. Trying to anticipate class loyalties and giving the defendant-employer its best shot by including the second largest class "Clerical" (17.9%) in the employer-sympathetic occupational camp,[44] the numbers would still be overwhelmingly in favor of the predictably worker-sympathetic camp.

PROJECTED JUROR BIAS BY OCCUPATIONAL CLASS, SPRING, 1921			
EMPLOYER SYMPATHETIC		**EMPLOYEE SYMPATHETIC**	
Executives	3.2%	Saloon Keepers, etc.	.8%
Technical & Artistic	2.6%	Domestic	11.1%
Contractors	1.6%	Service Employees	5.9%
Real Est. & Ins. Agts.	1.6%	Skilled Workers	7.9%
Clerical	17.9%	Needleworkers	1.8%
Merchants & Tradesmen	5.8%	Special Workers	4.2%
Farmers	2.1%	Engineers & Conductors	7.1%
Foremen	1.3%	Metal Workers	22.4%
Inspectors	2.9%	Sailors	.2%
Retired	.2%	———————	
Total	39.2%	Total	60.8%

Source: *Criminal Justice in Cleveland*

Table 9

This was the real problem with the jury system. Even when honestly administered, the cross section of the community that any good venire would gather for inclusion in the litigation decision making process would by definition include a fair and proportional representation of the entire community. Since that cross section would always include higher numbers from the bottom of the social and economic pyramid, it would never, from a corporate perspective, provide a dependable basis for submitting matters concerning the broader issues of wealth allocation and distribution. Unlike most matters submitted to the litigation process, worker injury suits cast the social and wealth paradigm in frighteningly stark terms and invited policy considerations into the decision making process that looked well beyond the constricting issues framed under the legal rubric concerning "liability" as between "masters" and their "servants."

* * * * *

Leaving Leffingwell's office, Stillwell drops by Schmiermund's, a well known political hangout, for a late dinner before returning to his boarding house. Nikopopulos' trial is set to begin in the morning. Enjoying an after dinner cigar while "lost in a depressing revery," Guy is joined by his grimy tutor, Henk, now sweaty and well in his cups.

It was Henk who approached my table. Along side of him stood a lithe, well-dressed, debonair man of about forty-five, with an indefinable expression of youth about his face. Perhaps it was the smooth shaven face of his, the skin of which seemed tightly drawn over the tissues, and his pleasant-looking brown eyes that gave him the appearance of a young man of thirty. I had heard of Frank Talcott. People speculated as to the source of his income. For awhile he was a lawyer with a well-equipped office, sumptuously furnished, and spent money liberally, scarcely any clients even intruded upon his privacy at his office, nor did he ever appear in Court. He had been in politics a decade before, and had held office, but at present he did not seem active in the field either. He was seen at Schmiermund's daily, with one foot on the foot-rest, leaning against the brass railing of the bar, with a whiskey or cocktail before him, chatting with someone. Judging by appearances, he was always drinking.

I shook hands with Talcott, who made a few desultory remarks and passed on. "So long," he said, as he turned to go. Henk edged in between the tables and the booth where I sat and joined me.

At a beckon from Henk, a waiter halted before our table.

"What's yours?" queried Henk, turning to me.

I declined.

"Don't be a mollycoddle," he urged. And without waiting for

my rejoinder, he dismissed the waiter with "two beers."

Henk lit a cigarette and began to talk. Although he could stand a good deal of drink, he seemed to have outdone himself that evening. His hair was damp and seemed plastered to his skull and his peeping little blue eyes appeared set deeper than usual. He was overflowing with loquaciousness.

"We've certainly had a narrow escape today, " he babbled on, with a toss of his head, and his upper lip curled back to emit a streak of smoke. "Tim double crossed us. I think the Nixon bunch must have slipped him something (the "Nixon bunch" was the legal firm of Nixon, Wright, Croak and Powers, counsel for the defending company in the Nikopopulos case). But believe me, Talcott will take care of the boys."

"What has Talcott to do with this?" I asked.

"Talcott is the best fixer in town—"

My look at Henk must have told him that his reference was lost on me.

"If you expect to ride easily, you must grease the axles— unde'stand?" he resumed. And suddenly checked himself (the waiter sat down two seidels of beer before us).

"Talcott has some machine! His Lieutenants operate in every ward and precinct, the same as when he used to be in politics—"

"You don't mean he bribes—"

Henk swallowed a mouthful of beer, threw his head back and laughed. "You should have been a preacher. You ain't cut out for a lawyer."

"You don't mean—"

"Say, you are guying me," Henk interrupted me again. "You ain't blind after hangin' around Mark nearly a year. Them corporation lawyers had their way long enough—it's our turn now. Say, Guy you had better get yourself a pair of good glasses—"

At this point Frank Talcott came up to our table again. "'T's al'right," he said to Henk laconically, with a jolly wave of his hand, and turned to leave.

"Wait a moment," Henk stopped him, rising from his seat. "So long, Guy."

Notes

1. The questionnaire listed six questions to employers and worker groups concerning their satisfaction with the current employer liability laws and their support for a compensation bill. The third question was "Is the court and jury system for fixing the responsibility for industrial accidents, now existing in the State, satisfactory in its operation?"

2. Although this Cleveland Foundation-sponsored survey of the criminal courts lies seven years outside the period of study, the report notes the persistence of many of the jury abuses exposed by the Cleveland Bar Association in 1914, confirming that in most respects the jury system had not changed substantially from the period under study. Further, the Cleveland Foundation Survey contains sociological information about the composition of juries that is invaluable for understanding their function within the courts during the pre-compensation era studied here.

3. Reginald Heber Smith and Herbert B. Ehrmann, "Juries," in *Criminal Justice in Cleveland*, ed. Roscoe Pound and Felix Frankfurter (Cleveland: The Cleveland Foundation, 1922), 340-53.

4. *James Reardon vs. The Lake Shore & Michigan Southern Railway Company* Cuyahoga County Common Pleas Court, Case No. 54887.

5. James Harrison Kennedy; Wilson M. Day *The Bench and Bar of Cleveland* (Cleveland: Cleveland Printing and Publishing Company, 1889) 280.

6. Ibid., 264.

7. "Into The Trap," *Cleveland Plain Dealer*, 24 November 1897, 1, 2.

8. George Irving Reed, ed. *Bench and Bar of Ohio* (Chicago: Century Publishing and Engraving Company, 1897) 296.

9. Cleveland Bar Association files, Western Reserve Historical Society, Cleveland, Ohio.

10. "Into The Trap," *Cleveland Plain Dealer*, 24 November 1897, 1, 2.

11. No names ever surfaced in connection with these other alleged bribes and no prosecutions were ever brought.

12. "By The Bar," *Cleveland Leader*, 29 December 1897, 1.

13. Ibid., 1. After the meeting, Judge Ong was contacted by the reporter for the *Cleveland Leader* and explained Judge Ingersoll's embarrassing recalcitrance by referring to a "personal matter" between them. When informed of Judge Ong's summary dismissal of his opposition at the meeting as a "personal matter," Judge Ingersoll replied, "Oh, its a personal matter,

is it? Well, you tell him that if he is so anxious to be investigated I should like to have the job."

14. "Bribery Cases," *Cleveland Plain Dealer*, 29 December 1897, 1, 6.

15. Ibid., "By The Bar," 1.

16. "$2,000 Bribe," *Cleveland Leader*, 12 December 1897, 1.

17. "Not By Neff," *Cleveland Leader*, 9 December 1897, 1.

18. The question was one of a number that each witness testifying before the Ohio Employers' Liability Commission was asked to answer. The response was from Stephen W. Tener, Manager of the Accident Department of American Steel and Wire, appearing before the Commission at the hearings in Cleveland, on November 1, 1910. Ibid., OELC, *Report*, Vol. II, 123-24.

19. We know little of Tener except that he was as an active participant in the company's safety and litigation management team. His name begins turning up in the company's court pleadings and affidavits in December of 1907. He apparently made an aristocratic appearance before the Commission. Revealing some of the tensions between the large and small employer groups, the witness who testified immediately after Tener, a "small employer," Mr. J. H. Van Dorn, began his remarks by declaiming, "Now, I am not going to be as gentle, as fine, and as nice as the gentleman who preceded me. It is not in me. I shall not undertake to borrow anybody else's ways or any educated gentleman or attorney or borrow from the gentleman who preceded me, because I have not his advantages, and I have got to go straight to the mark." Ibid., OELC, *Report*, Vol. II, 129.

20. Ibid., 127.

21. The company's Plan is reprinted as the "United States Steel Corporation, Voluntary Accident Relief Plan" in Appendix XI of the Ohio Employers' Liability Commission's Report. Ibid., Vol. I, 91.

22. See Purcell, Ibid., Chapter 3.

23. See Chapter V, Note 16, Infra.

24. The Civic League of Cleveland, "Report of Investigations Into Jury System," *The Municipal Bulletin*, January 1916 (Cleveland), 1.

25. Ibid.

26. Ibid., 11.

27. Ibid., 4.

28. The jury "venire" is the larger pool of jurors summoned to serve a term of court, or to be examined for selection in a particular trial.

29. Ibid., 5.

30. Ibid., 6.

31. Ibid., 6,7.

32. Ironically, the requirement for unanimity and the quotient verdict probably worked together to ameliorate the potentially harsher aspects of the local jury process, and may explain why the American Steel and Wire Company did not suffer any outrageous verdicts in the common pleas court. A single juror could refuse to agree to a verdict and the result would be a mistrial. The quotient could only be used with all the jurors' assent. Therefore, a single, strong-minded juror on a panel could wield great power in the deliberations. On the other hand, this same ability to "hang" a jury is precisely what Max Rosenblatt sought to sell to the Lake Shore & Michigan Southern Railway in the notorious Reardon case.

33. Ibid., 12.

34. Reginald Heber Smith and Herbert B. Ehrmann, "Juries," in *Criminal Justice in Cleveland*, ed. Roscoe Pound and Felix Frankfurter (Cleveland: The Cleveland Foundation, 1922) 340-353, 341.

35. Ibid., 340-353.

36. The famous survey *Criminal Justice In Cleveland*, contained different chapters about wide ranging topics related to the Cleveland area *criminal courts'* administration. The chapter reviewed here concerned the juries used in the common pleas court. In Cuyahoga County, the criminal and civil cases depended upon the same jury venire.

37. Ibid., 352.

38. Ibid., 352.

39. Ibid.

40. Ibid., 344.

41. Where many of American Steel and Wire's employees lived.

42. While they took East Cleveland to be a homogeneous, prosperous suburb, in fact, there were several working class neighborhoods in East Cleveland, adjacent to the mills and factories north of Euclid Avenue.

43. Given East Cleveland's strong showing and the aforementioned "industrial neighborhoods," it seems likely the "Colored, Shifting White & Foreign" representation on the Spring Term, 1921 jury venire actually exceeded their comprehension.

44. It seems improbable, given likely familial associations within the clerical "class," that the clerical group would favor, as a group, the employer camp in a work injury suit.

V

The Broad Ground

Writing to United States Steel subsidiary managers in December of 1909 Charles MacVeagh, General Solicitor of the Steel Corporation, explained why it was necessary to adopt the newly sanctioned, albeit still evolving, Voluntary Accident Relief Plan. The Plan was an alternative to the courts, and MacVeagh, head lawyer for the Corporation, made it clear why the state courts were no longer acceptable forums to resolve worker injury claims.

> Already many of the common law defenses have been done away within a large number of our states and the decision of most of the questions in accident litigation is left to the jury. This makes it more and more necessary to avoid litigation to the greatest extent possible by amicable settlements.[1]

Within the year, Stephen Tener, Manager of the Accident Department of American Steel and Wire, appeared before the Ohio Employers' Liability Commission to tout the plan and explain:

> The American Steel and Wire Company . . . has been dealing with the injured employes on the broad ground that all such are entitled to some compensation irrespective of questions of liability, and the result has proven the wisdom of this course. . .[2]

To extend the analogy, the "broad ground" began as a narrow path and steadily widened over an eighteen year period. The company's virtual abdication on the liability issues of worker injury claims resulted from the harrowing experiences its corporate counsel faced in the state courts fighting worker suits. And while this chapter will demonstrate that Cleveland's United States Steel subsidiary did strive to amicably settle most of the injury claims brought by employees, there was another "broad ground" that enabled that new company policy to succeed. The very immensity of the United States Steel Corporation, the first "Billion Dollar Corporation," provided its corporate managers with a unique opportunity to count, analyze, and accurately project the number and type of work injuries annually afflicting its 200,000 man work force. The broad actuarial experience of the subsidiary companies was intensively studied and produced the "Voluntary Accident Relief Plan," the private, corporate, in-house compensation scheme that anticipated and defined the national workmen's compensation reform by half a decade.

Prior to the Plan's public introduction in May of 1910, the subsidiaries fought a holding action against the worker suits in the local state and, when available, federal courts. For American Steel and Wire that litigation was handled by Cleveland's premier law firm, Squire, Sanders & Dempsey. A paradigm of the newly emergent corporate legal practice, Squire, Sanders & Dempsey performed their Thermopylaean assignment on behalf of the company with remarkable success. Beginning with the torrent of litigation in 1900 anticipating the final, Morgan-financed, deep-pocketed combine, they successfully stemmed the tide of suits and ultimately brought the number of worker actions down to a relative trickle. By the time the Ohio Employers' Liability Commission conducted its statewide hearings in 1910, Squire, Sanders & Dempsey, working closely with the company managers, had reduced the defense of worker suits to a predictable and rarely threatening routine of pleadings and trials. By 1915, following passage of Ohio's mandatory act—legislation actively supported by the firm's large corporate clients—the suits ceased altogether. The court house door was forever closed to the injured employees thus ending the need for corporate lawyers to defend the workers' lawsuits.

However routine those worker cases against their client were, between 1898 and 1915 an unmistakable trend developed in the injury litigation that suggests why the Steel Corporation (and most other large finance-capitalized corporations) chose to adopt an in-house plan that effectively conceded liability for worker injuries, the dreaded employer defenses notwithstanding. The rub was the trend in damages, and the Voluntary Accident Relief Plan and, later, workmen's compensation solved the corporation's nascent damage problem in a predictable, and permanent, fashion. But first let us return to our young and even still idealistic paraclete and pleader *extraordinaire,* the ever credulous Guy Stillwell and his soon-to-end professional side trip into the interesting, if ignoble, specialty of ambulance chasing "pippin" cases.

* * * * *

Our stalwart (albeit contemplative) hero had come to a very gloomy pass in his budding career. Working at "the game" as an associate in Mark Leffingwell's office was proving too demeaning, even depraved, for our earnest young dreamer. The frank exchange at Schmiermund's beer garden with the sweaty and nicotine-stained Henk proved the proverbial straw. As Henk so indelicately put it to Stillwell: "You ain't blind after hanging around Mark nearly a year. Them corporation lawyers had their way long enough—it's our turn now." This was sagacious Henk's final exhortation to Guy in his continuing practicum, The Majesty of the Common Law, Urban Torts.

It was the eve of Nikopopulos' trial. Leffingwell's "shop" had worked long and hard preparing it for court.

Leffingwell looked forward to the trial of the case with the anticipation, I imagine, of a confident jockey who is given the privilege of riding a "sure winner." The pathetic looking figure of the shrunken Greek; the five small children, the eldest eleven and the youngest in his mother's arms; the tear stained face of the poor wife with that foreign shawl over her head, and two small children clinging to her skirt—all these were patches of color that delighted the master painter. As the day of trial was drawing near Leffingwell spoke of these "fine points" with fiendish glee. Then began the drilling of witnesses (from one eye-witness the number had grown to nine), the examination, cross-examination (with traps and pitfalls laid to see how well the witness would stand up on the witness stand), suggestions, and corrections, with all the painstaking of a Belasco in staging a new play. My bewilderment during these rehearsals was so great that the iniquity of the whole business did not strike me quite forcibly until the day's work was over, when I returned to my lonely room and lost myself in my passionate pursuit of literature.

Whether it finally reduced to the jury tampering; or the perjurious rehearsals of dubious testimony (in halting and broken English); or to the rough and tumble solicitation of injured clients; or was it indeed, Henk's final and frank observation—that injury litigation was simply class warfare, a tortuous assault upon capital—or just all of it, is left unclear. So many of the past year's indiscretions clouded the brooding despair of our hero's long, dark and sleepless night. Whatever the final cause, upon the break of day, Guy decides to quit Leffingwell's office, effective immediately.

On his way to court to meet Leffingwell, Guy is joined by his fellow boarding house roomer, Virgil Tinker. Tinker (if you couldn't tell from his name) is a somewhat effete, but capable, young attorney and an associate in the powerful corporate law firm, Nixon, Wright, Croak & Powers. Tinker's firm is defending the very same American Tool Company against Nikopopulos' suit and he is evidently well informed about the particulars of Nick's case. "All the evidence is fabricated. We have absolute proof that this man Nikopopulos had a fight with a man by the name of Kolokolchik, who pushed the Greek against a machine in operation and caused the injury." Tinker's zealous effusions regarding the Greek's cause "rang true" to our already disillusioned hero—further confirmation, if any were needed, that injury suits were too much "the game" and too little, far too little, concerned with fairness, propriety or social justice.

Arriving at court, Guy sees Leffingwell, Henk, Nikopopulos, his wife and, of course, the interpreter, huddled in the rear corner of the courtroom. Nick appears agitated, shaking his head negatively. Clearly distressed, Henk rushes over to our grimly resolute protagonist and pleads for Guy to intercede with Nikopopulos, who was, according to Henk, "insisting on ruining his case." Stillwell declines, but gets Leffingwell to join him and Henk and then curtly informs them both of his intention to quit, effective immediately. Leffingwell's perennially sunny, albeit smarmy, disposition, darkens. Ever the courtroom tactician, Leffingwell takes up a position between the just-arrived American Tool Company counsel and his own now crumbling alliance—hiding his side's increasingly obvious disintegration from the enemy. Nikopopulos fires Leffingwell ". . . he no my lawyer . . ." and insists that Guy do what Leffingwell was theretofore refusing to do—communicate a desire to settle the case to the other side. "Tell Company's lawyers me want settlement, me no fight—." With Stillwell acting as intermediary, the case settles (for an unspecified amount) and Guy and Mark Leffingwell part professional ways, on sour and sullen terms. Leffingwell suspects treachery and accuses Guy of a double cross. Stillwell's next career move only serves to confirm his suspicions.

The sudden—and apparently highly principled—resignation from Leffingwell's "shop" impresses Virgil Tinker and his associates, and with

Tinker's warm and admiring recommendation, Guy begins as a new associate in the lofty realm of the preeminent corporate law firm of Nixon, Wright, Croak & Powers.

> It was quite a distinction for a young man without "influential connections," without an "uncle in the Senate" and with no prospect of bringing in business of any sort, to be taken into the offices of Nixon, Wright, Croak & Powers . . .
>
> Nixon, Wright, Croak & Powers were not a legal firm but an institution. Unlike most legal concerns it was now in its second generation. Nixon, a renowned lawyer of the old school, had died many years ago; Wright was still alive but was old and wealthy and was a sort of *emeritus*, spending his winters in Florida, sometimes in Egypt, and his summers in Maine, and showed himself at the office at rare intervals. Jimmie Croak was the son of Alonzo Croak, who laid the foundation of the firm with Rowland Nixon in 1869, and was the link between the concern and 'Big Business'. He rarely if ever, entered the sacred precincts of a court room . . . He had chosen the business end of the profession because it paid best. He well knew that he could hire a skillful "trial lawyer" and pay him for five years the price of a "merger" or a new organization which would only take part of his time of two months. People spoke of him as a slick lawyer. The profession looked at him askance. And yet the year I came to the office Jimmie Croak was president of the Bar Association.
>
> The Jupiter of this solar system, however, was John Powers . . . He was special counsel for several railroads and advisor of the largest banking institution in the city. He appeared in the State supreme court a few times a year and perhaps that often in the Federal supreme court. Earlier in his career he had waged many a legal battle in all courts—stories of his ingenious cross examination are still current among local members of the bar—but in recent years he, too, had been forced away from the trial table by more lucrative and more congenial work.

But the distinction between Mark Leffingwell's "shop" and Nixon, Wright, Croak & Powers lay deeper than in the nature of the work the two firms handled. The differences ran to the very norms of professional culture.

Nixon, Wright, Croak & Powers assumed the hierarchical operational structure and standards of its largest and most influential clients, finance capital business corporations. It was a culture thoroughly imbued with status and hierarchy, with senior partners, junior partners, senior associates, junior associates, law clerks, secretaries, receptionists, clerks, typists, and etc. Brudno couldn't resist a military analogy in describing the firm:

> Nixon, Wright, Croak & Powers, like a modern department store, handled all kinds of business, every branch entrusted to a "specialist." No business was too big for them, none too small. They floated "issues" and collected grocers' bills. They stood for influence.
>
> Had I penned these memoirs before the War I could hardly have been able to give an adequate description of the maze of offices that housed these lawyers without an architect's blue-print. But, now, the formation of trenches and dugouts having become so familiar, the reader can easily visualize it by calling to mind a long trench running about one hundred feet, with little dugouts branching off the main trench every ten feet, then turning sharply to the left, with more dugouts on either side, ending in a mysterious cave, where the commander Jimmie Croak, well sheltered from air raids, had his headquarters. Dispatchers and messengers were ever going up and down, from dugout to dugout, carrying orders, giving signals, demanding pass-words. As you entered the main trench an orderly (sometimes dozing but more often alert on the job) rose from his seat and demanded your name, which he put down on slip of paper and with that in hand disappeared and soon emerged to tell you to follow him. For this was no lawyer's office with clients in a waiting-room. You came by appointment, and the appointments were punctually kept.

Unlike Leffingwell's noisy and indecorous "shop," this was no polyglot staging area for the city's beshawled and grimy social dregs, the urban-industrial halt and lame. How utterly different Nixon, Wright Croak and Powers was from Leffingwell's rowdier domain, awash in monikers, but devoid of honorifics—save "runner" or possibly "fixer." Our gentle *picaro*'s experience of law practice is about to take a deceptive, even disorienting turn. But for the nonce, his new surroundings prove most congenial, indeed.

* * * * *

The earliest lawsuits against the American Steel and Wire Company date from May of 1898 (following the first Illinois-based merger engineered by Gates) and were a combination of divorce actions (collateral attachment proceedings against husband-employees that named the company so as to set up alimony levies of their wages); commercial, real estate and contract suits mostly devolving from the recent ownership restructuring; and work injury cases. By the fall of that year, only one firm's name appears in the court records on behalf of American Steel and Wire Company—no matter the nature of the proceeding—Squire, Sanders & Dempsey. The first case where Squire Sanders appears as counsel for the Company was actually (and atypically) filed by the company against the Wire Drawers Union in an effort to break a strike brought against the new owners ("Bet a Million" Gates, et al.) for recently imposed wage cuts. Whether the new owners were impressed with the manner in which Squire Sanders handled that case[3] or whether the law firm garnered the area's largest employer (well over 5,000 workers) by virtual default—is not evident. In any event, Squire Sanders remained American Steel and Wire's only counsel until, at least, the end of this study, 1915.

Founded in 1890, Squire, Sanders & Dempsey was one of the first corporate law firms in Cleveland and the only nineteenth century Cleveland firm to survive under its original name to the present day. Its "associational genealogy" traces back to the partnership of Estep & Squire, formed in 1878. In 1882 Judge Moses R. Dickey[4] joined the firm thus aborning Estep, Dickey & Squire. In 1884, the younger James H. Dempsey joined as a clerk and later as junior partner. Squire (b. 1850) and Dempsey (b. 1859) were the younger partners by "almost a generation" and, according to Squire, this ultimately led to them splitting off from the elder Estep and Dickey in 1890, joining with Judge William Brownell Sanders (b. 1854) to form the final transmutation of what remains to this day one of the preeminent Cleveland corporate firms.

All five of these men, witness-participants to the corporate transformation of American law and business, were Ohioans by birth, and, to the extent they had formal undergraduate educations, they were obtained from Midwestern colleges. From the elder generation, E.J. Estep was the oldest, born in Columbiana County in 1820. After studying for the Presbyterian ministry he took an interest in law and ultimately set up practice in Canfield, Ohio. Moving to Cleveland in 1853, he continued in practice until 1894 when his health began to fail. The second elder, Moses R. Dickey, was born in 1827 near Mansfield, Ohio and led an adventurous life prior to taking up the successful practice of law in Mansfield. A private in the

American forces in the Mexican American War, he returned to Mansfield where he taught school until he suffered a near fatal bout with Gold Fever. He traveled with a small party over the Rockies to California to pan for his fortune. Unsuccessful after two years, he returned to Mansfield by way of a "disastrous" detour to Central America. Soon after his return to Ohio, he began practicing law in the Mansfield area. He again took up arms—this time in the Civil War—abandoning his Mansfield practice. He was forced to retire from the Army before the end of the war because of failing health. This time he was discharged with a colonel's commission. He was eventually appointed to the common pleas bench in Richland County and was thereafter elected by popular vote at the end of his appointed term, but resigned in 1882 due to "business inducements" and joined with Messrs. Estep and Squire in Cleveland.

All three of the younger men obtained undergraduate degrees before going on to law (Squire, A.B. Hiram College, 1872; Sanders, A.B. Illinois College, 1873; and Dempsey, A.B. Kenyon College, 1882). Sanders and Dempsey both took post graduate law courses, Sanders from Albany Law School (Ll.D. 1875) while Dempsey studied for a year at Columbia Law School before joining Estep, Dickey and Squire where he read the law under Mr. Estep. These three law partners practiced on the very cusp of the modern Republic. In the words of Andrew Squire:

> No decade in my memory saw such changes in the practice of law as that from 1880 to 1890. The transaction of business through the means of corporations received great impetus during that period. Many old and well known business firms changed to corporations. Trial work, while always important and demanding the greater part of the lawyer's time and attention up to that time, had to take its place as one of the departments of his practice, for much time and attention were demanded in the organizing of corporations, in directing them, and in advising as to various phases of their operation.[5]

It was the end of the era when successful commercial enterprises, usually partnerships, were forged according to family kinships and marriage. The new corporate form of doing business eventually supplanted these powerful family alliances as ways of combining and structuring productive wealth. But the transformation was slow at first, and during the late nineteenth century, whom one knew or married, or whom one's father knew or married, often served as a defining influence on a person's social, professional and business prospects.

William Brownell Sanders was born in Cleveland, but moved with his family to Jacksonville, Illinois where his father taught rhetoric at Illinois College. He returned to Cleveland after obtaining a law degree from Albany Law School in 1875, and married Annie Otis, daughter of Charles A. Otis, Sr., in 1884. Charles Otis was from an "old" Western Reserve family and was a very prosperous banker and steel manufacturer.[6] Charles Otis' father, William A. Otis, began his career in Ohio in 1820 in Trumbull county selling wheat, produce and ash to settlers. Otis eventually entered the banking business and was instrumental in founding and managing the Society for Savings (with another transplanted New Englander, Samuel Mather) and other banks. When he wasn't trading, manufacturing iron or banking, William Otis was promoting railroads. One of the elder Otis' banking partners was Abner Brownell,[7] yet another New Englander and Mayor of Cleveland (1852-55).

James Howard Dempsey was first introduced to the firm of Estep, Dickey and Squire as a result of his father's longstanding friendship with Judge Dickey. Soon after starting at the firm he married Emma Norris Bourne, daughter of a prominent Cleveland businessman, Ebenezer Henry Bourne. E.H. Bourne came from a wealthy and old Cape Cod family and, although relatively late arriving to Cleveland (1866), he quickly established himself in successful iron and steel fabrication concerns and, of course, banking. Dempsey served on the board of one of those concerns, the Bourne-Fuller Company. Dempsey was the organizational genius of the three original partners and administrator of the firm, coordinating its various departments on a daily basis.[8]

Andrew Squire, the only founding partner of Squire, Sanders and Dempsey with no formal legal training, ran in prominent Republican political circles. Born in a small town outside of Cleveland he began his legal career after graduating from Hiram College. He arrived in Cleveland with a letter of introduction from a then-Congressman named James Garfield. (Garfield had earlier taught and served as President at Hiram). Although all three of the original partners of Squire, Sanders & Dempsey were staunch Republicans, Squire was the political mover in the firm, forming strong ties in both the local and national Republican party power structures. He was a friend and advisor to many locally prominent businessmen and politicians including Marcus Hanna, William McKinley (he attended the 1896 Republican nominating convention as a delegate), Samuel Mather and Governor Myron Herrick. Squire's first wife, Ella Mott, was the daughter of a Hiram, Ohio, shoe merchant. After she passed away, Squire married Eleanor Seymour. His second wife's father, Belden Seymour, came to Ohio City in 1848 and quickly rose to prominence through his real estate development efforts on the west side of the Cuyahoga River (Ohio City). Seymour went on to become involved in the People's Gas Light Company, People's Savings & Trust and Citizens Savings & Loan Association. Squire served as a director of the latter concern. It was Eleanor Seymour's second marriage as well as Squire's, and followed "an absence (from Cleveland) of about fifteen years, largely spent in travel."[9]

Between the three founding partners there was an abundance of wealth to be managed without even looking beyond their family holdings. However, these were three extremely capable men, and their influence and connections were soon felt city, state and nationwide. Their firm was not the mere transient partnership of convenience that so often characterized law practices of the day. They created a cutting edge service business and hired the best and brightest from the eastern law schools to staff their multifaceted efforts on behalf of corporations large and small. These fresh, properly educated (and bred) young associates obtained a training in modern law and business associations that couldn't be rivaled elsewhere in the country, and, if they "worked out," could look forward to eventually joining in the firm as partners. When their law partnership was formed, and for at least two generations following, Cleveland was a national center for steel, mining, manufacturing and lake and rail transportation. Thriving on the continent's seemingly insatiable need for the basic infra-structure development of nation building, these industries provided the wealth required to produce wealth. In the 1880's and 1890's local Republican politicians were at the forefront of national governmental affairs. The Tariff protected Cleveland's immense capital investments (what Judge Taft referred to as the "wealth of the East") and assured the continuing stability required by the huge capital markets forming to serve the needs of the new wealth. The corporate form, the legal rules and norms that governed this newly created and creating wealth, was literally forming itself from its own clay. It was a heady time to live in the city, and, presumably, a headier time still for its best and brightest corporate lawyers.

*   *   *   *   *

The genesis of American Steel and Wire's "Voluntary Accident Relief Plan" (The Plan)—the in-house, corporate devised and administered injury compensation system that predated, and arguably delimited, the Ohio Workmen's Compensation Act—lay in the simple task of counting. Counting lives and counting limbs, counting widows and counting orphans, counting days off and counting down time, counting lost staff time and counting new man training time, counting summonses and counting subpoenas, and, of course, counting surgeons' and lawyers' fees. When the Morgan merger went through, United States Steel's extensive interstate holdings presented an unrivaled actuarial laboratory to examine, and ultimately to anticipate, the injury experience of the almost 200,000 employees serving in the constituent companies of the huge combine. The merger brought not just steelworkers, but trainmen, sailors, miners and office workers, under one corporate federation. It was only a matter of collecting the relevant facts for the individual accidents comprising the annual corporate casualties, the ongoing aggregate mass of accident and claims experience, into one manageable body of "safety" statistics. At United States Steel, the subsidiary companies were instructed to start counting in 1906.[10]

Control of the massive information gathering process was delegated to the legal department headquartered in the New York corporate offices. Charles MacVeagh, general solicitor for the Steel Corporation, headed up and controlled the effort. He, with the continuing support of the executive officers and the omnipotent Finance Committee, began to hold meetings in New York with the casualty managers from the far-flung subsidiaries. At first the efforts to gather information were quite unsophisticated—how many deaths on the job corporation-wide in 1906?—was posited to the subsidiary presidents. Staff tallied up the grim toll and the presidents reported back to New York on the fatalities, "insofar as they have been brought to our attention."[11] All told, 405 men died in service to the Corporation that year. Eventually, a team of casualty managers from five subsidiary companies, including American Steel and Wire, were brought together in New York to meet with General Solicitor MacVeagh on a monthly basis. This "Safety Committee" met to consider common problems and to begin to attack some of the causes that led to the legendarily high industry accident rates. As noted by American Steel and Wire's Chief Safety Inspector, in a moment of rare public candor, it was actually the worker lawsuits that engendered the subsidiaries' new safety consciousness.

It is probably safe to say that the "casualty" or "accident" department has always preceded the "safety" department . . . What was originally a species of self defense has broadened out into more humanitarian lines, until at present it is being taken up on a scale that would not have been dreamed of in this country a few years ago.[12]

Prior to 1906 at U.S. Steel there was no discernable work accident policy. The principal concern was for each of the constituent companies to reduce injury and suit related expenses to the extent permitted by local conditions. In the Cleveland area that meant that American Steel and Wire removed as many cases as possible to the federal circuit court for the advantages offered by a sympathetic, appointed judiciary that was loath to allow jury determinations on liability. To the extent that the work injury cases were heard in the state common pleas court they were subject to jury determinations and the usual best route in defending the actions was to argue the damages, not liability.

* * * * *

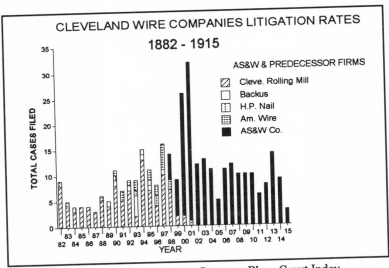

Figure 7 Source: Cuyahoga County Common Pleas Court Index

When Squire, Sanders & Dempsey was initially retained to represent American Steel and Wire in the local state and federal courts they were confronted with a veritable litigation avalanche. The recently announced formation of the first "Billion Dollar Corporation" and the local subsidiary manifestation of the Morgan monster, American Steel and Wire, lead to unheard of amounts of litigation being filed against the New Jersey-chartered wire combine. Figure 7 is a stacked bar graph that covers the years 1882-

1915 and shows all the litigation filed against the predecessor wire firms (1882 was the earliest year indexes for the common pleas court were available) and the American Steel and Wire concern through to the end of the period studied here. As Figure 7 makes clear, the final merger, rolling American Steel and Wire into the House of Morgan, encouraged a great deal of litigation.

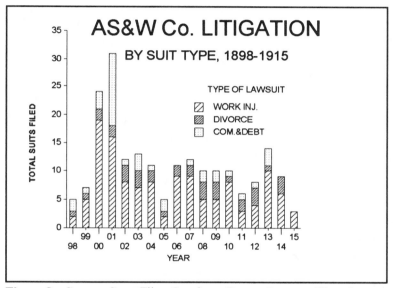

Figure 8   Source: Court Files, Cuyahoga County Common Pleas & Probate Courts & U.S. Circuit Court, Cleveland, Ohio.

Figure 8 is limited to the period under examination here, and therefore focuses only on the American Steel and Wire suits. Figure 8 breaks down the common pleas court suits into three case types. The divorce cases were really collateral actions intended to set up garnishment proceedings against husband-employees of the firm. The commercial litigation was varied, running the gamut from securities issues, to real estate, to simple collection proceedings. In 1900 and 1901 litigation involving the Company quadrupled, with the merger related commercial suits reaching their peak in 1901. Figure 8 suggests that work injury suits were not correlated to accident rates. Worker suits triple in 1900 and remain inordinately high in 1901, when the Steel Trust was officially established. Inasmuch as these were not particularly productive years for steel manufacture, it seems probable that these high rates were engendered by causes aside from, or in addition to, work injuries. As was clear from the walkout at two of the plants in 1898, these consolidations were not achieved without causing displacements and strife at the plant level. American Steel and Wire set wage rates at a national norm, cutting the Cleveland workers wages[13] as the mergers proceeded. [14] These kinds of deprivations and disruptions to the work force might explain the workers' increased predilection to file suits against the company.

The pleadings filed by Squire Sanders on behalf of the company reveal the firm's tactical and strategic responses to this deluge of litigation. The complex commercial matters were answered in a very individualized and thorough manner. Pleadings were lengthy and exhaustive and these cases often involved extensive motion practice. The divorce matters and injury suits, however, received a more abbreviated and repetitious response. The injury suits filed by the workers' attorneys were initiated with very wordy petitions replete with third person constructions, "party"s, "wherefore"s, "same"s, "aforementioned"s, etc. By contrast the Squire Sanders' responsive pleading was always short and succinct, reducing the company's answer to a seven page petition to seven or eight lines, free of the jargon and meaningless legalistic iteration that was standard in the plaintiffs's petitions.[15] The company had the advantage of experience in these injury suits—there were hundreds filed against their clients—and could effectively use the same simplified forms to respond to the droning verbiage of the workers' petitions, all to their advantage. Squire Sanders would, over the eighteen years that they represented the company, respond to over 130 injury suits on behalf of American Steel and Wire. Their abbreviated pleadings, short, succinct and sufficient without overstatement or bombast, imply an altogether new legal culture than traditionally held sway in the common law courts. Appointments made and promptly kept, phrases exact and exacting, these were the badges of the new corporate culture imbuing the practice of law. It was as if the pleadings communicated to the opposition and to the court—without, of course, actually saying it— "Yes, of course, we know all about this, can we just get on with it?"

By 1902 the flood of litigation drawn by the deep pockets of the House of Morgan was under control. After 1901 the year of the Morgan merger, the commercial litigation slowed to a trickle along with the one to three collateral divorce actions filed each year. The work injury cases that dominated the litigation against the company after the initial merger flurry diminished to an average of about six per year until the passage of the workmen's compensation act in 1915. These litigated cases represented a very small portion of the total industrial injuries sustained in the Cleveland plants. Given the number of men that worked in the Cleveland area properties of American Steel and Wire Company (conservatively over 5,000); the hazardous activities involved in all phases of steel making; and the statistically verified extra hazards present in wire drawing, six cases represented a mere sliver of the total number of potential suits each year.[16]

Part of Squire Sanders' task was to insulate the senior management of the Company from the nuisance of litigation. The principal involvement of the company managers was to sign the occasional "verified" legal pleading. Rarely, if ever, were the managers directly involved in the pre-trial discovery or actual trials of the lawsuits. But by 1908, the new company "Accident and Pensions Department" appears on record to play a greater and more direct role in the injury litigation. The Accident and Pensions Department was headed by Stephen Tener, who began to assume an increasingly prominent role in the litigation, signing verifications, affidavits and other miscellaneous court filings as and when needed by the Squire Sanders lawyers. Tener's role was not limited to working with the lawyers. As appears from his testimony before the Ohio Employers' Liability Commission, he was also responsible for evaluating the value of injury claims made by employees outside the courthouse context. His job brought him into personal contact with some of the most gruesome and awful injuries that occurred in the Cleveland plants. In responding to a question from one of the Commission members regarding amounts that should be paid for compensation to injured employees under the company's Voluntary Plan he replied:

> You will see injuries and death taken care of, except such catastrophes as both hands, both legs, both eyes, and these are too great to put a fixed amount. Circumstances would have to be taken into consideration. These are so dreadful we could not begin to get our minds down on what should be paid.[17]

*   *   *   *   *

At first our recently redeemed young hero's sojourn into the cozy corporate realm of law practice proves blissfully reassuring. Guy is again comforted by the embracing arms of "The Law," as he knew blind, wise Themis in his university days. All rigorous reasoning, along distinct lines defined by right thinking, sound professional ethics, equity and justice.

Happy months followed. My association with Mr. Powers rekindled my enthusiasm for the law. For there was nothing sordid about the matters he handled. No petty courts, no partisan judges, no bribed jurors, but principles of law and equity urged along lines as fundamental as the ten commandments. And the people I was coming in contact with (in contrast to Henk and his ilk) were clean, wholesome, congenial.

Stillwell's affection for Mr. Powers (the "Jupiter" in the firm's "firmament") is built upon more than mere professional admiration. Powers' niece, Mary Halstead, is Guy's old flame (or perhaps more accurately, ember) from his recently-passed Yale days. Mary haunted Guy from their very first meeting at a college football weekend. She was down from Wellesley, visiting her cousin in New Haven for the annual Harvard-Yale game. She has come to live with Powers, by sheer coincidence her "dear Uncle John," and our amorous hero's romantic aspirations rekindle and soar when he forms a regular evening chess date with his mentor at Nixon, Wright, Croak & Powers. Congenial duties fill his days as an associate at the firm, good company and glimpses of his love fill, and titillate, his evenings. It all ends soon enough—at least the congenial days.

A staff shortage in the "personal injury department" at Nixon, Wright Croak & Powers combined with Guy's experience in Leffingwell's "shop" gets him reassigned to work under the senior associate in that department, Nelson Brooks. At first things proceed smoothly enough, although, our hero can't help but notice that while receiving some practice pointers from his superior he, yet again, hears personal injury work referred to as "a game." In time, the shadow of his former practice will only lengthen.

Brooks takes care to explain to Guy that it will be his task to keep track of the jurors empaneled for an upcoming case. Brooks gives him a list of names . . .

. . . (he handed me a small book alphabetically arranged.) See whether—an "F" or an "H" or an "N" precedes it—like this or that (he pointed out the prefixes in the little book).

"What do the letters signify?" I asked him.

"'F' stands for friendly, 'H' for 'hostile' and 'N' for 'New'. You see, we have the record of all the jurors that have served in the past twenty years, and jurors in this county repeat themselves at least once in three years, unless they die. This book contains all the names that have been drawn for this term. We have a history of every prospective juror. Also for your own guidance let me tell you who of the Judges are friendly and who are hostile (and he named them) . . .

But if things were growing increasingly and discouragingly familiar within the consecrated halls of Nixon, Wright, Croak & Powers, worse was yet to come.

One morning Guy looks up from his desk to see the "grinning countenance" of that snaggle-toothed scoundrel, Henk—now a new Nixon Wright staffer! Henk explained that he, too, was "quits" with Leffingwell and had jumped to the other side for the "dough." In a huff, our offended junior associate goes to speak with Brooks about the firm's new employee. Brooks explains:

> . . . The fellow is worth his weight in gold . . . We need a fellow like Henk. In the first place his absence will cripple Leffingwell's machine, and, then think of the service he'll render us in defending cases against Leffingwell!"
>
> "But—" I could barely find my speech.
>
> "Well, we have got to fight fire with fire. Mark has practically monopolized the personal injury business in this part of the State—look at the court's calendar this term—we haven't won a case against him in two years! We practically pay him his price in cases where his clients haven't a shadow of a claim, because we are afraid of him—yes, just afraid of him and ashamed to admit it to our clients. We might as well close up shop in this department. Something must be done.

More ominous still, soon after Henk arrives, Frank Talcott, the debonair and nefarious "fixer" from Schmiermund's, begins hanging about the Nixon Wright offices.

But the worst comes when our despairing dreamer observes a juror, empaneled in a pending trial, enter and stay in Nelson Brooks office! Guy confronts Brooks, who suavely explains that the juror is only a "spotter," and assures Guy that nothing untoward is afoot. But, you see, they are trying to get Leffingwell to make a mistake . . .

A few days later Guy is switched to yet another department. This time it's bankruptcy. The Bankruptcy Department is managed by Colvin Hammersmith, a bloodless, myopic man who spoke "as if his tongue was too large for his mouth." Hammersmith is one of the five local attorneys comprising "The Clique" who together control all the substantial bankruptcy work in the city. Guy's first task in his new assignment is to go to the court clerk's office and copy down the names of the newly filed bankruptcy petitioners. Armed with these names Nixon Wright can contact its "correspondents" in other cities to notify them of the pending insolvency actions . . . and inquire whether they might require local representation? Guy and his fellow rooming house boarder, Virgil Tinker, disagree as to whether this isn't the same thing that was so often decried as base advertising and soliciting when practiced by the personal injury bar. Virgil takes the Bar Association (corporate firm position) on the issue:

> "You don't call this soliciting," he burst out indignantly.
>
> "What do you call it?" I insisted.
>
> "Representing our correspondents. We represent them and they represent us."
>
> "Then why do we advertise in The _____ and The _____" (mentioning well known monthly and quarterly and annual publications)? "In what respect is this method different from the method of the shysters who advertise in daily newspapers and offer advice free?"
>
> "Really you could try the patience of a saint!" Tinker was losing his temper. "One is legitimate advertising and the other isn't."
>
> "Wherein is the difference?" I persisted.
>
> He shrugged his shoulders and dropped the subject.
>
> Several days of depression followed. I had again grown pessimistic about my career. Disappointment was corroding my very heart . . .

Stillwell's career at the corporate bar culminates simultaneously with a delicious Clique-bred scandal of grand proportions.

A local merchant, Clinton Cornhill, owner and manager of the Cornhill Drygoods Company, comes to seek the advice of Hammersmith on how to hold off some of his most pressing creditors until the temporary cash flow problem the firm is having can be worked out. Little does Cornhill suspect that by consulting with Hammersmith (one of The Clique) he has committed a mistake that will prove fatal to his drygoods concern: "The Clique forced people into bankruptcy, if bankruptcy meant more remuneration; compromised, if that was more profitable for The Clique; or squeezed the unfortunate dry if the spoils justified such action . . ." The next day Cornhill returns to Hammersmith, a ruined man. Upon Cornhill's departure the day before, Hammersmith immediately notified his "correspondents" and set up a meeting with the Clique. This was a four million dollar case and the spoils had to be divided. Creditors, who the day before were content to wait, were now clamoring to drive Cornhill Drygoods into liquidation. Whatever time might have been available to work out the cash problem was lost. And so was Cornhill Drygoods . . .

At the first meeting of creditors the entire cast of the Clique are all present and involved—if not as counsel for the bankrupt then as receiver, if not as receiver then as counsel for the receiver, if not as counsel for the receiver then as counsel for the creditors . . . It had all been arranged, including the ultimate distribution of the fees. All that remained was the monotony of the mock trial where the "proofs" of the claims are presented for the record and tallied up for distribution

But just before the proceedings were to begin in earnest, Mark Leffingwell saunters into the court room. The members of the Clique are visibly perturbed. Who is he representing? This wasn't agreed upon in advance. He doesn't do this kind of work. What is he up to?

Vigorous procedural maneuvering ensues. Leffingwell is there to represent three small claims against the company. Making known his information about how the Clique had conspired to *cause* the Cornhill firm to go into bankruptcy, he sends the opposition into a disarrayed retreat. Ultimately, he gets himself appointed as the receiver's counsel, after raising the specter of numerous conflicts of interest among the cozy Clique members. Then he asks for time to serve subpoenas to compel witnesses to come testify regarding certain irregularities with the Cornhill books. He doesn't say whom he will call, only that he knows they won't appear voluntarily. The Clique harumphs and objects to the insinuations and then, reluctantly, joins in asking for a recess.

The next day, after having been subpoenaed, Jimmie Croak, President of the Bar Association and senior partner (and therefore technically counsel for) and stockholder in, Cornhill Drygoods is called to the stand by Leffingwell for cross examination. Croak testifies that as counsel he saw to it that all the corporate financial records were turned over to the receiver prior to the first meeting of creditors. Leffingwell inquires at length about some missing cash books. Croak responds that they were burned in a fire, four months previous. "They are not missing because it is in the interest of the stockholders to have them missing?" asks Leffingwell. "Your insinuations are unprofessional . . ." replies the increasingly restive Croak.

Leffingwell asks the bailiff to summon his next witness. "Call Mr. Henry W. McNamara." Now Croak, et al., are more than perturbed, they are panicked. Stillwell looks to the back of the court room wondering who this mysterious and fearsome Henry W. McNamara could be. In strolls "the grinning physiognomy of . . . Henk!" One of the Clique manages to sputter out a request for another recess. Shortly thereafter the Clique lawyers, with Leffingwell's acquiescence, arrange for a continuance until the next day. Back at the office, Stillwell is no longer privy to the urgent and gloomy partner conferences that fill the afternoon. He did, however, notice that "toward the close of day came the hush of an armistice, with the palpable sadness of defeat in our quarters."

A few days later, Henk and Stillwell meet at Schmiermund's where Henk and Talcott are obviously in the midst of a celebration. After Talcott leaves, Guy confesses to Henk that he still doesn't understand what happened. Surprised and amused, Henk explains the details—yet another lesson in his ongoing practicum on the Majesty of The Law:

> "You see them corporation guys were after Mark's scalp for some time and I admit he had some close shaves. At the time I left Mark it looked pretty bad for him, and for the whole bunch of us. Yes, sir, they caught us all in a sack and were about to tie its mouth. It certainly did look black for us. It was then that Nelson Brooks made me a proposition. The pact was to give Frank (Talcott) and I the immunity bath and hang Mark. We promised to produce the goods and save our own skins. And we strung Coit and Brooks and the rest of them along until the opportunity presented itself. If the Cornhill failure had not happened we would have sprung our surprise on Coit and Brooks in another matter—we hardly hoped to get as big a fish as Jimmie Croak. That was an accident."
>
> "How did you get the evidence?" I asked.
>
> "Give a fellow a chance and you'll hear the whole gag," Henk said proudly. "Back of Croak's private office, in the other wing of the building, is Pat Keegan's office. With Pat's assistance and one thousand dollars paid to the night watchman it was not difficult to install a dictaphone in Keegan's office and conceal the wires right under Croak's nose. So stenographic notes of the proceedings of the secret meeting between Croak and the other bankruptcy lawyers—their arrangements for the division of the spoils—were easily obtained. But it never rains but it pours. The day after we got the evidence of the meeting Mr. Croak called me to his office and ordered me to take a set of Cornhill books—the books Croak

testified were burned—to Chicago, where I myself helped place them in a vault as directed by Croak. The rest was easy. We have now sealed their lips forever. They'll never bother Mark no more, I can tell you. And I am back at Mark's."

"Did they also pay Mark any money?" I asked innocently.

"Did they? O, boy! One hundred and fifty thousand dollars in cold cash, which was divided in four equal parts after paying Pat Keegan ten thousand for his little job, and the other incidentals. We could have gotten half a million but we didn't want to blackmail 'em. And from now on the lion and the lamb shall lie down together, and the lion shall eat straw like the ox—isn't that what the Bible says?"

*   *   *   *   *

What does not immediately appear from the relatively few injury suits filed against American Steel and Wire between 1898 and 1915 is that the value of those worker claims was steadily increasing over the eighteen year period that preceded the compensation reform. Table 11 in the Appendix contains the known injury values for 55 of the 127 work injury cases filed against the company between 1898 and 1915. In these 55 cases the settlement amount (N=12) or verdict amount (N=43) appears in the public record. The injuries in the 55 cases are all inclusive, ranging in severity and permanence from broken bones to death. What is contained in this table is only the tip of the tip of the iceberg of worker injuries sustained at the American Steel and Wire Company over eighteen years. (See note 16.)

However, it is possible to take the settlement and verdict amounts from this limited sample of cases and look for a trend in the claim values over the eighteen years. By grouping the data into six 3 year spans and "extrapolating" from what is known, to what is probable, it is possible to project the cost trends encountered by the American Steel and Wire Company (and other employers) for worker injuries.

To understand Table 10 and how it attempts to establish a correlation between the value of work injury cases and the passage of time, it is necessary to work through some of the lines.[18] Starting with 1901 (the founding of U.S. Steel) and moving to the right, there were four cases located in the public record of the Cleveland area state and federal courts for which the verdict or settlement amount is known. Moving again to the right,

EXTRAPOLATED ANNUAL INJURY CLAIM VALUES IN THREE YEAR GROUPINGS 1898-1915					
Year	N= Cases of Known Value	Mean Value of Cases	Total Cases Filed	Extrapolated Annual Costs	Weighted Three Year Averages
1898	0	$0	2	$0	
1899	2	$66	5	$330	
1900	3	$0	18	$0	
Total	5		25	$330	$13.20
1901	4	$363	16	$5,800	
1902	6	$387	8	$3,100	
1903	4	$633	6	$3,800	
Total	14		30	$12,700	$423.33
1904	4	$375	8	$3,000	
1905	1	$750	2	$1,500	
1906	10	$678	10	$6,783	
Total	15		20	$11,283	$564.15
1907	7	$793	9	$7,140	
1908	3	$600	5	$3,000	
1909	2	$550	5	$2,750	
Total	12		19	$12,890	$678.41
1910	2	$575	7	$4,025	
1911	1	$450	3	$1,350	
1912	1	$400	4	$1,600	
Total	4		14	$6,975	$498.21
1913	2	$700	10	$7,000	
1914	2	$2,250	6	$13,500	
1915	1	$0	3	$0	
Total	5		19	$20,500	$1,078.95
1898-1915	55		127	$64,678	$509.27

Source: Court Files, Common Pleas, Probate & U.S. Circuit Courts, Cleveland, Ohio.

Table 10

the average value of those cases was $362.50. (See the Appendix for the cases listed in Table 11 for 1901) Moving again to the right, in 1901 the public record reveals that there were a total 16 work injury cases filed against the company (12 settled without a record of the sums paid to workers). Assuming that this number is correlated to the total number of claims against the company—claims is a more inclusive notion than "cases" (i.e. lawsuits)—it "weights" for the number of employees looking for compensation short of pursuing litigation. Taking the average known settlement and verdict value of the litigated cases and multiplying by the total number of cases filed in 1901 (values both known and unknown) one arrives at $5,800, or the "extrapolated" (projected) cost to either settle or pay the verdicts on all the cases filed that year. Note that no attempt is made to factor in the incidental costs for this litigation, court and lawyer fees, staff time, etc. The concern is only to discover the "market value" of the workers' injuries, not the "transaction costs" to the company to administer the claims handling process.

Taking that set of calculations and working up 1902 and 1903 and then combining them derives the three year total. There were 14 cases in the three years where the value of the settlement or verdict is known. The total number of work injury cases filed against the company of known and unknown value in 1901, 1902 and 1903 was 30. The total extrapolated annual costs for settling or paying the verdicts for those 30 cases over the three years was $12,7000. Finally, dividing that amount of three years settlement and judgment costs by the total number of work injury suits for the same period (30) yields $423.33 which is proposed as the "weighted average claim value" for all the cases filed in that triennium.

Dropping to the bottom line of the table derives the "extrapolated" weighted claim value for eighteen years of $509.27, but, more significantly, within the period there is a definite trend over time. That trend is revealed in the bar chart in Figure 9. There is a relatively strong correlation coefficient of .873 over the period and using a regression analysis to further smooth the data, (see the Appendix, notes 5 and 6) the "line of best fit" reveals a sevenfold increase in the value of worker injury cases between 1898 and the end of 1915.

Moving this line of best fit into a graph that compares the consumer price index, national manufacturing annual wages, and the Steel Corporation annual wages for the period 1902 through 1915, it is possible to see that there is no correlation between the value of the workers' injuries and either the adjusted cost of living or national wage trends. Accepting the assumptions underlying some of the data smoothing used to obtain the line

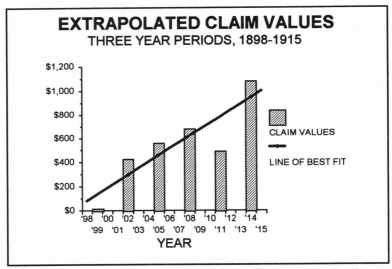

Figure 9   Source: Court Files, Common Pleas, Probate, U.S. Circuit Courts, Cleveland, Ohio.

of best fit, Figure 10 graphically illustrates the corporate employers' economic motivation to support the workmen's compensation reform. From what appears in the public record, American Steel and Wire's worker injury compensation amounts increased over 300% between 1902 and 1915, while wage rates barely increased by 30%. Work injury compensation amounts were rising at an accelerated rate—unrelated to the other costs of labor.

While Squire Sanders was doing an admirable job keeping some of the corollary costs of litigation (legal fees and court costs) contained for the company (and presumably other client corporations) the substantive costs of the workers' injuries, the injuries' "market values," were escalating beyond control, Squire Sanders' considerable legal and management acumen notwithstanding. It is this time-related dynamic that has been ignored by previous studies of the workmen's compensation reform movement. Public sympathies and a growing community awareness and understanding of the actual costs of industrial injuries led to an ongoing and ever upward re-calculation of the "value" of those injuries both upon the worker and larger community. What these figures roughly demonstrate is that in the Cleveland area, both juries and judges were more and more inclined to shift that social cost of work-sustained injury over to the corporate balance sheet.

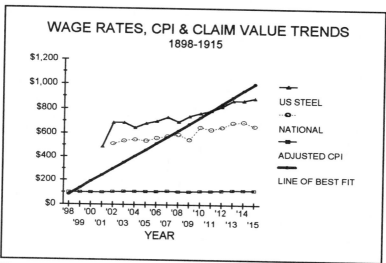

Figure 10 Source: Court Files, Common Pleas, Probate & U.S. Circuit Court , Cleveland, Ohio.

    This spiraling injury value phenomenon was well known to employers generally. The Cleveland Chamber of Commerce representative, U.B. Stewart, confirmed the trend to the Ohio Employers' Liability Commission when he testified before the panel the day after Tener's appearance. Responding to a question about the effects of the recently passed "Norris law" he referred to Tener's situation in sympathetic terms:

    Mr. Thomas: Mr. Tener, representing the American Steel and Wire Company, read an opening paper on this matter yesterday, and made the statement the that the American Steel and Wire Company had only two lawsuits for the past four or five years, or since the adoption of this compensation law. Has the Norris law increased lawsuits any?

    Mr. U.B. Stewart (of the Cleveland Chamber of Commerce): It has increased their liability.

    Mr Thomas: Has it increased their lawsuits any?

    Mr. Stewart: That does not necessarily follow. But he has had to increase his payments occasioned by the Norris Act. No question about that, but he does not like to go into court. He is a charitable gentlemen. I know, and their payments keep on mounting up, step by step, and they keep on paying.[19]

*   *   *   *   *

As the continuing saga of Mark Leffingwell and the corporate bar has suggested, the Cleveland (and national) legal community was sharply dividing between the new and thoroughly modern, large firm, corporate lawyers and their professional antecedents, the courthouse-oriented small firm and solo practitioners. In a sense, the so-called "ambulance chasers" were only the urban symbol of this old school, courthouse attorney, most of whom did not handle injury cases and many of whom never actually litigated cases of any kind. This split in the legal profession can be analyzed as a symptom of the larger divisions that began to rend the American social fabric in the late nineteenth and early twentieth centuries. Capital vs. labor, rich vs. poor, Republican vs. Democrat, employer vs. employee, native vs. immigrant, city vs. rural. None of these categories can be precisely aligned into a thorough, neat and cohesive Hegelian dichotomy that exactly parallels the division within the bar. But the split in the bar was very real and did reflect—and in some instances exaggerate—the divisions between the parties to work injury litigation.

It might even be suggested that, had the bar not split cleanly, dividing into two camps, with two separate cultures, and two separate sets of professional norms, the flood of litigation faced by employers might well have amounted to the merest trickle. At bottom, the profession that presumed to maintain the political-economic order, that is, the lawyers who prosecuted, and the lawyers who defended work injury cases, had to agree to disagree in order for there to be a "problem," or even, a single work injury lawsuit. Arguably that dichotomous professional dynamic was as responsible for the crisis in employer liability as any other underlying factor in the worker litigation.

If, then, at least part of the dynamic forces behind the workmen's compensation reform lay in the differences between the two professional types, the emerging and ascendant corporate lawyer and his professional antithesis, the antiquarian and descendant courthouse lawyer, it follows that the two types bear some deeper examination. The litigation attending the American Steel and Wire Company in Cleveland flushes out two individuals—lawyer-archetypes—who will serve well to illustrate the best, and worst, of the emerging professional ying-yang of urban lawyering..

There is a remarkable parallel between the fictional, soon-to-be-consummated romance between Guy Stillwell and Mary Halstead, John Powers' beloved niece in *The Jugglers*, and that of an actual young associate at Squire, Sanders & Dempsey and Mary Sanders, daughter of founding partner William Brownell Sanders. The associate, Harold Terry Clark, came to Cleveland in 1906 and in the spring of 1907 took over the American Steel and Wire litigation where he was responsible for defending all the injury suits until the passage of workmen's compensation stemmed the suits against the company in 1915. He married Mary Sanders in 1911 and in 1913 he made partner. Clark would go on to make major contributions in the city's civic and charitable realms. He was, in fact, a kind of Cleveland elite paradigm—Connecticut Yankee born and bred; successful, large firm corporate lawyer; philanthropist; care-taker of commercial and civic capital; institution founder and institution builder.

His career in Cleveland began in 1906 when he arrived fresh out of Harvard law school. He was admitted to both the Connecticut and Ohio bars but came to Cleveland to work at Squire Sanders. Born in Derby, Connecticut (New Haven County) he was educated in the public schools of Ansonia, Connecticut, and graduated from Yale undergraduate in 1903. It is not clear what brought him to Cleveland, but given the strong ties between Yale and Cleveland's many transplanted New England families, it seems likely he developed some social contacts with Western Reserve-born classmates while at Yale.

In 1907 Clark's own personal signature replaces the generic partnership "signature" of "Squire, Sanders and Dempsey" on the court filings—Clark is now signing as a representative of the firm. His personality does not appear in the public record of the injury cases. In one transcribed deposition filed with the federal court, he prevents two American Steel and Wire employees from giving testimony to the plaintiff's attorneys, although according to the transcript, the witnesses were properly subpoenaed. The transcript doesn't contain Clark's reasons for interceding, but apparently concerned whether the witnesses would be available for trial.[20]

During the First World War, Clark served a brief tenure as assistant to Bernard Baruch while Baruch served as chairman of the United States War Industries Board and then, in early 1919, accompanied Baruch to Europe when he served as a technical advisor to the American Commission to Negotiate Peace in Paris. While in Europe he was decorated as Chevalier of the Order of Leopold I, by King Albert of Belgium.

Clark was very involved in war-related concerns locally as well. He was appointed by the then mayor of Cleveland, Harry L. Davis, to head the Cleveland Americanization Council, a coordinating agency that worked with 68 local organizations and state and federal programs directed to securing the loyalty of the large unnaturalized immigrant populations in Cleveland. Clark worked closely with the public schools and pushed for the compulsory attendance of immigrant children until age 21. In 1937 Clark left Squire Sanders and set up his own practice, specializing in corporate and probate work. He created the corporate structure for Glidden Paints and other local concerns and served on the boards of numerous corporations and banks.

His philanthropic and civic efforts were extensive, if not herculean. In 1920 he helped found, and gathered the support of others, for the Cleveland Museum of Natural History and is said to have been instrumental in sustaining the museum during the lean Depression years. He was also instrumental in seeing to it that the museum carried out educational programs as well as serving as an institutional curator. He was involved in starting the Cleveland Metropark System and its Brookside Park Zoo. He served as president of the Cleveland Art Museum, and was very active in the Cleveland Society for the Blind. An avid tennis fan, he also promoted American involvement in the Davis Cup Tennis Competition.

In 1937, the same year he left Squire Sanders, Clark's first wife, Mary, passed away. They had six children. Clark married Marie Odenkirk in 1940. He lived in Cleveland Heights, and died in 1965, having left a tremendous mark upon the city.[21]

If Harold T. Clark serves as our corporate lawyer "thesis," Harry F. Payer, Clark's contemporary, is a near perfect antithesis. Payer practiced law in the Cleveland area, beginning eight years before Clark, in 1899, and continued in practice until 1950. There, any resemblance between the two Cleveland attorneys ends. Born in Cleveland in 1875, Payer was of Czech origin. He attended Cleveland public schools and worked his way through Western Reserve College graduating in 1897 with an A.B. degree. Unlike Clark, he attended Cleveland Law School, a proprietary "night law school" founded by local area judges. He graduated in 1899 and was thereupon admitted to the Ohio bar.

Payer immediately started doing personal injury work. In fact, two of his first cases were brought against American Steel and Wire. In all, he filed seven cases against the company before workmen's compensation was passed. Although the only recovery amounts against the company that appear of record are in his first two cases, and those were for a mere pittance[22]—he was renowned for getting good results from a jury. Nicknamed

"Demosthenes" for his oratorical abilities, most of his clients in the American Steel and Wire litigation were new immigrants. (Indeed, Payer might well have served as Brudno's model for his extravagantly eloquent and successful "Mark Leffingwell.")

He was a life-long Democrat, having started in his political career by serving as Tom Johnson's campaign manager. He served as an assistant city solicitor under Newton D. Baker between 1901 and 1907. In his private practice he specialized in criminal defense and personal injury suits. He was very active in the Cleveland Bar Association in the 1920's but later abandoned that organization to help found and serve as a three-term President of the Cuyahoga County Bar Association. The County Bar Association was the declared rival to the much older and more prestigious, corporate firm-oriented Cleveland Bar Association. The County or "common man's bar" was comprised of many of the ethnic, small firm and solo practitioners who depended upon the petty courts for their living and who often felt that the Cleveland Bar Association ill served their interests. Payer wrote an interesting editorial for the Association's publication in 1930 bemoaning the deplorable state of workmen's compensation in Ohio.[23] He belonged to the Czecho-Slovak Club of America and the Czecho-Slovak Chamber of Commerce. He made his living (and a very good one) opposing the corporate elite of the city and both suffered and prospered from his chosen social, political and professional alignments.

In 1939 Payer was embarrassed by a published opinion of the Ohio Supreme Court involving a fee dispute with one of his former clients. According to the facts recited in the high court's opinion, Payer was shamefully grasping and overreaching in his siphoning off the lion's share of a workmen's compensation recovery from his client, an unsophisticated and trusting widow.[24] He was an accomplished amateur linguist who could speak Czech, Polish, Italian, French and German, and maintained a reading literacy in Greek and Latin. He married Florence Graves, a kindergarten teacher, in 1902, and they had three children. He also lived in Cleveland Heights and died in 1952.[25]

*   *   *   *   *

By 1910 two of the major Morgan interests, International Harvester and the United States Steel Corporation, had sufficiently coalesced their in-house injury compensation policies into coherent "Plans" that could be submitted for public consideration. The United States Steel Corporation's Plan was released through its Cleveland-headquartered subsidiary, the American Steel and Wire Company, and it was published in Crystal Eastman's widely read *Work Accidents and the Law*. Its major features were as follows:

GENERAL CONDITIONS

1. The Company contributes 100% of the cost of the Plan.
2. The Company Manager shall have sole and final discretion in setting and paying claims.
3. No claim will be paid if the employee or his family files suit against the Company and the Company will not deal with an attorney.
4. Claims will be paid to any employee who is disabled while acting in the service of the company due to accidental injury.
5. No compensation will be paid for the first 10 days of disablement nor longer than 52 weeks.
6. The period of disability shall be determined by the Company surgeon.
7. No employee can receive both wages and disability compensation simultaneously.
8. The Company will provide treatment by Surgeons and Hospitals of its choosing.
9. The Company will provide artificial limbs and trusses when required.
10. To receive compensation a disabled employee must follow the instructions of the treating surgeon and if not confined to the house report to the surgeon as directed.
11. Compensation will not be paid for injuries caused by intoxication or resulting from illegal or immoral acts.
12. Receipt of compensation will be conditioned upon the employee signing a liability release to the Company.

TEMPORARY DISABILITY

13. Single Men with less than 5 years of service with the company shall receive 35% of their daily wages earned at the time of injury. Single men with more than 5 years service shall receive an additional 2% of their wages at the time of injury for each year of service over 5 years. In no event shall a single man receive more than $1.50 per day for 52 weeks.

14. Married Men living with their families who have been in the service of the Company for less than 5 years shall receive 50% of their daily wage rate at the time of injury. For each year of service over 5 years 2% shall be added to the daily wage rate earned at the time of injury. For each child under 16 years 5% shall be added to the compensation. In no event shall the compensation exceed $2.00 per day for 52 weeks.

PERMANENT DISABILITY

15. Compensation amounts for permanent injuries (such as loss of an arm or leg) will vary greatly depending upon the extent to which the disability renders further gainful employment difficult or unlikely. Broad discretion is left to the Company Manager to set compensation amounts corresponding as far as possible to the amounts stated below:

Loss of a hand	12 months wages
Loss of an arm	18 months wages
Loss of a foot	9 months wages
Loss of a leg	12 months wages
Loss of an eye	6 months wages

DEATH

16. Death compensation will be paid to the families of deceased employees as soon as certification of the cause of death and a legal release from the surviving family is given.
17. The Company will pay reasonable funeral expenses not to exceed $100.
18. The widows and children of deceased employees shall receive compensation as follows: For married men living with their families who had less than 5 years service with the company leaving a widow and children under 16 years the company shall pay 18 months wages at the rate at the time of death. For each additional year of service above 5 years, three percent shall be added to this relief. For each child under 16 years ten percent shall be added. In no event shall the compensation for death exceed $3,000.

Notes

1. Letter dated December 21, 1909, from Charles MacVeagh, General Solicitor of the United States Steel Corporation to William B. Dickson, First Vice President of United States Steel Corporation enclosing the Voluntary Accident Relief Plan. William Brown Dickson Papers, Pennsylvania State University Library, Historical Collections and Labor Archives, University Park, Pennsylvania.

2. Stephen Tener, testifying on behalf of American Steel and Wire Company before the Ohio Employers' Liability Commission, November 1, 1910. Ibid., OELC, *Report*, Vol. II, 124-25.

3. The Injunction Judge himself, William Howard Taft, then with the federal Sixth Circuit Court in Cincinnati, signed the temporary restraining order restricting the workers' demonstrations around the Cleveland wire facilities. The temporary injunction was later amended to a permanent order against the Union and strike breakers were brought in to defeat the Union. *American Steel and Wire Company vs. Wire Drawers and Die Makers Union No 1, et al.*, United States Circuit Court, Northern District of Ohio, Eastern Division, Case No. 5812, filed September 26, 1898.

4. The same Judge Dickey who represented the railroad in the jury scandal case *Reardon vs. Lakeshore & Michigan Southern Railway.*

5. William B. Neff, *Bench and Bar of Northern Ohio*, (Cleveland: The Historical Publishing Company, 1921), 239.

6. Otis' holdings in the manufacturing sector were extensive and included the American Wire Company which would join in the final set of mergers in 1901 that produced the American Steel and Wire Company of New Jersey. He was also, like so many successful manufacturers of his day, much involved in the creation and direction of area banking institutions. Samuel P. Orth *A History of Cleveland, Ohio* (Chicago: S. J. Clark Publishing Company, 1910) Vol. III, 55; Ibid., *Encyclopedia of Cleveland History*, 746.

7. It is unclear whether Abner Brownell was Sanders' middle namesake.

8. Samuel P. Orth *A History of Cleveland, Ohio* (Chicago: S. J. Clark Publishing Company, 1910) 55.

9. Ibid., Orth, 591.

10. Letter to subsidiary presidents from William B. Dickson, dated May 23rd, 1907, requesting information on fatalities for 1906. Ibid.

11. Letter from C. L. Taylor, Chairman of the Carnegie Relief Fund, to William B. Dickson, Senior Vice President of United States Steel, May 20, 1907. Ibid.

12. Ibid., Beyer, 205.

13. *American Steel and Wire Company vs. Wire Drawers and Die Makers Union No 1, et al.*, United States Circuit Court, Northern District of Ohio, Eastern Division, Case No. 5812, filed September 26, 1898.

14. It would be interesting to try to correlate the higher work injury litigation rates with the labor strife in the plants at the time of the mergers, but beyond the ken of this study.

15. The distinction between the plaintiff lawyers' pleading and the Squire, Sanders & Dempsey' pleading was palpable. For example, consider one sentence of a seven typed legal page Petition filed on behalf of an injured worker:

> . . . That on the said 23rd day of March 1900, said belt came partly off said pulleys as before described and for the reason above named and following the instructions of said foreman in that behalf and obeying his order theretofore given and relying upon the superior skill and knowledge, and experience of said foreman and his assurance that it was a safe thing to do, and not knowing or appreciating the danger incident thereto plaintiff proceeded, as before directed, instructed and ordered by said foreman, to replace said belt, using said stick of wood in the manner that the said foreman used it theretofore and in the manner being described . . .

And so forth and so on, for seven interminable pages. The Squire, Sanders & Dempsey Answer to the Petition is as follows:

> Now comes defendant, The American Steel and Wire Company of New Jersey, and for its answer to the petition of plaintiff filed herein, says that it admits that it is a corporation duly organized under the laws of the State of New Jersey. Further answering, defendant denies each and all the other allegations in said petition contained, and says that if plaintiff were injured as therein alleged, his own negligence contributed thereto.

> WHEREFORE, defendant asks to go hence with its costs.

Joseph Letmenski vs. American Steel and Wire Company, Case No. 6192,

Circuit Court of the United States, Northern District of Ohio, Eastern Division.

16. Some rough mathematics and basic information about accident rates, both industry wide and within wire drawing departments, can project what the accident frequency and severity rates would have been in the Cleveland area. In 1910, Stephen Tener testified that 7,500 men worked for the concern in the State of Ohio. The only properties in the state were in Cleveland with a minor property in Salem, Ohio. Conservatively estimating that 5,000 men worked in the Cleveland properties in all the departments; and knowing from Steel Corporation figures that the average work week during this period was 68 hours; and figuring a 50 week work year; there were approximately 17,000,000 man hours of exposure in a year in the Cleveland properties. Plugging in the industry-wide frequency rate of 39 accidents per 1,000,000 hours of exposure there would have been approximately 663 accidents in the Cleveland properties per year. According to the statistics regarding wire drawing frequency rates for permanent injuries (20.5 per 10,000,000 hours of exposure), of those 663 accidents 35 would have resulted in permanently disabling injuries. Thus, even using these conservative estimates, the "injury to suit ratio" for American Steel and Wire was only 1.5%. 98.5% of the lost time accidents never made it to the courthouse steps. Clearly, the company was working with considerable success to settle up with injured employees *before* suits were filed.

17. Ibid., OELC, *Report*, Vol. II, 128.

18. For a more detailed discussion of the strengths and weaknesses using this method, see the Appendix. There are some obvious limitations to this technique. The sample is small, and certain assumptions are required to build upon such a limited number of known claim values to "extrapolate" out what all claim values were doing over the course of nearly 20 years. The sample is too small to control for variations in the type of injury and any difference between the verdicts and settlements. However, the rounding technique used here attempts to compensate for some of the problems presented by the limited data and the results are suggestive, and confirmed by the limited statistical and anecdotal sources available. See Anthony Bale, "America's First Compensation Crisis: Conflict Over the Value and Meaning of Workplace Injuries Under the Employers' Liability System" in *Dying for Work* eds. David Rosner; Gerald Markowitz (Bloomington: Indiana University Press, 1987).

19. Ibid., OELC, *Report*, Vol. II, 168.

20. The deposition was given by a company employee to the plaintiff's attorneys "for the preservation of testimony," i.e. to be read into the record at trial in federal court. It is one of the rare cases where there was co-counsel on behalf of American Steel and Wire Company—Kline, Tolles & Goff. Perhaps the reason for the appearance of co-counsel can be deduced from the fact that the case resulted in the highest recovery amount of all the cases filed against the company by an injured worker—$6,200, paid in settlement. At the time the case was being prepared for trial Clark was only one and a half years out of law school. *Egnac Komorowski vs. American Steel and Wire Company*, U. S. Circuit Court for the Northern District of Ohio, Eastern Division. Case No. 7318.

21. Ibid., *Encyclopedia of Cleveland History*, 193-94.

22. Case Nos. 1 and 2 in Table 3.

23. Payer's 1930 editorial reads in part:

> The appalling situation already bared by the partial reports of the members of the Committee on Workmen's Compensation Law—reveals a conscientious personnel struggling with a cumbersome, inefficient and inexpert system which in seventeen years of trial has left countless numbers of industrial victims inarticulate and remediless . . .

Harry F. Payer, "Can Justice Forsake the Court?" Cuyahoga County Bar Association *Bulletin*, Vol. 1 (February, 1930), 1.

24. *McCamey v. Payer*, 135 Ohio St. 660, (1939).

25. Ibid., *Encyclopedia of Cleveland History*, 757-58; *Progressive Men of Northern Ohio* (Cleveland: Plain Dealer Publishing Company, 1906) 90.

V I

The Free Hand

. . . a stone to one who asks for bread.[1]

The constitutional and legislative history of the Ohio Workmen's Compensation Act began in earnest when, in early 1910, the Employers' Association of Cleveland suggested to Governor Judson A. Harmon that he appoint a commission to study, conduct hearings and recommend a compensation scheme for injured workmen in the State of Ohio.[2] Harmon, a conservative Democrat and former judge, ran on a platform that supported passage of a strong employer liability law, and needed little prompting to initiate the consensus building process required to pass a new industrial injury compensation system. In May of 1910, the Ohio legislature passed enabling resolutions for a commission "to make inquiry, examination and investigation into the subject of a direct compensation law or a law affecting liability of employers to employes for industrial accidents."[3] Harmon quickly appointed a five-member Ohio Employers' Liability Commission with two "employer" representatives, two "labor" representatives and an "impartial" attorney as chairman.[4] Inexplicably, the legislature didn't appropriate any money to fund the Commission's work so Harmon paid the initial costs for the Commission's investigative expenses out of his own pocket.

The time was ripe for a concerted push toward a new statewide compensation system. Nationally, reformers had been spreading the gospel of compensation beginning fully five years before the appointment of the Ohio Commission. 1910 was a pivotal year for the reform nationally as well as in Ohio. In November of that year, the Ohio Commission adjourned its hearings to attend a national conference with various other state liability commissions meeting in Chicago. A measure of the strength of the rising wave of reform fervor can be gathered from the number of states that were simultaneously investigating employer liability and compensation alternatives. In attendance at the fall conference in Chicago were the commissioners and their representatives from: the United States Employer's Liability Commission; the New York Commission on Employers' Liability; the Wisconsin Industrial Insurance Committee; the Minnesota Employees' Compensation Commission; the Illinois Employers' Liability Commission; the New Jersey Employers' Liability Commission;[5] the Employers' Liability Commission of Montana; the Massachusetts Commission on Compensation for Industrial Accidents; the State of Connecticut (by special delegate); the Special Committee of Commissioners on Uniform State Laws to prepare a Uniform Workmen Compensation Law; and the United States Commissioner of Labor, Charles P. Neil.

Throughout the next four years, until Ohio finally adopted the nation's first broadly inclusive and compulsory compensation law, the reform received the unflinching support of the state's large manufacturing employers.[6] Their group, the Ohio Manufacturers Association (OMA), ultimately joined the Cleveland Chamber of Commerce, and the Cleveland Employer's Association to lobby for and closely monitor passage of the statewide reform.[7] At least part of the impetus for pushing for the reform lay in the recent passage of the Norris Act, which severely delimited the employer defenses of contributory negligence and the fellow servant rule (assumption of the risk had its common law wings effectively clipped by the Ohio legislature in 1904 by the Williams Bill[8]). However, notwithstanding (or perhaps because of) the darkening horizon for employers in the courts and legislature, most smaller and proprietary concerns continued to fight the compensation reform in all its forms and permutations through, until and even beyond the year of its final adoption by the Ohio legislature.[9]

The Ohio Employers' Liability Commission held hearings in cities throughout the state in the fall of 1910. Most of the hearings involved taking prepared statements from various experts and representatives from local employer and labor groups who came to testify along well understood and clearly defined lines. Depending upon the witness, the Commission might then follow the testimony with specific questions to the issues addressed by the witness. Most, if not all, who testified before the Commission fulsomely decried the deplorable circumstances of injured workers cast, as they were, upon the treacherous waters of the employer-favoring common law and the corrupt and convoluted court-administered system of personal injury litigation. The principal variations in the testimony were in the suggested remedies to the despised tort system. Almost all the discussions and testimony before the Commission concerned the distinctions between the liability aspects of the work injury litigation system as compared to a reformed compensation scheme.

Strangely, there was very little discussion of the damages under the liability system, or proposed compensation amounts under a reformed system. However, while the public discussion and analysis of actual litigation recovery rates was practically nonexistent, the Commission did quietly set about to gather facts and figures regarding the dollar recovery amounts in worker injury cases filed in the local and federal courts of Cuyahoga County (Cleveland) between 1905-1909. Cuyahoga County was selected because it was the largest industrial county in the state.[10]

The Ohio Commission hired the former Illinois Employers' Liability Commission investigator, Emile E. Watson, for the Cuyahoga County litigation study. Watson, an actuary with a masters degree, was working as an investigator for the Illinois Commission of Occupational Diseases when he was hired away by the Ohio Commission. Watson (who later took a permanent position as the chief actuary of the Ohio compensation fund) brought his assistant at the Illinois Occupational Disease Commission, William P. Harms, to help gather and organize the data for the litigation study. A third member of the investigative staff, William Peacock, was law-trained at the University of Chicago. These three were assigned the task of investigating the actual "amounts of compensation paid by employers on account of the partial and total disability of married men injured and the compensation paid dependents of married men killed in industrial accidents during the years 1905-1909 inclusive" in Cuyahoga County, Ohio. The only completed portion of the study that appears in the published *Report* of the Ohio Employers Liability Commission concerned the fatal accidents in the Cleveland area during the five years studied. (See Appendix.) The results of the examination of the temporary and permanently disabling accidents were supposed to be completed in March of 1911[11] but, if completed, were never published. However, as will appear below, the study of fatal accidents proved crucial in defining the upper and lower limits of worker recoveries for all accidents in Ohio under the new Workmen's Compensation scheme.

The Commission completed its work quickly and submitted two proposed bills to the Ohio Legislature addressing the industrial accident problem. The majority bill was supported by the employer representatives, and by Chairman Boyd and by William Rohr, one of the employee representatives. The majority recommendation proposed that the state maintain a fund that would compete with private insurers; pay 60% of an injured employee's average weekly wage during the period of disability; and be funded by both employers (75%) and employees (25%). The majority bill set $3,400 as the maximum amount that could be recovered by an injured employee (except for permanently and totally disabled employees who would receive compensation for life), set a limit of $150 for doctor and hospital expenses and set a maximum of $150 for funeral expenses for fatally injured employees.

Some of the give and take during the Commission's deliberations can be gleaned from Commissioner Rohr's (a labor representative) addendum to the majority recommended "Employees' Compensation Code":

> On account of the concessions made by the majority members of the commission, namely that the employes should be compensated for so long as total disability lasts, and the maximum amount of compensation in permanent partial disability and death should be four hundred dollars ($400) more than agreed at the Chicago conference, and the waiting period only one-half of that decided by the Chicago conference and the minimum and maximum weekly allowance be raised from $4 to $5 and from $10 to $12, also, that the employe be given the right of appeal in the event he is denied any compensation by the State Board of Compensation Awards, I have signed my name to this Code, without exceptions.[12]

William Winans, the other labor representative, couldn't bring himself to join in recommending the majority bill, no matter how hard won the concessions from the employer representatives.

Winans, a trade unionist, submitted a minority recommendation that differed primarily in its provision for exclusive employer contributions to the fund and its preservation of the employees' right to elect to bring a court action in lieu of a compensation claim—even against employers who subscribed to the compensation fund. Winans' bill included relaxed employer defenses in an employee-elected court action but provided that if the employee won a verdict against a subscribing employer, the employer would be entitled to apply for reimbursement from the fund up to the maximum of $3,400 upon proof of payment of the employee's judgment. Winans also upped the weekly wage percentage to a full 66.6% over the slightly reduced 60% proposed in the majority bill. Remarkably, Winans' minority bill is better remembered for its exemption of employee contributions to the fund than for its preservation of the employees' right to sue in lieu of applying for compensation.[13]

Early in 1911 Ohio's first elective compensation law was drafted by George B. Okey of Columbus, acting as retained counsel for the Ohio Federation of Labor (OSFL).[14] The legislative process that followed seemed a veritable paragon of social harmony[15] with the Federation of Labor and the just-formed Ohio Manufacturers Association (OMA) working closely together on the proposed bill. After a crucial compromise caucus between the OSFL and OMA working out differences between the House and Senate versions of the bill, then state senator William Green (of the United Mine Workers, and later, American Federation of Labor fame) introduced the elective Act and it passed by a wide margin in both houses. The bill as finally passed compromised the majority and minority proposals of the commission by reducing the employees' contribution to 10% while completely barring workers from filing suit against an employer who elected to subscribe to the fund.

Ohio's first compensation Act was "elective" or voluntary, due in no small measure to the recently announced decision of New York's highest court in the famous *Ives* case, which invalidated New York's compulsory compensation law on the grounds that it deprived employers of property without due process of law. In an effort to avoid the *Ives* objection and thereby pass constitutional muster, the Ohio law provided that employers need not necessarily join in the state compensation fund, *but* would suffer gross disadvantages in the courts if they chose to remain outside the new compensation scheme's purview. The elective Act provided that if an employer so chose, and was sued by a work-injured employee, they could not avail themselves of any common law defenses to employee negligence suits. However, if the employer elected to join the fund, then the injured employee would lose all rights to pursue court action and would only have recourse under the compensation scheme. The participating employer effectively bound the injured employee under the Act by serving notice on the employee of the firm's election to pay premiums to the state fund. If an employee who received notice stayed on with that employer, he was held to have "waived" any rights to court process for any work-related injuries sustained after receiving the notice.[16] The employees anted up their 10% contribution to the fund through employer payroll deductions authorized by the Act.

Although the elective Act only operated through 1912 and 1913, it set the pattern for the final compulsory Act passed by the Ohio legislature in 1913. The elective law stipulated a quintessentially progressive tripartite State Liability Board of Awards. Governor Harmon appointed Morris

Woodhull, a retired manufacturer from Dayton, as the employer representative. Thomas J. Duffy, of East Liverpool, was the labor representative. He was a member of the OSFL and president of the National Brotherhood of Operative Potters. The "neutral" member, a representative of the "public interest," was again a lawyer, Wallace D. Yaple of Chillicothe.

The elective law provided the Board with authority to hire staff and promulgate procedures for administering the new compensation scheme. The Board was to classify employment and set premium rates sufficient to pay claims and fund a surplus. The Act provided for payment of doctor and hospital expenses (raised to $200) through the fund. The Act further provided for the payment of funeral expenses and defined a one week waiting period before an injured employee would qualify for compensation. (As pointed out by Rohr, the Chicago conference recommended a two-week waiting period.)

As for compensation amounts, the elective act set the standard that all payments were to be measured according to 2/3rds of the average weekly wage of the injured employee at the time of injury with mandated minimum and maximums of $5 and $12 per week respectively. Certain injuries (amputations, loss of an eye, etc.) were presumed to have specific periods of disability (e.g., 60 weeks for an amputated thumb, 35 weeks for an index finger, etc.). Death benefits were again measured according to the 2/3rds of average weekly wage rule for a maximum of six years following death or $3,400 ($1,500 minimum) in the event the deceased employee left dependents. If not, the law only provided for hospital and doctor bills and funeral expenses. For the very rare instances of total and permanent disability, the employee was entitled to 2/3rds of his average weekly wage at the time of injury for the duration of his life.

Although never discussed or addressed in a public forum, the compensation amounts that were established in the elective, and thereafter the compulsory Act, were based upon the actuarial study performed by E.E. Watson of the fatal cases litigated in the Cuyahoga County courts. (See Appendix.) In testimony presented to the Ontario Board of Employer Liability, Ohio Commission Chair James Harrington Boyd explained how the Ohio Act's compensation figures were determined. Answering a question from the Ontario Board concerning the Ohio law's upper limit for recovery, Boyd explained:

> There was a slight compromise on the $3,400, you see . . . They had 370 fatal cases that were investigated in Cuyahoga County during the period from 1905 to 1910. Now, there were 135 of these

cases that received something up to $300, for an average of $163.83. Then there were 107 of those cases received something between $300 and $1,000 or an average of $519.81. There were 71 cases that received something between $1,000 and $2,000, or an average of $1,269.98. There were 42 cases that received something between $2,000 and $4,000, or an average of $2,582.13. There were 15 cases received something above $4,000 or an average of $4,991.66. These were the 15 best cases of the 370. Take one quarter off $4,991 and you get $3,740, and $150 in doctor bills off that, and it would leave a little less than $3,600. In other words it brought it down below the $3,600, and they compromised on it and called it $3,400, and the workmen's organizations all agreed to that.[17]

Although the 1911 elective Act would change some features before the 1913 passage of the final compulsory Act, the parameters for employee compensation amounts was not revisited. Thus, did Watson's study of the fatal cases[18] brought under the "common law of unhallowed memory" set the monetary terms of settlement between the employers and injured employees of Ohio for generations to come.

Ohio's elective Act set another extraordinary precedent that would hold in Ohio for generations. The Act set up an exclusive state fund for compensation, effectively freezing out the stock liability insurance companies from a formerly lucrative line of business. The liability companies were involved in the compensation reform efforts since the beginning of the national compensation movement, providing testimony, and facts and figures to most of the employers' liability commissions set up in the various interested states. Reformers were often merciless in criticizing the insurance firms for their heartless and cruel techniques in exacting low settlement amounts from the needful and disabled employees facing the desperate straits of lost income and continuing disability. Yet most states eventually turned the business of workmen's compensation over to the same industry that handled it before the reform, by way of employer-purchased liability insurance policies. Exceptions to this general rule were states that set up competing state funds that operated alongside the private carriers in providing workmen's compensation coverage. Rarer still was the case in Ohio, where insurance firms were prohibited from writing any workmen's compensation coverage of any kind.

The feeling was very strong among Ohio workmen's groups that it was abhorrent for profit motivated concerns to come into the realm of compensation. Insurance industry participation would set up the inevitable conflict of interest between the insurance firm's owners—wanting to reduce settlement amounts with injured employees—and the munificent intentions of the statute—to fairly compensate injured workmen irrespective of corporate balance sheets, whether the employers' or the insurers'. Others argued it was simply repulsive for "profit" of any kind to be derived from the misfortunes of workers who were injured on the job. Governor Harmon, and his successor in office in 1912, James M. Cox, both supported the exclusive state fund. Cox stated his objection as follows:

> Liability insurance, in its very essence, is opposed, if not repugnant to the principle of compensation. The former gave very uncertain relief to the toiling masses . . . conditions of social unrest, of impatience with, if not a resentful feeling toward the courts, and glaring injustice in every community where there was located shop, mill or mine, grew out of the practices of liability insurance . . . A co-operation with the injured . . . is too holy a trust to be transferred to any business enterprise.[19]

In an extraordinary compromise with the state's large employers (represented by the OMA), Cox secured the insurance industry's exclusion from the State's workmen's compensation "business" in 1913. The OMA finally supported the exclusion of liability insurers from participation in the compensation scheme as part of a deal to get self-insurance provisions inserted into the compulsory Act. That is, large firms with sufficient reserve capital could provide direct compensation to their injured workmen so long as the firm agreed to pay claims according to the minimum, state-mandated schedules and terms. This feature allowed firms such as American Steel and Wire to handle most worker claims without the intercession of the Industrial Commission—or a liability insurance carrier—an obvious management and administrative advantage to the company. Once this self-insurance feature was secured, the OMA backed the insurance industry's exclusion from the compensation "business" in Ohio.[20]

It was well understood by reformers and "stand patters" alike that the elective law had to be tested for constitutional muster in the state's highest court. The Act was brought before the Supreme Court of Ohio in February of 1912 (two months following its effective date) and was held constitutionally sound. *Yaple v. Creamer*, 85 Ohio St. 349, (1912). Further constitutional support was provided for a *compulsory* act when, in 1912, Ohio held a constitutional convention to hammer out no less than forty-two propositions to change and amend the Ohio Constitution, last amended in 1856. The constitutional amendment authorizing the compulsory compensation laws was not debated by the convention and received unanimous voice vote approval at the convention.[21] The proposed amendment to the Ohio Constitution read as follows:

> For the purpose of providing compensation from a state fund, to workmen and their dependents, for death, injuries or occupational diseases, occasioned in the course of such workmen's employment, laws may be passed establishing a fund to be created and administered by the state and by compulsory contribution thereto by employers; determining the terms and conditions upon which payment shall be made therefrom and taking away any and all rights of action or defenses from employees and employers but no right of action shall be taken away from any employees when injury, disease or death arises from failure of the employer to comply with any lawful requirement for the protection of the lives, health and safety of employees.

The proposed amendments to the state Constitution were submitted to a popular vote in November of 1912, each amendment being subject to separate electoral consideration. The compulsory, exclusively employer-funded, and exclusively state administered workmen's compensation amendment to the Ohio Constitution passed by a popular vote of 321,558 to 211,772.

The constitutional path was now cleared for passage of Ohio's compulsory workmen's compensation law. On February 26, 1913, both houses passed the new compulsory law, unanimously. The new Act was effective January 1, 1914 and required participation from all firms that employed five or more persons. The statute consolidated previously independent state departments under the new Industrial Commission. The Commissioner of Labor Statistics, Chief Inspector of Mines, Chief Inspector of Workshops and Factories, Chief Examiner of Steam Engineers, Board of Boiler Rules and the State Board of Arbitration and Conciliation were all joined under the new Industrial Commission. The Commission replaced the elective act's State Liability Board of Awards. Again, the initial appointments to the Industrial Commission maintained the tripartite form. Yaple and Duffy were held over from the original Board of Awards while the employer representative, Woodhull, was replaced by Professor M.B. Hammond, from Ohio State University's Department of Economics.

Workmen's Compensation was now the constitutionally mandated statutory law of Ohio.

* * * * *

And what of Guy Stillwell? When last we joined him, Henk had just delighted in drawing his attention to yet another frayed and unseemly "rope." And this one, dangling indecorously from the professional petty coats of the Clique and Nixon, Wright, Croak & Powers, was far too slippery for Guy to hold any longer. This time Guy resolves to give up law altogether, the Cornhill case having shattered the beautiful "house of cards" he had misapprehended for the corporately-redeemed majesty of The Law. He determines to move on and forsake the whole mendacious lot—inconstant Themis and all her toady minions! On the way to his office at Nixon Wright for his last day at the firm, he passes a construction site:

> I paused to watch the structural iron workers, drilling and pounding, pitching and catching red hot spikes as if they were mere balls; the masons and the carpenters and the hod-carriers bending under the weight of their loads—I watched them all with unshed tears in my eyes and shame in my heart because of my cowardice, of my indolence, of my insincerity. I passed a grocery store on the corner, and I envied the clerk—he too, was a cog in the world's industry. What was I—indeed, what was I? A humbug, a parasite, pursuing a career of sophistry, of mental jugglery, living by my wits.

Yes, he must pursue an honest line of work, even though it probably means giving up all hope of winning John Powers' comely niece, his love, Mary.

Arriving at the office, he notices a letter from a publisher in New York, the seventeenth to receive his completed manuscript, and, yes, they would undertake to publish it. Saved by his avocation, Stillwell no longer must face a bleak future as "a cog in the world's industry." Mary is excited by his avocational triumph. Indeed, happier for him even than he had dared hope! Clearly, she feels for him, maybe not as much as he for her, but Guy is encouraged. And now his resignation from the Nixon Wright needn't raise questions about her dear Uncle John's firm.

His first novel is a success. At Mary's suggestion he goes to Europe to study and travel and, upon returning to New York, stops by his publisher with his just completed second effort. He returns the next day to his publisher's office to get his editor's reaction. Sadly, he is informed that yes it is very good, it rings true to life, but who wants to read about life? The publisher declines to take his second novel. Soon Guy finds another publisher who is eager to take on his second work, given that his first was so successful. The reviews are glowing, even in the *London Times*, but as his first publisher predicted, the book doesn't sell. The royalty checks from his first novel have tapered to a mere trickle. Soon Stillwell is back in town visiting old friends and associates, looking for a position in law. He and Mary have kept up a warm and very encouraging correspondence.

Mike Toner, a recently elected common pleas judge, alcoholic and boyhood friend of his father's, is willing to get him a "berth" on the Republican slate for the legislature. Toner, a Democrat, is owed a favor by Pat Keegan, a "turn-coat Republican." Guy is a Republican (and *always* has been) and, trading on his local notoriety from having published two novels, he is elected in a Republican landslide. So it is off to the capital where are pending a plethora of "Bills": the Usurer's Bill, the Liquor Bill, the Anti-Liquor Bill, the Mortgage Bill and, of course, the Compensation Bill. On Guy's first trip to the capital he is staying at the Great Western Hotel where all the legislators and lobbyists gather for the annual legislative sessions. Guy has taken up a position in the corner of the lobby to scan the scene:

"Hello, Guy! Good old boy, I haven't planted my eyes on you since you left for parts unknown," Henk burst out as he approached me . . .

"What are you doing here?", I asked.

"I'm working ag'in the compensation bill."

"What's wrong with it?"

"It'll kill our business—That and nothing else"; and he displayed a mouth of gold in place of decayed teeth.

His candor amused me and I joined in his laughter.

"You see I am straight goods," he further elucidated, and leaned toward me in semi-confidentiality. "I come out with the colors. I'd rather be a burglar than a sneak pick pocket—you get me?"

Together they survey the hotel lobby. They spot Pat Keegan, in town ostensibly to push for the salary raise legislation for the judges (but really to lobby for the Usurer's Bill); and there's Nelson Brooks from the Nixon Wright personal injury department ("a good scout," allows Henk) but even though Brooks says he's down state on behalf of the judges, he's really working for a railroad in need of special legislation; and, of course, Frank Talcott whose business is, as always, unstated.

Stillwell soon discovers that the Usurer's Bill is a terrible piece of legislation that appears benign, even favorable, towards debtors, but will actually cause no end of mischief with its harsh foreclosure provisions so grossly in favor of creditors. As soon as he speaks out about it, Guy is offered a thinly disguised bribe by an evil money lender who is ostensibly looking for Guy to represent him on a "private matter." Guy ultimately discerns his purpose and, of course, refuses the inducement but makes an enemy of the man, one Ignatz Beitel. Stillwell sees that the bill is getting lost in the session's legislative shuffle, and fearing that he is too new to gain the ear of the legislative body, he contacts Hapgood Hooper,[22] a sympathetic reporter at the *City Daily,* for help in defeating the bill. When the *City Daily* throws its full weight against the new law it is defeated, but in the process, Stillwell makes a mortal enemy of the mean spirited Keegan and his associate and client Ignatz Beitel.

Following his short tenure in the legislature, Hooper gets Guy a job working as an assistant prosecuting attorney where he uncovers a scandal involving his old nemesis, Judge Silas Screech. Later while serving an administrative "sentence" in the Grand Jury Room (where errant assistant prosecutors are assigned for punishment) for having angered Screech, Guy learns that his boss, Prosecutor Ferret, is as corrupt and open to improper "influence" as the next politician. Finally, Guy resigns to take up private practice again.

But alas, his past is not serving him well in the courts.

> I must own that aside from the enemies I had made in my mad pursuit of the legal rights I had championed—and my enemies were not a few and quite powerful—my bluntness, my impetuosity, my innate candor antagonized even those I could have counted as friends. If in no other respects, I resembled Whistler in "the gentle art of making enemies." And that, I declare, is no negligible art.
>
> My present difficulties were twofold. Besides the natural difficulty of building up a paying practice I encountered antagonism in the courts. Unlike jurors, who have a keen admiration for a fighting lawyer, judges detest him, unless he is a political power in the community . . .

Guy gets by as a "poor man's lawyer" and builds his practice slowly as a
strident advocate "who would rather fight than eat!"

Soon he is again battling Ignatz Beitel, the wicked money lender, on
behalf of a former business associate of Beitel's, who has fallen out with
him. Guy hates Beitel, and fights long and hard to frustrate him at every turn
in the ongoing and shifting litigation against his client. Soon he makes a
mistake in his ardor for his client, a Mr. Fairchild:

> While I was in the midst of one of Beitel's lawsuits against
> Fairchild my journalist friend, Hap, rushed into my office, closed
> the door of my private room, with a troubled look on his face.
>
> "I think they have trapped you—you had better look out," he
> said.
>
> I stared at him nonplussed. I did not grasp his meaning.
>
> "I mean Keegan and his bunch," he continued sorrowfully.
> "They had bought Fairchild and purposely made him hire you to
> defend him against those judgments and now have him to testify
> against you."
>
> I still did not fathom.
>
> "What of it?" I asked.
>
> "You see, they can prove that although you knew Fairchild
> owned part of his partner's assets you defended and shielded him
> and prevented the satisfaction of Beitel's judgment."
>
> He paused to let the seriousness of it penetrate my mind. After
> a moment's thought I realized that the fact that lawyers are daily
> instrumental in shielding fraudulent debtors against the honest
> claims of creditors it did not make the act right. In my zeal I
> followed the old jesuitic doctrine that the end justifies the means.
>
> "Keegan and his crowd will make capital of this," Hap soon
> continued. "In fact, he has just boasted to me that he has got you
> where he wanted. He hoped I'd make a story of it."
>
> After a momentary lapse he added, "Your friend—that white
> livered baboon on the bench (Old Screech)—will jump at the
> chance of humiliating you. You had better get some cool-headed
> lawyer friend to guide your steps through this muddy puddle."

Stillwell gets Judge Toner to his side and is advised to sit tight and weather
the Keegan-engendered recriminations that were beginning to fill the
courthouse hallways.

The next day Guy is leaving his office when,

> . . . Henk came in, his hat cocked on one side, a cigarette in the
> corner of his mouth, one shoulder hoisted higher than the other,
> and, sniffing the air, shambled in with, "Hello, old man! I've just
> heard them guys are circulating nasty reports about you—"and let
> loose a volley of epithets descriptive of Keegan.
>   Presently he sat down and, offering me a cigar, continued.
> "You've always thought I was agin' you but you are mistaken. I've
> always liked you. You can't play the game because you are on the
> square. Even Mark has a high regard for you. When he heard of
> this Mark says to me, 'Go and tell Guy,' says he, 'if he needs any
> help I'll give it to him.'"
>   "I thought Leffingwell disliked me," I said.
>   "He doesn't like you because you won't play in his
> yard"—Henk displayed his golden teeth and tittered—"but he has
> a great opinion of you. He'll do anything to help you."
>   I thanked him rather wistfully.
>   "I know what Keegan wants," Henk said, moving closer to me.
> "He isn't after revenge—blackmail is his game—and his
> blackmailing is always within the law, you may be sure of
> that—nothing for which you could get him indicted. He plays the
> game right: Crook in the inside, reformer on the outside—you get
> my point? At Bar meetings he is always has some scheme for
> purifying the Bench and Bar—just like his friend Judge
> Screech—and incidentally get a write up in the papers and is put
> on all sorts of civic committees. No one knows Pat better than I do.
> I've worked with him; and I'll deliver him into your hands as
> Delilah delivered Sampson into the hands of the Philistines."
>   "You are quite the Bible scholar," I remarked jocosely,
> wondering at his frequent references to the Bible.
>   "I've learned it from Pat"; and laughing, displayed his
> golden teeth . . .

Henk is good on his word, and recounts Keegan's undoing to Guy
several days later. He invites the black-hearted Keegan over to Leffingwell's
private office "to discuss an adjustment" of the Stillwell matter. There Henk
gets Keegan to speak candidly about the whole affair. Keegan admits that he
has paid Guy's client to set him up and then gets Keegan to state that either
Guy comes up with $5,000 or he will get "ten thousand in notoriety."

Whereupon, Henk throws open the door to Mark's office and there, holding three dictaphone receivers are Mike Toner, the Judge, a county prosecutor (one of Stillwell's friends from his short tenure at that office), and a court stenographer. The fixer foul is foiled. Henk continues:

> "Keegan got up, his shifty eyes moving from side to side, and muttered, `You dirty whelp!'"
> "'Look out.' says I, giggling like a school girl, 'this, too, gets into the dictaphone. You might as well take your medicine like a man,' says I, 'the same medicine you have administered to others.'"
> "You should have seen Pat strut out of the office without another word. I can still hear the slam of the door!"

Out from under Keegan's cloud, Guy goes over to dine with his fiancé, Mary. After dinner he learns that Mary is aware of the whole tawdry Fairchild embroglio (Keegan sent her an "anonymous" note to besmirch Guy's reputation on the eve of their wedding). She falters not in her faith and love for Guy. Many "unshed tears" don't fall. They are married.

Soon Guy prospers. He still hates law . . . but, "Before long, instead of the poor man's lawyer, I had become a little brother of the rich." On Armistice Day, November 11, 1918, he has an epiphany. Guy learns that his best client, a businessman, retained him only because he had heard the rumors of Guy's having "turned a sharp corner" in the Fairchild case. This, his client explains, is why he hired him. To do what needed to be done, to get the client what the client wanted! Stillwell is shocked, then angered, then contritely ashamed. He looks out over the celebrating city from his office, and resolves "I must declare an armistice with myself. Let the tens of thousands play a game of chess with the courts as the chess-board. I must look elsewhere for a career, a career that would give me peace with myself."

Guy wanders home through the boisterous crowds. He feels lighthearted and when he gets home to Mary and their little one, he tells her he wants to quit the law and build houses. She is not surprised but overjoyed, knowing full well the spiritual compromise law required of her husband. She has been taking a course in interior design and architecture. They work together. They are happy.

And the Jugglers? Yes they are still juggling, and quite profitably. I see by this morning's paper that Judge Silas Screech waxed very eloquent at the Bar meeting the other day and delivered a scathing harangue (and undoubtedly grew red in the face and foamed at the mouth and stuttered from excitement) against the iniquities of the profession, and that the Honorable Pat Keegan followed Screech with a speech bristling with invectives against the prevalence of crime due primarily to the loose methods of certain judges (presumably those who do not truckle to Pat Keegan) and especially to the reprehensible methods of so many members at the Bar. Thereupon the president of the Bar Association, Virgil Tinker, appointed a committee of three, with the Honorable Pat Keegan as Chairman, to investigate the causes of the regrettable conditions of the Bench and Bar.

Poor Mike Toner! He died of apoplexy the day following his reelection, and his good wife has since reopened Schultze's rooming and boarding house.

Mark Leffingwell is still casting pearls before the "swine of twelve," and is shedding crocodile tears when the occasion demands it, and wrests as large verdicts as ever in spite of the valiant efforts of his formidable opponents, Luther Coit and Nelson Brooks. Yes, our old friend Henk is still with Mark. Instead of a mere "runner" he is now chief of Leffingwell's organization. He is attending Night Law School and when "admitted" hopes to be taken into the "firm."

*   *   *   *   *

Any study of the past is necessarily burdened by the verities of the present. The hope is that the substantive issues chosen for historical examination might act as a prism does upon a shaft of light—to break down the too bright illumination into its various parts, casting color and richer understanding of the past, and present, where there was formerly only stark light and shadow. Workmen's compensation is just such a temporal prism. The change wrought by the compensation reform reached deeper and more severely into the egalitarian American ideal than is generally conceded or understood. Workmen's compensation was, and is, far more than a system of work injury recompense. It was a fundamental change in the American political economy—of constitutional proportions—that accompanied and institutionalized the coming of the age of a corporate, capital-favoring social hierarchy; the disestablishment of even nominal equality between formerly coequal citizens; and the abandonment of the American quest for the republican ideal of individual autonomy and democratic control over the basic social, economic and political equities that define and balance American life. Some of the constituent spectral colors of workmen's compensation follow.

LINES OF DIFFERENCE DRAWN

. . . On the other hand, the line drawn between the natives and the southern and eastern European races is very decided. The sections of the city in which these races live are quite separate from the native section, and the native population knows practically nothing about these immigrants beyond what they read in the daily newspapers about crimes, etc., committed in the foreign section and beyond what little contact they have with them in the way of hiring a few individuals as servants, washerwomen, etc. Many interviews and conversations with representative members of the native population substantiate the above statement as to their ignorance not only of what races live in the foreign section, but also of their general welfare. Another evidence as well as a cause of this indifference is seen in the almost entire absence of any effort on the part of native religious, charitable, and civic organizations to assist the immigrants in assimilation or to better their religious, civic, and living conditions . . .

On the other hand, the attitude of the employers is somewhat different. A general statement of attitude may be made as follows: There is no prejudice against German, Welsh, Swedish, English, and Irish immigrants, but there are frequent indications of an unfavorable attitude toward southern and eastern European immigrants. With reference to the latter, the majority of employers seem to regard the presence of immigrants of these races as a necessary evil . . .[23]

At least part of what happened related to the surge of east and south European immigration that washed over the United States, especially its industrial and urban centers, between 1880 and 1920. The newcomers to America simply didn't fit into the older immigrant assimilation patterns. They arrived too late to partake of the great western "barbecue" (or if one prefers a nobler characterization, frontier "ethos"). They were often just visiting, and even when they intended to stay, their strong agrarian cultures, mysterious languages and Roman Catholicism limited their social, economic and political aspirations and retarded their assimilation into the dominant American Protestant cultural hegemony.

They were perceived as a malleable and servile lot and were considered dispensable by the American natives who saw them, and treated them, and fretted over them, as constituents of a world apart. They were not-nearly-Americans who would require firm guidance and direction if they were to ever become integrated into the American social fabric. Brudno's shawled denizens were, as a practical matter, mere shadows on the American political and economic landscape, unknowns with unknowable names, multitudes of mutable servitude. America had known many immigrant waves and types before, but these predominately Roman Catholic agrarians (unlike the Irish of the early nineteenth century) couldn't even speak English. Prior tides of immigrants didn't spark Americanization Committees, concerned and xenophobic burghers nervously overseeing the "tired and poor"'s hurried transformation into dependable fodder for the new corporate-industrial order molded by finance capitalism. On balance, it can fairly be said that if immigrants were not a sufficient condition for the establishment of the workmen's compensation reform, they were a necessary one. Moreover, it seems doubtful that the American courthouse door would have forever slammed shut to workers, even industrial workers, had they been the only "slightly" different Welsh, or English, or German, or Swedes, or even Irish.

It is perhaps misleading to discuss the new immigration in isolation from another social and corporate fact of the period. The tendency to separate out groups of people according to status, to create hierarchies and stratified systems for structuring and analyzing and managing complicated institutions, preexisted and evolved independently of the new immigration. Mimicking the military model of organization, this stratifying tendency created an accommodating context in which to discriminate against the lower echelons of society in general, and the lower echelons of corporations in particular. Perhaps, had these newcomers arrived earlier, to an American shore that had as yet not come to be dominated by large business corporations, had they arrived in a preindustrial America, to a still open frontier—perhaps, then they would not have been perceived as lawsuits waiting to happen, mere distractions to their corporate betters. Distractions from the serious business of business, creating predictable environments for capital aggregation and preservation. But arriving when they did, and crucially, flocking as they did to a leadership industry in the compensation reform movement, meant that in the minds of their corporate superiors, the

Steel Corporation managers, they served to distance the mass of industrial workers from the republican ideal of coequal citizens sharing in mutual civil rights and privileges independent of their relation to the means of production.

REFORM BY STASIS

One of the ironies of the workmen's compensation reform was that it changed so very little of the derided common law as it was practiced before, and applied by, juries. So while the theory of employer liability law severely limited worker recoveries, bludgeoning worker claims with the unholy trinity of employer defenses, the practice of employer liability law in jury trials emasculated the fearsome threesome and imposed a de facto strict liability against employers years before the legislature enacted the compensation reform. In the Ohio state courts, where the scintilla rule assured jury predominance over the judiciary, the American Steel and Wire Company only secured one defense verdict in eighteen years of litigation before juries and judges—a win rate of about 2%. Even discounting for an aberrant effect probably caused by the well known (and likely resented) deep pockets of the Steel Corporation's subsidiary, the gross disproportion of worker-favorable verdicts over the course of eighteen years indicates an abiding reaction to, and adjustment for, the manifest inequities between the two parties to *any* work injury suit.

The further irony within irony (our prism turns into a hall of mirrors!) is that employer liability law, as a subset of tort law, did humble workers, but not by undermining the fault-based substance of their negligence claims against employers. Rather, it was the tort law of damages and wrongful death that limited the workers' recoveries for injuries. The law of damages and the only recently created wrongful death cause of action, severely proscribed substantial recovery for *all* injuries and death. The common law of damages, essentially the "make whole doctrine," effectively measured the value of bodily integrity with a yardstick of wages. Those wages were a measure of the loss of support capability, not just for the injured workers but for their dependents. Thus, dead children and single, childless men were accounted as virtually valueless, while gainfully employed married men with children were limited to some derived fraction of their wages. At a juncture in time when all life was measurably shorter and meaner, lacking in antibiotics and effective physical therapies, a severe industrial injury's long-term debilitating effects were often discounted as too speculative and tenuous for consideration. It was rare to convince a jury to extrapolate an injury's disabling effects beyond a decade into the future, never mind that a man might survive for another four decades. Yes, there was the possibility of "ringing the bell"[24] for pain and suffering, but by and large juries were more practical men than was conceded by the era's reformers, and more often they measured their awards according to straightforward considerations of income replacement and support. Looking at the American Steel and Wire cases, it was rare for juries to indulge sympathetic feelings spurred on by the plaintiff's pathos and discomfort. In short, under the common law, a man was only rarely going to recover more than some time-limited allocation of the prospective wages he would have earned, but for the accident. Ergo, a day laborer's life was quite literally, and measurably, less valuable than the life of a skilled workman.

While hedonic damages were more often than not minimized by the trial courts, those matters were submitted to judges and juries for recompense and did provide for an evolving and dynamic "ethos of injury."[25] Over time the workers' claims increased in value at a rate that far exceeded their incrementally increasing wage rates. One possible way to explain this effect is to assume that over time the larger community began to recognize and attach greater importance to maintaining simple bodily integrity. This was the genius of the common law as tempered by the democratizing influence of juries and an elected judiciary. It could and did change with evolving community standards and values.[26]

Thus, the compensation reform's substantive law of "strict liability" against the employer didn't substantially change the rules prevailing in the Cleveland litigation before the reform. And when the employer groups effectively bid for, and won, the right to fund (and therefore control) the compensation pool of capital, while agreeing to pay only a percentage of the workers' demonstrable lost wages—usually for a limited period of time—they effectively and permanently capped the value of all workers' lives and limbs. In short, they reformed the system by freezing it in stasis.[27]

The Ohio Employers' Liability Commission recognized that there was a pre-compensation "market value" for worker lives and paid for an actuarial study of the Cuyahoga County employer liability litigation between 1905 and 1910 to determine those values. The maximum death case values derived from that study determined the basic formulas and amounts for compensation recoveries for the next 86 years. That formula, 2/3rds of wages, usually for a limited period of time, permanently shifted a tremendous burden onto the injured employee and his dependents and deprived him of the only "humanizing" element of the common law of damages—pain and suffering—that could address the irreversible suffering and indignity of losing a limb, or ambulation, or life.

However cheap and demeaning the common law's rules of damages were, the value of industrial injuries *was* rising under the jury's tutelage—by 1915 damages increased nearly seven fold for the American Steel and Wire Company from eighteen years before. With the passage of workmen's compensation, employers were out from under those value trajectories,[28] dealing thenceforth with a mere time-limited percentage of a worker's earnings. A formula that was not just relatively inexpensive, better still, it was predictable, providing an excellent "market environment" for the private insurance industry and large self-insured corporations such as American Steel and Wire. Ohio proved the American anomaly by providing for an exclusive state fund,[29] but the palpable deference to the institution that taught the concept of compensation to the body politic—the large, capital-intensive corporation—was codified into the Ohio act by the "self-insuring" provisions of the compensation legislation. For the state's largest employers, such as the American Steel and Wire Company, the new system provided production line-to-dispensary-to claims office protection in a self-contained circuit that rarely involved meddling interventions by the Industrial Commission. No more plague of injury lawyers and "runners" scamming their way past the factory gate to "sign up" "pippin" fresh cases. Workers and their injuries just weren't worth the trouble anymore.

JURIES VIOLATE

Workmen's compensation might also be considered as a dark and foreboding chapter in the history of the American jury system. While the Ohio Constitution promised to maintain the right to jury trials as "inviolate," in order to work, the compensation reform required nothing less than a constitutional reordering of the political economy, and, in what was to become a pattern in modern American history, the jury trial system gave ground to the corporate sector's percieved needs. Anticipating the reform, juries had already begun imposing strict liability against employers. After the reform, juries would never again have the issue of work injury damages submitted to them. Thenceforth in Ohio, and in most other states, the only matters relating to worker injuries that juries would (rarely) hear were appeals on procedural issues under the Act. The corporate reformers who so disparaged the very commonness of the urban jury pools effectively deprived juries of any say over employee-employer relations as they were affected by workplace—workers'—safety and health. In essence, this aspect of the reform deposed community standards, and replaced them with corporate standards for defining and managing safety-related work conditions and the implicit social equities affected by occupational safety and health. It can be justly said that in Ohio, workmen's compensation was a victory of the corporate sector against the perceived tyranny of the urban juries—so often comprised of the very same social groups that sector sought to dominate both within the work place and in larger political economy.

The fact is that, the reformer's heady "social insurance" rhetoric notwithstanding, the switch to workmen's compensation was nothing less than the common law as practiced before juries, frozen to an arbitrary percentage of the cost of labor, reduced to statute form, and handed over to corporate managers for interpretation and enforcement. This transfer of power to the private, corporate realm has in turn had tremendous and mostly deleterious implications for public as well as occupational health. Workmen's compensation soon ceased to be an impetus to drive workplace safety efforts and expenditures and was transformed instead into an inexpensive liability shield used to forestall and inhibit safety expenditures.[30]

In the courts, the simple, mathematical formulation tying wages to damages was beginning to give ground to broader subjects for damages. Juries, perhaps only reacting to and reflecting the growing litany of reform rhetoric about the cruel corporate predilection to shift the costs of industrial injuries off the corporate balance sheet and onto the shoulders the injured workers and the larger community, began to increase the awards given to injured workmen well beyond the contemporaneous growth in worker wage rates. Pain, suffering, the costs of continuing care, extended calculations for recompense for workers who survived longer with what were formerly fatal injuries, all these matters were driving the principal "market indicator" for injuries, jury verdicts, ever and alarmingly upward.[31] Undoubtedly, if juries had remained in place, they would have remained the forum of choice for worker-plaintiffs to bring their occupational disease claims.

And while the corporate jury reformers spoke openly of the "lower class" of citizenry willing and able to participate in jury service, the jury reform rhetoric stopped just short of what arguably really frightened the corporate sector litigants. While it was certainly true that juries were predominantly drawn from the lower social echelons, the real problem was the tendency of the jury's power and sympathies to derive from extra-corporate clan and ethnic sources. Recall that what facilitated the Reardon jury scandal was one *landsman* approaching another (albeit the road's claim agent) to suggest a mutually convenient "arrangement." The power to reach, or subvert, a verdict did not run according to corporate or even party lines. Rather, it was a matter between fellow countrymen, *paisan', landesleute.*

These were sources of power and loyalty that lay in kinship and other social forms of "uncertain learning," tight, ethnic and community-based affinities, quite beyond the reach of mere political parties, wealth, corporate affiliations or esoteric legal theories of liability. For a time urban juries ascended to the status of demigods, virtual rulers of the pre-corporate common law, and were targeted (along with the other older vestiges of court-based power, the Justices of the Peace[32]) early on in the capital finance-led legal reconstruction of the American political-economic order.

THE CORPORATE DE-CONSTRUCTION OF THE REPUBLICAN IDEAL

The rise and predominance of the American business corporation as the chosen institutional form for aggregating, managing and distributing productive wealth, radically transformed the tacit and explicit norms of the American political economy. The large business corporation, beginning with the railroads, set the rules for the most basic "features of life" for its employees. The point and power of corporate culture is not whether it literally touches each and every citizen as a corporate employee, but rather, whether its polices toward employees ultimately set the minimum standards for all employed citizens, whether or not they are actually on a corporate payroll. An early case in point was American Steel and Wire's in-house plan for employee injury compensation that was eventually aped by the Ohio legislature in its Compensation Act. Nowhere in the contemporaneous literature, reform-based or otherwise, was it ever suggested, or even implied, that merely mimicking the corporate response to the work injury problem was to betray the supposedly needful subjects of the reform, the injured employees. By extending in the corporate hand the "bread" of compensation in lieu of the "stone" of litigation it seemingly didn't occur to even the most radical and ardent of the reformers that the bread was hard won—and won with a stone.

Part of the genius of workmen's compensation was that it was conceived, promoted and instituted without the larger issues of balance, social equity and evolving community standards being discussed or even raised in the public debate. Part of the answer to this "but what about" riddle, might lie in what has been called the corporate hegemony. Why were business corporations—vast self serving, commonweal-undermining organizations—exempted from civil and criminal conspiracy law, while labor unions were constantly harassed under both federal antitrust and state level conspiracy prosecutions? Whatever the explanation (consensus, oppression, social control, skills and resources of a corporately-incubated American elite?) the American corporate hegemony has prevailed.

And too, there were very mundane and practical reasons for the corporate dominance over the national policy formulation that culminated in the various state compensation systems. The large industrial, transportation and insurance corporations conducted operations large enough to amass the actuarial data required to come to an understanding of the predictable course of employee injuries, examined over time. And while the small businessman feared the lone, hobbling, former employee together with his ambulance-chasing lawyer conspiring to "ring the bell" with a wayward and punitive jury, the larger concerns and insurance companies knew full well that the occasional large verdict was just that—occasional—and not really the problem. The large concerns knew that the vast majority of employee actions were small-time affairs that could usually be managed at the plant level and reduced into a predictable and affordable, if annoying, nuisance, rather than a real threat to the balance sheet. That experience led to the further realization that with relatively small investments in administration, the entire cost of work injuries could be reduced to a manageable, and more importantly, predictable, cost of doing business.

To the extent that this study focuses upon the American Steel and Wire Company, it is an examination of the effect the corporate form has had upon the most basic economic and social equities in American life. If the corporate form was ascendant in the nineteenth century it has proved predominant in the twentieth, and its influence on the course of American political and social development has been too little examined in the American historical literature. None of this is to say that corporations "caused" workmen's compensation. However, it can be fairly said that corporations, especially large, capital intensive corporations, encouraged and accelerated the process of work injury compensation reform and it was effected in their own image. The genius of the corporate sector's contribution was that workmen's compensation was first and foremost a solution to its problems, which even to this day, is perceived as a publicly, as opposed to privately, administered system, meeting public, as opposed to private, needs.

The corporate form not only serves to create and manage wealth (and in the American experience with extraordinary success) but also, and more importantly, it serves to distribute wealth. How that wealth is divvied among the participants in the corporation, from the mere employee on through to the officers, board members and stockholders, is a matter of crucial importance to understanding the larger American political economy. An examination of the corporate solution to work injuries—formulated as increasingly polar shadows began to fall across the American social order—transcends mere egalitarian concerns and strikes at the heart of the distinction between American ideological rhetoric and American social and economic reality.

To simplify, the problem could be stated this way. In the political realm, there is at least a theoretical input from every American into the governing system through the voting process. One person, one vote. But in the economic realm (to the extent that it can be sorted from the political realm) the vast majority of Americans—mere employees—do not vote for their supervisors, or officers, or directors, or owners of the firm that employs them. That lack of meaningful input is reflected back down through the corporate hierarchy as indifference to, and devaluation of, labor as a primary contributing factor in the creation of wealth. More importantly, it flows out into the larger social landscape in the form of calloused indifference to entire communities that have been legally and constitutionally disenfranchised within the realm of corporate governance.

Having shifted the jurisdiction and control over worker safety and health from the public to the private, corporate sphere, workmen's compensation evolved from a reform into a reaction. Arguably, any meaningful reconstitution of that increasingly problematic system would require looking not to the public realm, but to the private institutional form that tacitly, but increasingly, governs not just worker safety and health, but the larger share of American wealth and life.

Notes

1. *Borgins v. The Falk Company*, 47 Wis. 327, (Wisconsin 1911). The quote refers to the dubious efficacy of using a negligence action to recover for work injuries.

2. Robert Asher, *Workmen's Compensation in the United States, 1880-1935*, Ph.D. Diss. (University of Minnesota, 1971), 546. Asher's chapter on the Ohio law focuses on the war between the insurance industry, which was "read out" of the act, and the proponents of an exclusive state fund. It is one of the best and most thoroughly researched of the various Ohio histories of the compensation reform.

3. Senate Bill 250, 1910.

4. George W. Perks of Springfield and John P. Smith of Cleveland represented the employers. William J. Rohr of Cincinnati and William J. Winans of Galion represented the employees. James Harrington Boyd, of Toledo was the "neutral" lawyer member of the Commission and elected its chair at the first meeting in August of 1910.

5. The Chairman of the New Jersey Commission was William B. Dickson, Vice President of the United States Steel Corporation and a home office point-man for the Steel Corporation's in-house Voluntary Accident Relief Plan.

6. Ibid., Asher; Patrick D. Reagan, "The Ideology of Social Harmony and Efficiency: Workmen's Compensation in Ohio, 1904-1919," *Ohio History* Autumn 1981, 317-31.

7. Ibid., Asher, 546.

8. H.R. Mengert, "The Ohio Workmen's Compensation Law," *Ohio Archaeological and Historical Publications* XXIX (1920): 1-48, 5.

9. Ibid., Mengert, 21. Part of the resistance to the compensation reform was actively fomented by the insurance industry which continued to try to exploit (unfounded) employer concerns about the "socialistic" exclusive state fund.

10. Thomas J. Duffy, "The Industrial Commission," in (1934)*A History of the Courts and Lawyers of Ohio*, ed. Carrington T. Marshall (New York: American Historical Society, 1934) Vol. II, 537-546.

11. Ibid., OELC, *Report*, Vol. I, lxxxviii.

12. Ibid., lxxviii.

13. Mengert, Duffy, and Asher all neglect to mention that the minority bill provided for injured employees to bring suit in lieu of direct compensation. They emphasize only that Winans' bill put the entire premium upon employers, instead of sharing the burden with employees as had been formulated by the majority bill.

14. Ibid., Mengert, 10.

15. See Reagan, passim.

16. Raymond Ratliff, "The New Ohio Workmen's Compensation Law," *Ohio Law Reporter* IX (1912) 207-24, 213.

17. Sir William Ralph Meredith, *Final Report on Laws Relating to the Liability of Employers to Make Compensation to Their Employees for Injuries, etc.* (Toronto: 1913), Minutes of Evidence, 332. Boyd doesn't explain why the highest paid group of death cases was selected as the standard, nor does it appear why that figure ($4,991) was cut by 25%. However, in his next answer to a question from the Ontario commissioners regarding the elective Act's 10% employee contribution feature, Boyd explained that there was agreement among Ohio's original Commission members that employees should be interested in the fund. His answer to the Ontario Commission also throws some light on the back and forth negotiations between the labor and employer groups interested in the Act.

> . . . The employers insisted on it (employee contributions) being 25% and then we came back at them and made them agree to total disability as long as it lasted, under those higher terms. The legislature would not take the position of not making them (employees) contribute but they would not take the position to make them contribute 25%, and they compromised on 10% in a Conference Committee between the Senate and the House.

Ibid., *Final Report*, Minutes of Evidence, 333.

18. By working off the recoveries for workers' *fatal* accidents the actuaries excluded awards for pain and suffering from the compensation baseline. Court awards for death were bound by the proscriptions of the wrongful death statute which denied any recovery for suffering.

19. James K. Mercer, *Ohio Legislative History, 1909-1913* (Columbus: Edward T. Miller Company, 1914), 266, 270.

20. Ibid., Asher, 548.

21. Ibid. Mengert, 16.

22. Many of the characters in the book invite comparisons with actual Clevelanders from the period. Hapgood Hooper, might well be a cross between Norman Hapgood and Erie C. Hopwood, *Plain Dealer* reporter and editor. Hopwood's tenure at the paper (1903-1928) coincides with Brudno's novel and his slogan, "Justice in the News Columns," is consistent with the continuing role Hapgood Hooper plays in *The Jugglers*.

23. Ibid., Immigration Commission, 387. The writer was reporting on conditions and attitudes toward immigrants drawn to iron and steel manufacture in one of the unnamed mill towns in the East.

24. Tort lawyer jargon for obtaining a large damage award in a personal injury case.

25. G. Edward White's term describing the amorphous but very real "place of injury in American life."

26. In his study of tort suits in the turn of the century New York courts, Randolph Bergstrom puts this evolving dynamic this way:

> Injury victims came from the same body of people that jurors did. Those who were deciding responsibility and reasonable care in the cases of others met injury themselves, and an increasing portion of them elected to seek compensation in the court. The change in their response to injury shared origins with the change in juries' behavior. The seedbed for both was the shift in public conceptions of responsibility and reasonable care.

Bergstrom also found that in New York City, work injury cases were increasing in value between 1890 and 1910. Randolph E. Bergstrom, *Courting Danger: Injury and Law in New York City, 1870-1910* (Ithaca: Cornell University Press, 1992).

27. So it is that today workers injured on the job will be advised by counsel to look to possible tort suits to circumvent or at least supplement the modern workers' compensation system. "Absolutely the first thing you look at when an injured worker comes in for help is, 'Can we get out of the workers' comp system and into tort?'" Mark Rust, "New Tactics for Injured Workers", Vol. 73 *American Bar Association Journal* (Oct. 1987) 77, quoting a personal injury and workers' compensation specialist from Illinois.

28. One area of modern tort law that may provide an "out" for an injured employee from the workers' compensation system is products liability, usually for a manufacturer's design "defect" in a machine causing the work injury. Whether a worker can recover under a "products theory" can mean the difference between real and nominal recompense. A study done for the

U.S. Department of Labor in 1980 defined the extent to which the modern compensation system has fallen behind the tort system in awards for serious injuries:

AVERAGE AWARD FOR PRODUCT LIABILITY CLAIMS vs. WORKERS' COMPENSATION CLAIMS		
Severity of Injury	Workers' Compensation Award	Product Liability Award
Death	$57,000	$133,000
Permanent Total Disability	$23,000	$255,000
Permanent Partial Disability	$6,000	$157,000
Temporary Total Disability	$2,000	$17,000

Nationally, the tort system has advanced in award levels beyond the compensation system by factors ranging from two to twenty six times the work injury payment schedules. U.S. Department of Labor, Assistant Secretary for Policy Evaluation, and Research (ASPER), "An Interim Report to Congress on Occupational Disease," 94 (1980).

29.   Although recent "reforms" of the Ohio compensation system are moving the administration of the claims handling apparatus over to private insurers.

30.   The sad history of asbestos is a glaring case in point. One suspects that what makes the asbestos epidemic so sad is not that it was atypically extensive and horrible, but rather, that it was atypically brought under public scrutiny. When workers were thrown out of court, so was the incentive to incur the "transaction costs" associated with discovering, proving and prosecuting occupational disease claims. While the asbestos industry knew what was happening to workers it had no incentive to deal with it and even less to divulge its privately acquired and maintained information concerning the pulmonary disorder endemic to the industry. See: Paul Brodeur, *Outrageous Misconduct* (New York: Pantheon Books, 1985).

31.   One writer noted that when the Ohio Constitution was amended in 1912 to allow for non-unanimous jury verdicts in civil trials, the effect was for personal injury awards to climb higher than was true when unanimity was

required: Carrington T. Marshall, *A History of the Courts and Lawyers of Ohio*, Vol. I, Pg. 157. Former Industrial Commission member and lawyer, Thomas J. Duffy, noted a rise in jury verdict amounts for injured workers following passage of the reform. Such cases were very rare, based upon unusual exceptions to the Act's blanket protections to employers, but could be discerned in "third party" suits and the trickle of "safety violation" cases brought before the 1924 amendment to the Act prohibited such actions. Thomas J. Duffy, "The Industrial Commission", in *A History of the Courts and Lawyers of Ohio*, Vol. I, 543.

32. The acronym for Justice of the Peace, "JP," was said to actually stand for "Judgement for Plaintiff" and led to their being replaced, in 1910, by the Cleveland Municipal Court, a Cleveland Bar Association-led reform. Samuel H. Silbert, *Judge Sam* (Manhasset, N.Y.: Channel Press, 1963).

Appendix

The primary quantitative data used in this study was gathered from the state and federal court records of all the litigation involving the American Steel and Wire Company in Cleveland, Ohio, between 1898 and 1915. Of the 201 cases located for this study, 127 were "probable" work injury cases. Although the sample is too small to provide a reliable source for rigorous statistical analytical purposes, it does provide a telling description of the reality of the work injury litigation that preceded the passage of Ohio's mandatory workmen's compensation act in 1914. While the data is statistically highly problematic because it is not random and because of its small size, observed patterns in the American Steel and Wire litigation are confirmed in other, more extensive contemporaneous quantitative studies of work injury litigation. The findings of the Ohio Employers' Liability Commission's study of worker suits in the Cleveland-area county and federal courts between 1905 and 1910 (hereafter referred to as the "Watson Study," for its principal author) confirms many of the important features and patterns in the American Steel and Wire sample and suggests that the American Steel and Wire data is more typical than exceptional of Cleveland-area work injury suits during the period studied.

PRIMARY SOURCE DATA
THE AMERICAN STEEL AND WIRE CASES
1898-1915

The principal litigation forum for work injury claims in Cleveland during this period was the Cuyahoga County Common Pleas Court. The court's docket indexes[1] were used to locate case numbers for all the civil litigation involving American Steel and Wire between 1898 and 1915. The court docket books were then examined and additional information gathered from the docket entries for each case. The docket record for a case included the plaintiff's name, defendant's name, plaintiff's attorney, defendant's attorney, the date the case was filed, and listed any procedural responses and counter-responses, (pleadings, briefs, written motions, etc.). If a case went to trial, the docket indicated whether it was heard by a judge or jury, which party prevailed, and if there was a plaintiff's verdict, the amount. If a case settled, the docket ordinarily only indicated the date of the settlement and which party paid the court costs (almost always the defendant).

If the docket showed promise that a suit was a work injury case (typically these cases were instituted by an individual male plaintiff against American Steel and Wire as the only defendant and were categorized by the Clerk as "Money Only" actions) and the docket indicated that the case went to trial, the micro-filmed "court file"[2] was examined to review the filings of the parties. The court file always included the plaintiff's "Petition," the narrative that formally initiated the lawsuit, setting out the plaintiff's "cause of action." For work injury cases the petition usually recited the date of injury; the plaintiff's job at the American Steel and Wire facility; the nature of the injury; allegations as to its cause; a statement of medical treatment received; if the injury was permanently disabling, a prognosis; and finally, a "prayer" for monetary damages. If a docket book indicated a jury trial, the court file usually contained a "jury verdict" form listing the petite jurors' names and their verdict. A search of the micro-filmed file was always done when a case went to trial. In some instances, when the case was settled with no record of the amount paid, the court file was examined to confirm it was a work injury suit and to try to detect settlement patterns that might not appear from the docket entries. No distinctive characteristics appeared in the settled case files that distinguished them as a group from the cases that went to trial.

One of the first patterns to appear in the common pleas dockets was that in some cases the American Steel and Wire Company moved to transfer the plaintiff's lawsuit to the federal circuit court sitting in Cleveland. The motion for removal was invariably granted. In all cases where the docket indicated that the lawsuit was transferred to federal court, the common pleas court file was examined. During the period involved here, the American Steel and Wire Company tried to litigate as often as possible in the federal circuit court. The reasons for this preference will appear quite vividly once the data set is examined in more detail. The majority of cases that ended up in federal court were initiated by workers in state court and later transferred to federal court on the company's motion.

A similar method was used to gather the information in the federal court records. The American Steel and Wire Company was indexed, and the docket records[3] examined in those cases where American Steel and Wire was a party. The federal court docket books were, as a rule, more complete and revealing than the comparable state court records, but as in common pleas court, court files contain the narrative documents. The federal court files are stored at the Chicago facility of the National Archives.

The best overview of the data is provided by Figure 8 and Table 11. As stated above the "probable work injury" suits included all those cases filed against the company by males which were marked on the docket by the Clerk as "Money Only" actions. The "Money Only" classification (used by the Clerk's office for record keeping and case assignment) could include cases other than work injury actions, but of the 89 "probable work injury" court files examined, only three proved to be non-work related injury cases. Divorce actions were easily identifiable because they were invariably brought by a female plaintiff against both their spouse and American Steel

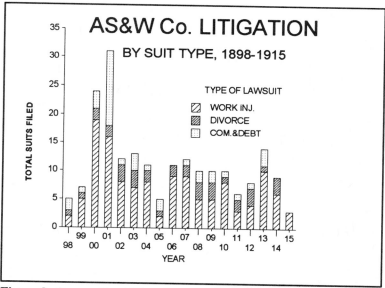

Figure 8   Source: Court Files, Common Pleas, Probate & U.S. Circuit Court, Cleveland, Ohio.

and Wire Company. The Clerk's classification for these actions was "Divorce, Alimony and Equitable Relief" or some combination of those three. American Steel and Wire was named as a defendant in these actions because the husbands were employees of the company and the wife was seeking a wage attachment against the husband. Finally, included under the category of "Commercial & Debt" are all debt collection, commercial and real estate actions and miscellaneous (non-employee) injury actions involving American Steel and Wire as a party. Typically, these cases were marked by the Clerk's office as "Money Only with Attachment" or "Real Property" or, in some instances, as "Money Only with Injunction Relief." Commercial litigation was easily identifiable from the docket because the other party was typically a business entity of some kind.

Work injury cases constituted anywhere from 40% to 82% of the litigation filed against the company in any given year. The most remarkable peak in the work injury case load occurred at the turn of the century. During only two years (1900 & 1901), 27% of the eighteen year total of work injury cases were filed against the company. The same two year period was also the peak for debt and miscellaneous cases with 43% of the eighteen year volume of those cases concentrated in that short span of time. 1901 was the year American Steel and Wire joined the Steel Trust and the reorganization engendered considerable litigation. The work injury peak during those years is not so easily explained, but might have been related to the perceived "deep pocket" of the ever re-capitalizing and consolidating steel industry. Of the total number of cases located (201), 63% were work injury cases (127), 19% were debt collection and miscellaneous cases (39) and 17% were divorces (35).

Of the 127 probable work injury cases filed against the company, 66% (84 of 127) were resolved without a trial. For the settled cases there is ordinarily no way to determine how much was paid to reach an agreement with the injured worker. However, it was possible to determine the amount paid to settle some of the cases that were transferred to federal court (because of the practice of the federal court to regulate plaintiff-attorneys' fees). Two additional wrongful death settlements were obtained by searching the Probate Court records for the deceased workers' estates. Thus, for a limited number of the settled cases (N=12), and for all the cases that went to trial (N=43), recovery amounts are known.

The workers who brought suit against American Steel and Wire were both "old" and "new" immigrants. Exclusively male (unless it was an action brought by a wife or mother on behalf of a deceased spouse or minor son) all the plaintiffs in the work injury group of cases were working at American Steel and Wire at the time of injury. Unfortunately, it is impossible to

No.	Year	Worker Occupation	Nature of Injuries	Court	Decided By	Recovery
			AMERICAN STEEL AND WIRE COMPANY WORK INJURIES—KNOWN RECOVERIES 1898-1915			
1	1899	Laborer	Fractured skull and spine	Federal	Settled	$63
2	1899	Laborer	Fractured shoulder	Federal	Settled	$69
3	1900	Wire Drawer	Dislocated right knee	Federal	Judge/DV	$0
4	1900	Laborer	Fell 30 feet, "made sick and sore"	Federal	Judge/DV	$0
5	1900	Electrician	Burned face and arms	Federal	Judge/DV	$0
6	1901	Laborer	Fractured skull	Federal	Judge/DV	$0
7	1901	Laborer	Injured right hand	State	Jury	$150
8	1901	—	—	Federal	Judge	$500
9	1901	Laborer	Amputated right leg above knee	State	Judge	$800
10	1902	Pipefitter Helper	Two broken wrists	State	Jury	$400
11	1902	—	—	Federal	Judge	$600
12	1902	Wire Drawer	Amputated right leg below knee	State	Judge	$700
13	1902	Nail Machine Helper	Fractured right arm	State	Judge	$150
14	1902	Hooker, rod mill	Crushed right foot, amputated big toe	State	Judge	$125
15	1902	Scale Messenger	Amputates left leg, fractured spine and leg	State	Judge	$350
16	1903	Laborer	Fractured spine and leg	State	Jury	$1,800
17	1903	Hooker, rod mill	Left foot amputated above ankle	State	Judge	$2,000
18	1903	Hooker, rod mill	Left foot "torn of at the ankle"	Federal	Judge/DV	$0
19	1903	Ladle car oiler	Gas poisoning, partial paralysis	Federal	Judge/DV	$0

Source: Court Files, Common Pleas, Probate & U.S. Circuit Court, Cleveland, Ohio.

Table 11

No.	Year	Worker Occupation	Nature of Injuries	Court	Decided By	Recovery
			AMERICAN STEEL AND WIRE COMPANY **WORK INJURIES—KNOWN RECOVERIES** **1898-1915**			
20	1904	Machinist	Scalded to death	State	Jury	$500
21	1904	Laborer	Amputated index finger	State	Jury	$350
22	1904	Nail Machine Helper	Nail in right eye, blinded	State	Jury	$400
23	1904	Switchman	Right & left index fingers amputated	State	Jury	$250
24	1905	Machinist	Scalded to death	Federal	Settled	$750
25	1906	Wire Drawer	Left arm "torn from body"	Federal	Settled	$2,200
26	1906	Laborer	Fractured left knee	State	Settled	$200
27	1906	Laborer	Four fingers amputated, left hand	State	Jury	$175
28	1906	Roller, wire mill	Fractured left arm, injured right foot	Federal	Judge/DV	$0
29	1906	Laborer	Fractured right leg	State	Jury	$175
30	1906	Laborer	Amputated 4th finger, injured 3rd finger right hand	State	Jury	$275
31	1906	Laborer	Amputated two toes, right foot	State	Jury	$105
32	1906	Hooker, rod mill	Fractured left ankle, burned left side	State	Jury	$100
33	1906	Laborer	Fractured left leg	State	Jury	$1,600
34	1906	Hooker, rod mill	Burned tendons, right leg	State	Jury	$250
35	1906	Switchman	Amputated four fingers, right hand	State	Jury	$1,200
36	1907	Scrapman	Blinded, right eye	State	Jury	$100
37	1907	Helper, nail mill	Fell from bridge, severe injuries	State	Jury	$50
38	1907	Laborer, rod mill	Killed, boiler explosion	Federal	Judge	$3,000

Source: Court Files, Common Pleas, Probate & U.S. Circuit Court, Cleveland, Ohio.

Table 11 (Cont.)

No.	Year	Worker Occupation	Nature of Injuries	Court	Decided By	Recovery
			AMERICAN STEEL AND WIRE COMPANY **WORK INJURIES—KNOWN RECOVERIES** **1898-1915**			
39	1907	Laborer	Killed, crushed by crane	Federal	Judge	$1,060
40	1907	Wire Drawer	Blinded, right eye	Federal	Settled	$400
41	1907	Laborer	Severe multiple burns	Federal	Settled	$6,200
42	1907	Carpenter	Injuries to back and leg	State	Settled	$150
43	1908	—	—	Federal	Settled	$1,400
44	1908	Laborer	Burned right foot and leg	State	Jury	$300
45	1908	Helper, nail mill	Fractured left arm	State	Jury	$100
46	1909	—	—	Federal	Settled	$850
47	1909	Loader	Fractured left leg	State	Jury	$250
48	1910	Laborer, rod mill	Burned eye	State	Jury	$250
49	1910	Laborer	Fractured left arm and leg	State	Judge	$900
50	1911	—	—	Federal	Settled	$450
51	1912	Laborer	Killed, caught in machine	State	Settled	$400
52	1913	Laborer	Left leg lacerated and infected	State	Jury	$200
53	1913	Laborer	Fractured left ankle	State	Jury	$1,200
54	1914	Electrician Helper	Fractured left arm	State	Jury	$1,500
55	1914	—	—	Federal	Jury	$3,000

Source: Court Files, Common Pleas, Probate & U.S. Circuit Court, Cleveland, Ohio.

Table 11 (Cont.)

determine whether any given plaintiff was employed at American Steel and Wire when the suit was filed. If it was the policy of the company to discharge an employee who brought suit, it would have had an obvious "chilling effect" upon the workers' inclination to litigate. No such company policy emerged from the data set (or narrative sources). From the limited figures available, the "old" verses "new" immigrant status of the worker doesn't seem to have had an effect on the value of a case or its probable outcome. However, it does appear that the old immigrants were much more inclined to take their claims to trial than the new immigrants. While the old immigrants elected to go to trial as often as settle, the new immigrants accepted 46 settlements while only taking 21 cases to trial. It should be pointed out that the vast majority of cases which went to trial in the common pleas court involved minor plaintiffs under 21 years of age. Of the 31 trials in common pleas court, 27 involved minors. Why every case brought by a minor went to trial is not clear.[4]

As a rule, the plaintiffs' attorneys were a varied group of semi-autonomous practitioners who relied upon contingency fee arrangements for payment. Those lawyers who appear more than once as attorneys for plaintiffs often fell into, and out of, partnerships over the course of the years examined. There was a limited amount of switching over from plaintiff representation to defense work on behalf of liability insurance companies, but as a rule, plaintiff attorneys did not defend corporate clients in work injury cases and vice versa. Their contingency fees were in the range of 23% to 50% of any recovery, with the bulk of fees at the lower end of the range. (See Table 15 below.) Although the state common pleas court made no apparent attempt to regulate the payment of plaintiffs' attorney fees, in federal court, it was routine to pay the settlement or judgment amount owing to the worker directly to the court Clerk. Then, by judicial order, a portion of the recovery was released to the worker's attorney.

During the period of time under consideration, all formal court pleadings were "verified" by clients. Clients were required to read and verify the lawyer-drawn suit documents for factual accuracy. This personal involvement of the client rendered litigation more intrusive upon the time and concerns of corporate managerial personnel. Although the lawyers could handle much of the suit, they had less autonomy in litigation than is permitted by modern court practice. Worker petitions that alleged the legal basis for the suit in paragraph after paragraph of allegations, read as exhaustive (and iterative) factual narratives as compared to modern pleading practice. Rigid rules governing the sufficiency of pleadings necessitated that petitions recite facts and very specific allegations of the employer's negligence. This focus

	EXTRAPOLATED ANNUAL INJURY CLAIM VALUES IN THREE YEAR GROUPINGS 1898-1915				
Year	N= Cases of Known Value	Mean Value of Cases	Total Cases Filed	Extrapolated Annual Costs	Weighted Three Year Averages
1898	0	$0	2	$0	
1899	2	$66	5	$330	
1900	3	$0	18	$0	
Total	5		25	$330	$13.20
1901	4	$363	16	$5,800	
1902	6	$387	8	$3,100	
1903	4	$633	6	$3,800	
Total	14		30	$12,700	$423.33
1904	4	$375	8	$3,000	
1905	1	$750	2	$1,500	
1906	10	$678	10	$6,783	
Total	15		20	$11,283	$564.15
1907	7	$793	9	$7,140	
1908	3	$600	5	$3,000	
1909	2	$550	5	$2,750	
Total	12		19	$12,890	$678.41
1910	2	$575	7	$4,025	
1911	1	$450	3	$1,350	
1912	1	$400	4	$1,600	
Total	4		14	$6,975	$498.21
1913	2	$700	10	$7,000	
1914	2	$2,250	6	$13,500	
1915	1	$0	3	$0	
Total	5		19	$20,500	$1,078.95
1898 1915	55		127	$64,678	$509.27

Source: Court Files, Common Pleas, Probate & U.S. Circuit Court, Cleveland, Ohio.

Table 10

upon the sufficiency of pleadings in a case led to the filing of some particularly obnoxious and confrontational, as well as repetitive, petitions.

Table 10 attempts to breakout the limited amount of information concerning recovery amounts over time. The first column, contains all the years of the study broken into three year groupings. The second column contains the number of cases in a given year for which the recovery amount is known. Referring to the Table, for worker suits filed in 1899 there are two known recovered amounts ($63 and $69). The average known recovery then is $66.00 which appears in the third column, "Mean Value of Cases." The fourth column contains the total number of work injury suits filed against the company in that year, and is almost always higher than the second column because of the high settlement rate. In 1899 there were a total of five work injury suits filed against the company. The fifth column, "Extrapolated Annual Costs," is the product of multiplying the "Mean Value of Cases" by the "Total Cases Filed" for that year. For 1899 that calculation is 5 x $66 or $330. This "smoothing" technique is intended to assist in assessing the overall cost trends in work injury litigation as they might have been analyzed by the company. It is based upon the inference that known case values can be used to predict total case values if they are factored by the total number of injury suits filed against the company. Finally, for each three year period,

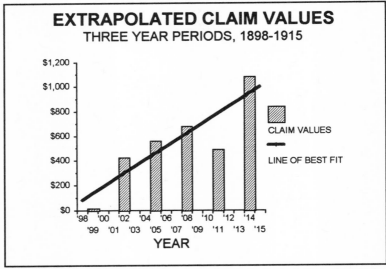

Figure 9 Source: Court Files, Common Pleas, Probate & U.S. Circuit Court, Cleveland, Ohio.

the "Extrapolated Annual Costs" are added and divided by the total work injury suits filed for that three year period. This then is intended to provide a "Weighted Three Year Average" claim value. This technique has the effect of smoothing the annual data to reveal a time series trend.

It must be emphasized that this technique is subject to several methodological problems. First, the sample is not random. Second, the sample group for the entire period of eighteen years (N=127) is very small. When that non-random sample is further diminished to include only those cases where recovery amounts are known (N=55), the sampling reliability is further reduced. Finally, breaking down the known recovery amounts into yearly groups, and then re-combining the figures into three year periods, though arguably helpful in establishing trends, diminishes the statistical reliability of the sample even further. However, notwithstanding all of those problems, this smoothing technique offers at least descriptive possibilities, is intuitively appealing, and taking the results with a very large grain of salt, leads to some interesting conclusions. When reduced to graphical form, the resulting three year groupings of weighted claim values delineate a very strong trend of increasing values over the eighteen year period. See Figure 9. Moreover, these three year weighted claim value numbers yield a

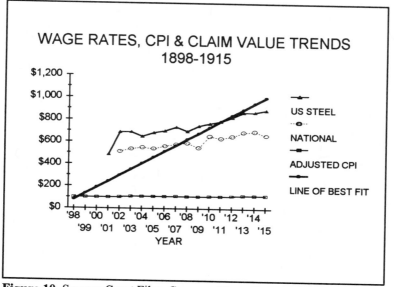

Figure 10 Source: Court Files, Common Pleas, Probate & U.S. Circuit Court, Cleveland, Ohio

relatively high correlation coefficient[5] of .873. From there is it a simple matter to further smooth the data by solving for the line of best fit.[6]

Finally, Figure 10 adds in available data for the average annual national manufacturing wages[7] (1901-1915), the average annual United States Steel Corporation wages[8] (1902-1915), and the consumer price index for the period[9] (1898-1915). It is now possible to see the trend that was so alarming to the large employers who had access to these aggregated time-related claim costs. While Figure 10 relies upon the much manipulated and limited data being smoothed, other quantitative and narrative sources confirm the trend.

As a final intuitive check on the argument that claim values were rising over time, Figure 11 is a scattergram of the 55 known recoveries in the American Steel and Wire litigation plotted over the pre-compensation time

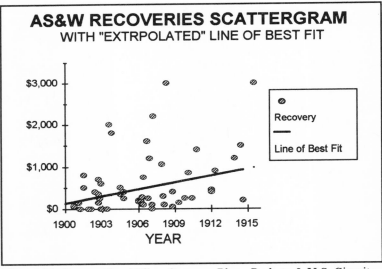

Figure 11 Source: Court Files, Common Pleas, Probate & U.S. Circuit Court, Cleveland, Ohio.

period. Then, imposed over those claim value dots is the "extrapolated" line of best fit used in the smoothing technique discussed above. This graph brings together the data in its "purest" raw form—the individual recoveries as dots on the scattergram—and then superimposes the most manipulated and "smoothed" version of the data, the Line of Best Fit derived from the "extrapolated" claim values in Table 10. The graph is, in essence, a check on the data smoothing techniques to see if there is a correlation between the raw and manipulated data. It is submitted that such a correlation is confirmed by Figure 11.

SECONDARY SOURCE DATA
THE WATSON STUDY
1905-1910

As part of its investigation into then existing conditions around the state, the Ohio Employers' Liability Commission hired Emile E. Watson to do a statistical study of the employer liability litigation in the Cuyahoga County area courts between 1905 and 1910. It was this study that provided the baseline for negotiations between the employer and employee groups in the legislative wrangles setting benefit levels under the new workmen's compensation act. Watson's work was broken up between fatal and non-fatal cases. His most complete work was done on fatal cases, but some information was also gathered and reported concerning non-fatal cases in the county. Watson worked from a much larger and "concentrated" (five as opposed to eighteen years) sample, and the numbers gathered should be a more reliable reflection of existing conditions in the courts. This section will first discuss the findings, as aggregated and presented by Watson, and then compare some of Watson's data with the American Steel and Wire data to see if the latter is on its face inconsistent with the Watson findings. This approach assumes that if the American Steel and Wire data is grossly inconsistent with Watson's, then the company data (and the company's experience in the courts) was presumably atypical of the prevailing conditions in the courts during the period.

While the Watson team did gather data on 500 non-fatal injury claims, they were more confident of the fatal case data. It should be pointed out that the tables that follow attempt to capture the "feel" of the original tables provided in the Ohio Employers' Liability Commission *Report*. However, some liberties have been taken in an effort to clarify the original Watson tables. As will appear below, the sample sizes for many of the tables provided by the Watson team changed from table to table, usually without any explanation. To the extent that explanations are provided regarding the sampling of cases, it is clear that the Watson team did not attempt to obtain random samples.

Watson begins with a summary of the familial consequences following a fatal work injury accident. "In all cases" of fatal accidents 36% of the workers' dependents received a settlement; the average amount those dependents received was $838.61; the average cost for attorneys and court costs was 24% of the recoveries; the delay in settlement was from one year to one and one half years; 56% of surviving widows went to work; 18% of all dependent children went to work. However, as is clarified later in the *Report*, the sample used to compile the percentages for widows and children was one of the smallest in the study, 86 households. The percentage of cases receiving settlement was derived from a sample of 175 cases, with many claims still pending at the time the figures were compiled. The average recovery in death cases was taken from a still larger sample of 285 cases, while the attorney fee amounts (discussed below) was derived from a smaller sample of 106 cases. Watson's sample sizes changed from feature to feature and practically no explanation is provided to differentiate the different data sets and methodologies.

Watson and his team confirmed that single and married workers were treated very differently by the tort system for fatal injuries.

AVERAGE AMOUNT RECEIVED IN SETTLED FATAL CASES 1905–1910		
Civil Status	N=	Recovery
Married	176	$1,056.51
Single	109	$485.87
Totals	285	$838.61

Source: OELC, *Report*, Vol. I, xxxviii.

Table 12

The investigators also confirmed that the employer-hated "Norris Bill," just passed by the Ohio legislature, eviscerating the employer defenses, had a measurable impact upon worker recoveries after its effective date in May of 1910. The overall value of death cases in the sample of 285 suggested a 16% increase in claim value due to the passage of the Norris Bill.

Effect of The Norris Act Upon Settlement Value of Fatal Cases 1905–1910						
Date of Death	Avg. Recovery	N=	Married	N=	Single	Total N=
Before 5/12/10	$829	164	$1,046	101	$480	265
After 5/12/10	$958	12	$1,220	8	$564	20

Source: OELC, *Report*, Vol. I, xxxix.

Table 13

Although it is not stated in the *Report*, it appears that Tables 12 and 13 were obtained from Probate Court records, only. The largest sample group obtained by Watson's team included the 285 probated cases together with the common pleas and federal circuit court recoveries totaling 370 fatal cases. However, no explanation is given for excluding the common pleas and federal circuit court cases in Tables 12 or 13.

As Table 14 makes clear, the amount and percentage of recoveries were heavily skewed to the lower end of the compensation spectrum with the largest number of dependents sharing in the smaller awards. As Watson pointed out, almost 90% of the claimants received under half of the total awarded sums, while about 10% of the claimants received over half the total awarded. Watson's figures in this particular table formed the basis for all the ensuing discussions between the interested parties leading up to the final compensation schedules incorporated into the mandatory Ohio act in 1914. As the head of the Ohio Commission, James Harrington Boyd, testified to the Ontario Employers' Liability Commission, it was the average amount in the highest category of the death recoveries ($4,991.66) that provided the starting point in the negotiations for the Ohio statute's maximum recovery limit for any work injury except full and permanent disability.

This table will also provide a check on the American Steel and Wire litigation experience. Watson's breakout of recovery frequency rates within broad ranges of award sums, allows for a comparison between the data Watson found in his study of work injury suits in Cuyahoga County and the fifty five known recovery amounts in the company litigation between 1898 and 1915. See the discussion below.

AVERAGE RECOVERY FOR FATAL CASES AS APPEARED IN COURT RECORDS 1905-1910			
Amount	Court	N=	Average Recovery
$1-$300	Common Pleas	15	$178.93
36% of Sample	Federal	4	$187.50
6.3% of All	Probate	116	$161.05
Recoveries	**Total**	**135**	**$163.83**
$301-$1,000	Common Pleas	14	$542.85
29% of Sample	Federal	10	$587.54
15.8% of All	Probate	83	$507.78
Recoveries	**Total**	**107**	**$519.81**
$1,001-$2,000	Common Pleas	8	$1,231.25
19% of Sample	Federal	14	$1,290.00
25.6% of All	Probate	49	$1,270.59
Recoveries	**Total**	**71**	**$1,269.98**
$2,001-$4,000	Common Pleas	6	$2,241.67
11% of Sample	Federal	7	$2,364.28
30.9% of All	Probate	29	$2,704.31
Recoveries	**Total**	**42**	**$2,581.13**
$4.000>	Common Pleas	1	$4,500.00
4% of Sample	Federal	6	$5,419.17
21.3% of All	Probate	8	$4,687.74
Recoveries	**Total**	**15**	**$4,991.66**
	Common Pleas	**45**	**$915.20**
Averages	**Federal**	**40**	**$1,775.26**
By Court	**Probate**	**285**	**$838.61**
	Total	**370**	**$949.19**

Source: OELC, *Report*, Vol. I, xl.

Table 14

Watson's team looked at attorneys' fees in a limited sample of cases and found that in Cuyahoga County, the courts and bar tended to police attorney fees in personal injury cases. They also pointed out that interviews with local attorneys indicated that the going rate to take a case to trial (as opposed

ATTORNEY FEES IN ALL COURTS				
Court	N=	Total Fees	Fee %	Avg. Fee
Common Pleas	53	$20,650.00	26.3%	$390.00
Federal	13	$14,100.00	24.6%	$1,085.00
Probate	88	$19,919.00	20.3%	$226.00
Totals	106	$45,669.00	23.4%	$516.00

Source: OELC, *Report*, Vol. I, xli.

Table 15

to settling before trial) was 33% of any award. Court costs were one of the distinguishing features between the state common pleas court and the

COURT COSTS STATE, FEDERAL & FEDERAL APPEALS			
Court	Settled	Judgment For Plaintiff	Judgment Appeal
Common Pleas	N=33, $9.06	N=14, $17.93	----------------
Federal	N=45, $29.37	N=10, $84.62	N=4, $573.65

Source: OELC, *Report*, Vol. I, xlii.

Table 16

federal circuit court. At the trial level, the federal circuit court costs were 3 to 4 times higher than in the state courts, and the costs for appeals within the federal system were extremely high—about the same as a year's wages for most workers.

As for delays in settling cases, the Watson group presented two sets of figures. The first tabulation was for settling "out of court," presumably through Probate Court, without the necessity of bringing suit. These cases settled relatively quickly, in about 8 months. On the other hand, litigated wrongful death claims took far longer, at least in the common pleas court.

Out of Court Delay in Settlement of Fatal Cases			
Amounts	Civil Status	N=	Average Delay
$0-$300	Married	48	6 months, 13 days
	Single	53	12 months, 27 days
$301-$1,000	Married	40	8 months, 13 days
	Single	33	7 months, 1 day
$1,001-$2,000	Married	27	8 months, 16 days
	Single	12	3 months, 6 days
$2,001-$4,000	Married	22	10 months, 10 days
	Single	4	9 months, 17 days
$4,001 >	Married	5	8 months, 3 days
	Single	----	
Totals	Married	142	8 months, 3 days
	Single	102	7 months, 26 days
	Total	**244**	**8 months, 1 day**

Source: OELC, *Report*, Vol. I, xliii.

Table 17

Delay in Litigated Fatal Cases Settled and Court Judgment		
Court	N=	Average Delay
Common Pleas	36	25 months
Federal	87	9 months, 9 days

Source: OELC, *Report*, Vol. I, xliv.

Table 18

By way of comparison, for the settled work injury cases brought against the American Steel and Wire Company (N=84), the average length of time a case was pending was 12½ months, with a median duration of 9½ months.

For all the cases, whether they went to trial or were settled , the average time to conclude an action was 10½ months, with a median pendency of 7½ months. The Watson report noted that there was a local rule of court in Cuyahoga County that provided for urgent cases to be advanced on the court's calendar. This might explain how it was that the American Steel and Wire cases that went to trial—many brought by minors—actually concluded more quickly than the settled cases. The trial sample (N=43) averaged a little over 6 months in court.

The Watson study addressed the limited data from the approximately 500 *non-fatal* injuries brought to court between 1905 and 1910. The researchers presented two tables to summarize their data on the non-fatal cases. The first presented the recovery rate in the litigated (filed in 1906 and 1907) non-fatal cases.

RECOVERY RATES IN STATE AND FEDERAL COURT, NON-FATAL CASES 1906–1907		
Resolution Mode	Common Pleas	Federal
Judgment for Plaintiff	N= 58 **26.6%**	N= 29 **22.0%**
Settled	N= 139 **57.6%**	N= 70 **53.6%**
Judgment for Defendant	N= 28 **12.6%**	N= 30 **22.7%**
Overall Recovery Rate in Court	N= 188 **84.2%**	N= 89 **75.6%**

Source: OELC, *Report*, Vol. I, xlvi.

Table 19

At least in the sample of cases filed in 1906 and 1907, the recovery rate was quite high. Watson took great pains to discount the high worker recovery rate of over 80%, cautioning that these cases represented only 20% of all the work injuries in the county during the period, as "four-fifths of the non-fatal industrial accident cases never come into court at all." That statistic is, unfortunately, not attributed to any source.

Finally, the Watson team presented a table of 199 non-fatal injury cases where the recovery amount was known:

Appendix

		DELAY IN RESOLUTION, NON-FATAL CASES, STATE & FEDERAL COURTS 1905-1910		
Amount	Court	Resolution	N=	Average Delay
$1-75 N=7 3.5% of Sample	Com. Pleas	Judgment	3	12mon,8day
		Settled	4	8mon,10day
	Federal	Judgment	----	----------------
		Settled	----	----------------
$76-200 N=35 17.6% of Sample	Com. Pleas	Judgment	16	6mon,5day
		Settled	16	13mon,14day
	Federal	Judgment	2	16mon,27day
		Settled	1	2mon,9day
$201-500 N=53 26.6% of Sample	Com. Pleas	Judgment	18	11mon,26day
		Settled	24	15mon,11day
	Federal	Judgment	2	13mon,6day
		Settled	9	25mon,21day
$501-1,000 N=42 21.6% of Sample	Com. Pleas	Judgment	13	15mon,23day
		Settled	13	16mon,22day
	Federal	Judgment	9	25mon,16day
		Settled	7	25mon,10day
$1,001-2,500 N=35 17.6% of Sample	Com. Pleas	Judgment	10	13mon,25day
		Settled	6	12mon,16day
	Federal	Judgment	11	33mon,12day
		Settled	8	26mon,2day
$2,501-5,000 N=13 6.5% of Sample	Com. Pleas	Judgment	3	14mon
		Settled	1	5mon,4day
	Federal	Judgment	8	21mon,12day
		Settled	1	16mon,9day
$5,001> N=14 7% of Sample	Com. Pleas	Judgment	2	13mon,29day
		Settled	3	21mon,6day
	Federal	Judgment	6	22mon
		Settled	3	14mon,15day
Totals	Com. Pleas		132	15mon,13day
	Federal		67	21mon,17day
	All Courts		199	17mon,16day

Source: OELC, *Report*, Vol. I, xlvi, xlvii.

Table 20

Although Table 20 was intended to illustrate the delays in litigation, it also incidentally provides information concerning recovery rates. Unlike Table 14, the investigators did not figure average recoveries within any given dollar range, but Table 20 does provide specific information about the percentages of claimants who obtained dollar amounts within certain ranges.

It is therefore possible to check three different sets of data to look for commonalities to validate the typicality of the American Steel and Wire litigation experience. One measure of the numbers (that requires a minimum of assumptions, manipulations and "smoothing") suggests that the American Steel and Wire, and Watson Fatal and Non-Fatal data sets are reasonably consistent, and therefore are—taken together—fair and accurate representations of the work injury marketplace that existed prior to passage of Ohio's workmen's compensation law.

Charted below are modified Watson fatal injury recovery numbers. The fatal numbers in Table 21(W) are derived from Table 14, above. The only modification of the original tabulations has been to extend the possible recoveries to $7,500. We are not told what the maximum recovery for wrongful death was in the Watson sample, but we know that the top 4% of cases *averaged* $4,991.66. Table 21(W) and the graph representation of the information in the table in Figure 12, assumes a $7,500 maximum. Because of the manner in which Watson switched sample sizes, we cannot determine how many of the death cases that were brought as claims against employers ended in no recovery for the workers' dependents. What is included in Table

WATSON STUDY, FATAL CASES 1905-1910 N=370		
Recovery Range	Percent of Claimants	Mean Recovery Within Range
$1-$300	36%	$163.83
$301-$1,000	29%	$519.81
$1,001-$2,000	19%	$1,269.98
$2,001-$4,000	11%	$2,581.13
$4,001-$7,500	4%	$4,991.66
$7,500>	0%	$7,500.00

Source: OELC *Report*, Vol. I, xl.

Table 21(W)

21(W) then, is only those death cases that received some settlement or recovery.

Turning to the American Steel and Wire data, Table 21(AS&W) takes the Watson "fatal case format" (i.e. the recovery ranges defined in Table 14) and plots all the company's historical figures—fatal and non-fatal— into the same ranges. Note that the seven company-favorable verdicts were not used in this table, because there is no comparable range in the Watson data presented in Table 14. Because there are only five fatal, known-recovery cases in the company data, *all* the known recovery amounts for the company cases (excepting the company verdicts) is included in Table 21(AS&W).

AMERICAN STEEL AND WIRE CO. 1898-1915 ALL RECOVERY CASES, WATSON FATAL FORMAT N=48		
Recovery Range	Percent of Claimants	Mean Recovery Within Range
$1-$300	44.0%	$166.05
$301-$1,000	31.3%	$556.67
$1,001-$2,000	16.6%	$1,470.00
$2,001-$4,000	6.3%	$2,733.00
$4,001-$7,500	2.0%	$6,200.00
$7,500>	0.0%	$7,500.00

Source: Court Files, Common Pleas, Probate & U.S. Circuit Courts, Cleveland, Ohio.

Table 21(AS&W)

Although, it may seem suspect to include the American Steel and Wire non-fatal cases in the fatal format, it will become clear why that was done when the two tables are plotted on a graph, Figure 12. The point of these comparisons, is to illustrate the recovery frequencies within given ranges. What becomes clear is that, whether the worker claims were for injuries or death, there was a compensation curve: the bulk of all recoveries, for death *and* injury, ended up on the lower end of the compensation scale and share a very well-defined (and therefore predictable) relationship between recovery amounts and the percentage of claimants who receive those sums for their injuries.

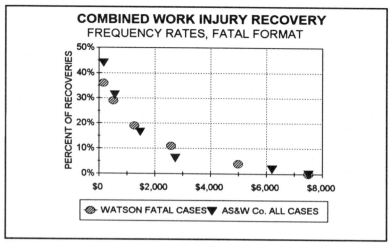

Figure 12   Sources: Court Files, Common Pleas, Probate & U.S. Circuit Courts, Cleveland, Ohio; OELC *Report*, Vol. I, xl.

Because the fatal and non-fatal cases that Watson tabulated were broken out into different recovery ranges, it becomes necessary to set up a different pair of tables for the non-fatal cases. The Watson non-fatal numbers are taken from Table 20. In Table 22(W) the "Mid-Point of Range" numbers are derived by assuming a "central tendency" within any given range—that the halfway point between the extremes of a range will approximately reflect the mean or average of the range as a whole. Further, unlike the fatal cases, Watson noted in the *Report* how many of the non-fatal cases actually brought by workers concluded with no recovery. Referring to Table 19, it appears that 58 cases of a total of 354 ended in favor of the employer, or 16.3% of all the claims were "no recovery" cases. In the text of his report, Watson notes that the highest award in all the non-fatal cases was for $12,000 (for the loss of both arms).

Thus, Table 22(W) takes the basic information in Table 20 and then adds 38 "no recovery" cases to the 199 in Table 20 to create a sample of 237 cases. This manipulation produces a 16% (38/237) "no recovery" rate blended into the recovery cases in Table 20. Finally, using the maximum non-fatal award figure provided by Watson, $12,000 is reflected as the highest limit for all the non-fatal recoveries. This combined set of figures in Table 22(W) then, is derived from data, facts, and figures that Watson discusses without actually putting into one table or summary form. But they are all "real" contemporaneous data from the 1910 *Report*.

WATSON STUDY, NON-FATAL CASES 1905-1910 N=237		
Recovery Range	Percent of Claimants	Mid-Point of Range
$0	16.3%	$0.00
$1-$75	3.0%	$38.00
$76-$200	14.7%	$163.00
$201-$500	22.4%	$350.00
$501-$1,000	17.7%	$750.00
$1,001-$2,500	14.7%	$1,750.00
$2,501-$5,000	5.4%	$3,750.00
$5,001-$12,000	5.9%	$8,500.00
$12,000>	0.0%	$12,000.00

Source, OELC, *Report*, Vol. I, xlvi, xlvii.

Table 22(W)

Finally, Table 22(AS&W) is all the non-fatal American Steel and Wire cases with known recovery amounts tabulated according to the Watson non-fatal case format. Here, the seven "no recovery cases" in the company sample are reflected in the table, and although the highest known recovery in the company sample was $6,200, the Table goes out to $12,000 to keep the format consistent with the Watson recovery ranges in Table 22(W). Note that unlike the Watson non-fatal sample, the tabulation for the non-fatal company cases calculates an actual mean recovery amount within each range rather than using the mid-point technique required by the lack of information in the Watson data set. While the total number of known recovery cases in the company data set is fifty-five, the five fatal cases have been taken out of Table 22(AS&W) so as to keep the non-fatal format consistent between the Watson and company figures. Therefore, in Table 22(AS&W) N=50.

American Steel and Wire Co. 1898-1915 All Cases, Non-Fatal Format N=50		
Recovery Range	Percent of Claimants	Mean Recovery Within Range
$0	14%	$0.00
$1-$75	6%	$60.67
$76-$200	24%	$144.16
$201-$500	26%	$340.38
$501-$1,000	10%	$770.00
$1,001-$2,500	16%	$1,612.50
$2,501-$5,000	2%	$3,000.00
$5,001-$12,000	2%	$6,200.00
$12,000>	0.0%	$12,000.00

Source: Court Files, Common Pleas, Probate & U.S. Circuit Courts, Cleveland, Ohio.

Table 22(AS&W)

When these two paired tables (Table 22(W) and Table 22(AS&W)) are plotted as frequency polygons in Figures 13(W) and 13(AS&W) it appears that the American Steel and Wire sample is, again, consistent with the Watson data. Note that in both graphs the "x axis" is not a linear scale, but almost approaches logarithmic scaling. As was suggested above, death cases are not more valuable than severe injury cases. In fact, the recovery frequencies for death cases look very similar to non-fatal cases. In both the fatal and non-fatal comparisons the company data is skewed somewhat to the left (lower values) reflecting the decreasing case values as the company data goes back to 1898 while the Watson data only goes back to 1905. Finally, all the graphs demonstrate the "compensation curve:" the vast bulk of work injury claimants are awarded relatively small sums, while the largest awards comprise the smallest fraction of cases.

It is suggested that the correlations between the more extensive and contemporaneously gathered Watson data and the more limited American Steel and Wire data, argues for the acceptance of the American Steel and Wire litigation records as more typical than extraordinary of the pre-compensation state of affairs in the Cleveland, Ohio, courts. While all the problems incident to the small, non-random, American Steel and Wire data set cannot be brushed aside, neither can its descriptive validity, given

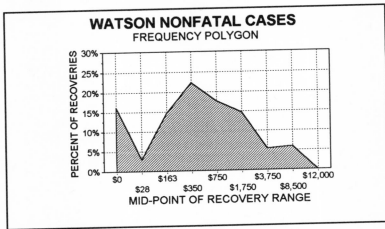

Figure 13(W) Source: OELC, *Report*, Vol. I, xlvi, xlvii.

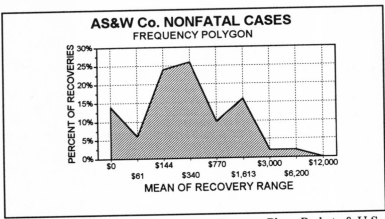

Figure 13(AS&W) Source: Court Files, Common Pleas, Probate & U.S. Circuit Courts, Cleveland, Ohio.

these statistical correlations and the narrative sources that support the main argument of this study: that work injury case values were rising over time, at a rate unrelated to the other costs of labor.

THE EVOLUTION OF REFORM

The table below attempts to trace the workmen's compensation reform in Ohio from the earliest efforts to modify the common law, through to the corporate response to the problem of employee litigation circa 1910, on to the "public" response to worker injury lawsuits, the compulsory workmen's compensation act passed in Ohio in 1914. Discussion of the compensation reform focuses on the early years of the Ohio system, not its modern version. The table is an effort to trace continuities as much as draw distinctions between the three stages in the development of workmen's compensation.

The injury awards and settlements under the various schemes are based upon certain assumptions. The litigation awards do not deduct out the court costs and attorney fees. The company Accident Relief Plan amounts were derived from the 1910 average annual wage levels for workers employed by the United States Steel Corporation subsidiaries—$766. The sums for the Ohio compensation system were calculated using the average annual national wage levels (not specific to any given industry) in 1915—$661.

FROM COMMON LAW TO COMPENSATION		
Common Law In The Cleveland Courts 1898-1915	**AS&W Co., "The Accident Relief Plan" 1910**	**Ohio Workmen's Compensation Law 1914**
LIABILITY ISSUES		
Theory: Fault based, employer negligence required, employee due care required. Employer defenses, assumption of the risk, fellow servant rule, and contributory negligence frustrate employee recovery. Death recovery limited to loss of support for dependants as permitted by statute, if no negligence on behalf of deceased worker.	Theory: No Fault, only issue: Was employee accidentally injured or killed while acting in service to company or while protecting its property? Only reasons for denying recovery are for self-inflicted injuries, or those sustained while intoxicated or taking part in illegal or immoral acts.	Theory: No Fault, only issue: Was employee injured or killed "in course of employment"? Injury or death not self-inflicted. Claim made to State Industrial Commission, unless employer is self-insured, in which case claims handled by employer according to state standards.

Table 23

FROM COMMON LAW TO COMPENSATION		
Practice: Juries (and many judges) tend to ignore and ameliorate harshness of common law rules, and create a "common law compensation" standard that practically assures employee recovery. Appeals to higher (judge only) courts, where there is greater deference to employer defenses. Federal court initially hostile to worker claims until about 1906-1907. Thereafter, federal court more inclined to force settlements with workers.	**Practice:** Same as theory, employee must waive suit and sign release to recover from Plan. No appeal of company manager's decisions.	**Practice:** If employer pays into fund or self- insures, no right to sue employer. Appeals to court only on issues of whether injury sustained in the "course of employment."
Disease and "toxic" claims not recognized, but are being advanced under negligence theory in suits.	No provision for disease or toxic claims.	While Ohio constitutional amendment anticipated coverage for occupational disease, the final statute does not include diseases in the compensation schedules.
DAMAGES, COMPENSATION AMOUNTS		
Injury: "Make whole" doctrine is overarching principle governing verdict amounts. Damage award ordinarily related to loss of income, future earning ability; medical and doctor bills; and directly related incidentals.	**Injury:** "Temporary Disablement" for injuries that prevent working up to one year: Single men 35% of wages with additional 2% for each year of service over 5 years service $1.50/day maximum; Married men, 50% of wages with 2% kicker for every year over 5 years service, $1.50/day maximum.	**Injury:** "Temporary Disability" 66.6% of wages for up to 6 years, $3,750 maximum "Partial Disability" 66.6% of wages; $3,750 maximum.

Table 23 (Cont.)

FROM COMMON LAW TO COMPENSATION		
Common law made no formal distinction between temporary and permanent injuries; "make whole" governs all injuries.	"Permanent Disablement" somewhat discretionary with Plan Manager, who was guided by presumptive amounts listed below.	"Permanent Total Disability" 66.6% of wages until death; $12/week maximum, $5/week minimum All awards payable in installments, not lump sums.
Damages for injured employees are increasing over time, but are often tied to wages (see below).	Compensation strictly tied to wages over a limited period of time.	Compensation tied to 66.6% of wages for up to 6 years, unless a permanent, total disability, then for life.
Pain and Suffering are permitted as a compensable items, but not clearly separated out from single sum awards.	No Pain & Suffering recovery.	No Pain &Suffering recovery.
AS&W Suit Recoveries:	**AS&W Plan presumptive amounts:**	**W.C. compensation schedule:**
No Data	**Loss of hand**: 12 months' wages--$766	**Loss of hand**: 66.6% 150 weeks' wages--$1,270
Loss of arm: 1906, fed. court settled--$2,200	**Loss of arm**: 18 months' wages--$1,150	**Loss of arm**: 66.6% of 200 weeks' wages--$1,693
Loss of foot: 1903, state judge--$2,000; 1903, fed. judge--$0	**Loss of foot**: 9 months' wages--$575	**Loss of foot**: 66.6% of 125 weeks' wages--$1,058
Loss of leg: 1901, state judge $800; 1902, state judge $700; 1902, state, judge $350.	**Loss of leg** : 12 months' wages--$766	**Loss of leg**: 66.6% of 175 weeks' wages--$1,481
Loss of eye: 1904, state jury $400; 1907, state jury $100; 1907, fed. settled $400; 1910, state judge $900.	**Loss of eye**: 6 months' wages--$383	**Loss of eye**: 66.6% of 100 weeks' wages--$846

Table 23 (Cont.)

FROM COMMON LAW TO COMPENSATION		
Loss of big toe: 1902, state judge $125	No Data	**Loss of big toe:** 66.6% of 30 weeks wages--$254
Loss of 4 fingers: 1906, state jury $175 (left hand); 1906, state jury $1,200 (rt hand).	No Data	**Loss of 4 fingers:** 66.6% of 100 weeks' wages--$846.
Loss of index finger(s): 1904, state jury, 1 finger $350; 1904, state jury, 2 index fingers $250.	No Data	**Loss of index finger(s)**: 66.6% of 35 weeks wages $296 - 1 finger, $592 - 2 fingers
Death: Single Men: Medical and funeral expenses Married Men: Reasonably expected wages, less personal usage, maximum of $10,000 (until 1912); no pain and suffering or bereavement damages.	**Death:** Single Men: Funeral Expenses up to $100. Married Men: Funeral Expenses: 18 months wages; plus 3% additional for every year of service over 5 years and 10% additional for every child under 16; Maximum of $3,000.	**Death:** Single Men: Funeral expenses up to $150; medical & hospital expenses up to $200. Married Men: 66.6% of wages for 6 years following date of injury; Maximum recovery $3,750; Minimum recovery $1,500; payable in installments.
Five AS&W recoveries: 1904, machinist, jury verdict--**$500**; 1905, machinist, settled federal court--**$750**; 1907, laborer, fed. judge verdict--**$3,000**; 1907, laborer, fed. judge verdict--**$1,060**; 1912, laborer, settled state court--**$400** Avg. **$1,142**	Example---Married man, 10 years service, 3 children under 16: Funeral expenses $100 18 months wages $1,150 5 years x 3% $172 3 children x 10% $345 Total $1,767	Example---same AS&W married man: Funeral expenses $150 Medical expenses $200 $766 x 66.6%x 6 $3,060 Total $3,410 (Paid in installments)

Table 23 (Cont.)

FROM COMMON LAW TO COMPENSATION PROCEDURAL FEATURES		
Suit must be filed or threatened with apparent ability to carry out threat of litigation. Attorney required, can be hired without retainer, payment of fee under contingency agreement for 25-33% of recovered amount.	**Make claim to company** claims office, waive filing suit and sign release. Company will not deal with attorney.	**Make claim to state or company** claims office. Attorney can be, but is not required, for use with compensation claim. Attorneys who practice compensation law move to specialized, high volume practices, and are sought increasingly to help workers against large, self-insured employers who begin fighting more claims as part of cost reduction efforts.
Waiting Period: From 1 to 2 years.	**Waiting Period**: 10 days	**Waiting Period**: 7 days
Worker chooses doctor. Doctor and hospital bills covered if verdict or settlement reached, and they are notified. Doctors usually peripheral to litigation---in theory. Volume personal injury attorney practitioners often developed a mutually beneficial relationships with "plaintiff's doctors."	**Company chooses doctor** and hospital and has control over course and duration of treatment for injury if worker is to recover from the Plan.	**Doctors play a major role** in managing care for injured workers and making determinations regarding extent and/or duration of injury for determination of claim amount and type. Industrial Commission can require worker to submit to examination by its own physician for determination of disability.
Doctor & hospital bills included in damages, but no assurance doctor paid if worker recovers.	**Doctor & hospital bills** paid by company.	**Doctors & hospital** can recover up to $200 directly from the Industrial Commission.
Recovery, if any, paid in lump sum, with costs of suit and attorney fees (25-33%) taken out.	**Recovery** may be in lump sum or in weekly installments, no deduction for costs or attorney fees.	**Recovery** always paid in installments for duration of injury, six years or life depending on injury type and dependants.

Table 23 (Cont.)

FROM COMMON LAW TO COMPENSATION		
Employer risk reduction options: Private liability insurance; self-insurance; employer sponsored (possibly employee funded) benefit plans.	**Company was self-insured**: Paid for lawyers, as needed; safety and claims management staff; and paid any verdicts or settlements out of corporate funds. Did not carry liability insurance.	**Employer risk reduction options**: If employed five or more workers, mandatory participation in State Fund or comparable self insurance system meeting state standards. Employers not paying premiums into state fund or self-insuring within guidelines were subject to worker suit without benefit of legal defenses. Ohio prohibited the sale of private insurance to cover workmen's compensation risk, but most states turned over the underwriting to private insurers.

Table 23 (Cont.)

Notes

1. The indexes and the docket books for the common pleas court during the period of this study are kept at the Cuyahoga County Archives.

2. These records are still in the custody of the Clerk of the common pleas court.

3. The United States Circuit Court indexes and docket books are currently kept by the Clerk for the federal District Court, Northern District of Ohio, Eastern Division, in Cleveland.

4. When testifying before the Ohio Employers' Liability Commission, Stephen Tener noted in passing that "settlements with minors . . . must be made a matter of court record." Ibid., OELC, *Report*, Vol. II, 125. However, the twenty-seven hearings in common pleas court involving minors were not *pro forma* settlement proceedings, but full-blown jury trials taken to verdicts.

5. Where: x = Triennium Periods
y = Weighted Claim Values
N = 6 (Triennium Periods in 18 years)

x	y	x-x	y-y	(x-x)²	(y-y)²
1	13.	-2.5	-528.5	6.25	279,312.25
2	423.	-1.5	-118.5	2.25	14,042.25
3	558.	-.5	16.5	.25	272.25
4	678.	.5	136.5	.25	18,362.25
5	498.	1.5	-43.5	2.25	1,892.25
6	1,079.	2.5	537.5	6.25	288,906.25
21	3,249.			17.5	603,057.5

Mean Year = 21/6 = **3.5**
Mean Cost = 3249/6 = **$541.50**
Standard Deviation of x = 17.5/6 = 2.916 = **1.708**
Standard Deviation of y = 603,057.5/6 = 100,509.6 = **$317**

Co-Variance of x+y:
    (x-x)*(y-y)
1   1321.25
2   177.75   2837.5/6 = **472.908**
3   -8.25
4   68.25   Therefore, the Correlation Coefficient is:
5   -65.25
6   1343.75   472.908/(1.708*317) = **.873**
     2837.5

6. To solve for the "Line of Best Fit," assuming it is a straight line:

The Regression Coefficient is:
    b = 427.908/1.708^2 or 472.908/2.917 = **$162.106**

The Regression Constant is:
    a = 541.5 - (162.10 * 3.5) or 541.5 - 567.35 = **-$25.85**

Solving for y: y = bx + a

Where x = the first triennium or 1: y = (162.10 * 1)-25.85 = **$136.25**
Where x = the second triennium or 2: y = (162.10 * 2)-25.85 = **$298.35**
Where x = the third triennium or 3: y = (162.10 * 3)-25.85 = **$460.45**
Where x = the fourth triennium or 4: y = (162.10 * 4)-25.85 = **$622.55**
Where x = the fifth triennium or 5: y = (162.10 * 5)-25.85 = **$784.65**
Where x = the sixth triennium or 6: y = (162.10 * 6)-25.85 = **$946.75**

7. U.S. Bureau of Census, *Statistical Abstract of the United States 1991*, 111th Edition (Washington: 1991) Table 740/664.

8. Douglas A. Fisher, *Steel Serves the Nation: The Fifty Year Story of the United States Steel Corporation* (New York: U.S. Steel Corp., 1951), 224.

9. Ibid., *Statistical Abstract*, Series E 135-166.

Bibliography

Manuscript and Primary Sources

Clerk of Court, Cuyahoga County Common Pleas Court. Cleveland, Ohio. Records of the Cuyahoga County Common Pleas Court.

Clerk of Court, United States District Court for the Northern District of Ohio, Eastern Division. Cleveland, Ohio. Records of the Federal Circuit and District Courts.

Cuyahoga County Archives. Cleveland, Ohio. Records of the Cuyahoga County Common Pleas Court.

National Archives, Great Lakes Region. Chicago, Illinois. Records of the United States Circuit and District Courts.

Pennsylvania State University Library. University Park, Pennsylvania. William Brown Dickson Papers.

Western Reserve Historical Society. Cleveland, Ohio. Cleveland Bar Association Papers.

Newspapers and Periodicals

"Jury Bribery." *Cleveland Plain Dealer*, 23 November 1897, 1.

"Into the Trap." *Cleveland Plain Dealer*, 24 November 1897, 1,2.

"Will Sell." *Cleveland Leader*, 5 December 1897, 1.

"Ong's Jury." *Cleveland Leader*, 7 December 1897, 1.

"Not by Neff." *Cleveland Leader*, 9 December 1897, 1.

"$2,000 Bribe." *Cleveland Leader*, 12 December 1897, 1.

"A Mystery." *Cleveland Leader*, 20 December 1897, 1.

"Will Meet." *Cleveland Leader*, 23 December 1897, 1.

"Bribery Cases." *Cleveland Plain Dealer*, 29 December 1897, 1,6.

"By the Bar." *Cleveland Leader*, 29 December 1897, 1.

Beyer, David S. "Safety Provisions in the United States Steel Corporation."
    The Survey, 7 May 1910.

Hard, William. "Making Steel and Killing Men." *Everybody's Magazine*
    XVII, No. 5 (November 1907): 579-591.

Government Publications

Chaney, Lucian W. *Causes and Prevention of Accidents in the Iron and
    Steel Industry, 1910-1919.* Bulletin No. 298. Washington D.C.: Bureau
    of Labor Statistics, June, 1922.

Employers' Liability Commission of Ohio. *Report to the Legislature.* Report
    and Proceedings of the Employers' Liability Commission. Columbus: F.
    J. Heer, 1911. 3 vols.

Hayhurst, E. R. *Industrial Health-Hazards and Occupational Diseases in
    Ohio.* Columbus: Ohio State Board of Health, 1915.

Immigration Commission. *Immigrants in Industries, Iron and Steel
    Manufacturing.* Senate Document No. 633. Washington D.C.:
    Government Printing Office, 1911. 2 vols.

U. S. Bureau of Labor Statistics. *The Safety Movement in the Iron and Steel
    Industry, 1907-1917.* Bulletin No. 234. Washington D.C.: Government
    Printing Office, 1918.

United States. Congress. Senate. *Accidents and Accident Prevention. Conditions of Employment in the Iron and Steel Industry.* vol. IV. Washington D.C.: Government Printing Office, 1913.

Encyclopedic and Reference

Bench and Bar of Ohio. Edited by George Irving Reed. Chicago: Century Publishing and Engraving Company, 1897.

The Book of Clevelanders. Cleveland: The Burrow Brothers Company, 1914.

Representative Clevelanders: a Biographical Directory of Leading Men and Women in Present Day Cleveland. Cleveland: The Cleveland Topics Company, 1927.

The Cyclopedia of Medicine, Surgery, Specialties. Philadelphia: F. A. Davis Company, 1969.

Encyclopedia of Cleveland History. Edited by David D. Van Tassel and John J. Grabowski. Bloomington: Indiana University Press, 1987.

Prosser and Keeton on the Law of Torts. Edited by W. Page Keeton. St. Paul: West Publishing Company, 5th Ed., 1984.

Duffy, Thomas J. "The Industrial Commission." In *A History of the Courts and Lawyers of Ohio,* vol. II, edited by Carrington T. Marshall. New York: American Historical Society, 1934.

Kennedy, James Harrison; Day, Wilson M. *The Bench and Bar of Cleveland.* Cleveland: Cleveland Printing and Publishing Company, 1889.

Marshall, Carrington T. "Constitution--Part V." In *A History of the Courts and Lawyers of Ohio,* vol. I, edited by Carrington T. Marshall, 147-165. New York: American Historical Society, 1934.

Neff, William L. *The Bench and Bar of Northern Ohio.* Cleveland: The Historical Publishing Company, 1921.

Orth, Samuel P. *A History of Cleveland, Ohio.* Chicago: S. J. Clark Publishing Company, 1910.

Books and Pamphlets

Adam, Alastair Thomas. *Wire-Drawing and the Cold Working of Steel.* London: H. F. & G. Witherby, 1936.

Baldwin, Simeon E. *The American Judiciary.* New York: The Century Co., 1905.

Bell, Thomas. *Out of This Furnace.* Pittsburgh: University of Pittsburgh Press, 1941.

Bergstrom, Randolph E. *Courting Danger: Injury and Law in New York City, 1870-1910.* Ithaca: Cornell University Press, 1992.

Berkowitz, Edward, and Kim McQuaid. *Creating the Welfare State: the Political Economy of Twentieth Century Reform.* New York: Praeger, 1980.

Bodnar, John. *Immigration and Industrialization: Ethnicity in an American Mill Town, 1870-1940.* Pittsburgh: University of Pittsburgh Press, 1977.

Brody, David. *Steelworkers in America, the Nonunion Era.* New York: Harper & Row, 1960.

Brudno, Ezra. *The Jugglers.* New York: Moffat, Yard & Company, 1920.

Bureau of Safety, Sanitation & Welfare. "The Safety Provisions of the United States Steel Corporation." Bulletin No. 7. New York: United States Steel Corporation, December, 1918.

Chandler, Alfred D., Jr. *The Visible Hand: the Managerial Revolution in American Business*. Cambridge: The Belknap Press, 1977.

Cotter, Arundel. *The Authentic History of the United States Steel Corporation*. New York: Moody Magazine and Book Company, 1916.

Eastman, Crystal. *Work Accidents and the Law*. New York: Russell Sage Foundation, 1910.

Eggert, Gerald G. *Steelmasters and Labor Reform, 1886-1923*. Pittsburgh: University of Pittsburgh Press, 1981.

Fisher, Douglas A. *Steel Serves the Nation*. New York: United States Steel Corporation, 1951.

Forbath, William E. *Law and the Shaping of the American Labor Movement*. Cambridge: Harvard University Press, 1991.

Friedman, Lawrence M. *A History of American Law*. New York: Simon and Schuster, 2d ed., 1985.

Galford, Justin. *The Foreign Born and Urban Growth in the Great Lakes, 1850-1950*. Ph.D. Diss. New York University, 1957.

Graebner, William. *Coal-Mining Safety in the Progressive Period: The Political Economy of Reform*. Lexington: University Press of Kentucky, 1976.

Hogan, William T. S.J. *Economic History of the Iron and Steel Industry in the United States*. Lexington, Massachusetts: D.C. Heath and Company, 1978.

Hofstadter, Richard. *The Age of Reform*. New York: Vintage, 1965.

Horwitz, Morton J. *The Transformation of American Law, 1870-1960: The Crisis of Legal Orthodoxy*. New York: Oxford University Press, 1992.

Keller, Morton. *Regulating a New Economy: Public Policy and the Economic Change in America, 1900-1933*. Cambridge: Harvard University Press, 1990.

Key, Marcus M., et al., ed. *Occupational Diseases, a Guide to Their Recognition.* Washington D.C.: U.S. Department of Health, Education and Welfare, 1977.

Kolko, Gabriel. *The Triumph of Conservatism: a Reinterpretation of American History, 1900-1916.* London: Free Press of Glencoe, 1963.

Licht, Walter. *Working for the Railroad: the Organization of Work in the Nineteenth Century.* Princeton: Princeton University Press, 1983.

Lubove, Roy. *The Struggle for Social Security, 1900-1935.* Cambridge: Harvard University Press, 1968.

Mercer, James K. *Ohio Legislative History, 1909-1913.* Columbus: Edward T. Miller Company, 1914.

Purcell, Edward A., Jr. *Litigation and Inequality: Federal Diversity Jurisdiction in Industrial America, 1870-1958.* New York: Oxford University Press, 1992.

Reed, Jewett V., and A. K. Harcourt. *The Essentials of Occupational Diseases.* Springfield: Charles C. Thomas, 1941.

Silbert, Samuel H. *Judge Sam.* Manhasset, N.Y.: Channel Press, 1963.

Silverman, Robert A. *Law and Urban Growth.* Princeton: Princeton University Press, 1981.

Smith, J. Bucknall. *A Treatise Upon Wire, Its Manufacture and Uses.* New York: John Wiley & Sons, 1891.

Smith, Reginald Heber, and Herbert B. Ehrmann. "Juries." In *Criminal Justice in Cleveland,* edited by Roscoe Pound and Felix Frankfurter, 340-353. Cleveland: The Cleveland Foundation, 1922.

Steinfeld, Robert J. *The Invention of Free Labor: the Employment Relation in English and American Law and Culture, 1350-1870.* Chapel Hill: University of North Carolina Press, 1991.

The Civic League of Cleveland. "Report of Investigations Into Jury System." *The Municipal Bulletin*, January 1916. Cleveland.

Tomlins, Christopher L. *The State and the Unions: Labor Relations, Law, and the Organized Labor Movement, 1880-1960.* Cambridge: Cambridge University Press, 1985.

Walker, Charles R. *Steel: the Diary of a Furnace Worker.* Boston: Atlantic Monthly Press, 1922.

Warshow, Robert Irving. *Bet-A-Million Gates, the Story of a Plunger.* New York: Greenberg, 1932.

Watson, Archibald R. *Damages for Personal Injuries.* Charlottesville: Mitchie Company, 1901.

Wendt, Lloyd, and Herman Kogan. *Bet-A-Million! The Story of John W. Gates.* New York: Bobbs Merrill, 1948.

Weinstein, James. *The Corporate Ideal and the Liberal State, 1900-1918.* Boston: Beacon Press, 1968.

White, G. Edward. *Tort Law in America, an Intellectual History.* New York: Oxford University Press, 1980.

Wilgus, Horace L. *A Study of the United States Steel Corporation.* Chicago: Callaghan & Company, 1901.

Journal Articles

Alger, George. "Address to the New Jersey State Bar Association". 10 Ohio Law Bulletin, 375.

Asher, Robert. "Failure and Fulfillment: Agitation for Employers' Liability Legislation and the Origins of Workmen's Compensation in New York State, 1876-1910." *Labor History*, Spring 1983, 198-222.

———. *Workmen's Compensation in the United States, 1880-1935.* Ph. D. Diss. University of Minnesota, 1971.

———. "The Limits of Big Business Paternalism: Relief for Injured Workers in the Years Before Workmen's Compensation." In *Dying for Work: Workers' Safety and Health in Twentieth-Century America,* edited by David Rosner and Gerald Markowitz, 19-33. Bloomington: Indiana University Press, 1987.

———. "Business and Workers' Welfare in the Progressive Era." *Business History Review* XLIII (Winter 1969): 452-475.

———. "Radicalism and Reform: State Insurance of Workmen's Compensation in Minnesota, 1910-1933." *Labor History,* Winter 1973, 19-41.

Craven, Paul. "Law and Railway Accidents, 1850-1880." Paper presented at the Canadian Law in History Conference. Ottawa, Ontario, June, 1987.

Croyle, James L. "Industrial Accident Liability Policy of the Early Twentieth Century." *Journal of Legal Studies* 7, no. 2 (June 1978).

Downey, E. H. "The Present Status of Workmen's Compensation in the United States." *American Economic Review,* March 1922.

Epstein, Richard A. "The Historical Origins and Economic Structure of Workers' Compensation Law." *Georgia Law Review* 16, no. 4 (Summer 1982): 773-819.

Friedman, Lawrence M., and Jack Ladinsky. "Social Change and the Law of Industrial Accidents." *Columbia Law Review* 67 (January 1967): 50-82.

Krasity, Kenneth. "The Role of the Judge in Jury Trials: The Elimination of Judicial Evaluation of fact in American state Courts from 1790-1913." *University of Detroit Law Review* 62 (1985): 595-632.

Mengert, H. R. "The Ohio Workmen's Compensation Law." *Ohio Archaeological and Historical Publications* XXIX (1920): 1-48.

Milic, Louis T. "Inflation, Consumers and the CPI." *The Gamut*, no. 36 (Summer 1992): 19-29.

Munger, Frank. "Social Change and Tort Litigation: Industrialization, Accidents, and Trial Courts in Southern West Virginia, 1872 to 1940." *Buffalo Law Review* 36 (1987): 75-118.

———. "Law Change, and Litigation: A Critical Examination of an Empirical Research Tradition." *Law and Society Review* 22 (1988): 58-101.

———. "Trial Courts and Social Change: The Evolution of a Field Study." *Law and Society Review* 24 (1990): 217-26.

Posner, Richard A. "A Theory of Negligence." *Journal of Legal Studies* 1, no. 1 (1972).

Ratliff, Raymond. "The New Ohio Workmen's Compensation Law." *Ohio Law Reporter* IX (1912): 207-224.

Reagan, Patrick D. "The Ideology of Social Harmony and Efficiency: Workmen's Compensation in Ohio, 1904-1919." *Ohio History*.

Schwartz, Gary T. "Tort Law and the Economy in Nineteenth-Century America: a Reinterpretation." *Yale Law Journal* 90, no. 8 (July 1981): 1717-1775.

Tripp, Joseph F. "Progressive Jurisprudence in the West: the Washington Supreme Court, Labor Law, and the Problem of Industrial Accidents." *Labor History*, Fall 1983, 342-365.

Weinstein, James. "Big Business and the Origins of Workmen's Compensation." *Labor History* 8 (Spring 1967): 156-174.

Wesser, Robert F. "Conflict and Compromise: the Workmen's Compensation Movement in New York 1890-1913." *Labor History*, Summer 1971, 345-372.

Reported Cases (In Order of Reference)

Yaple v. Creamer, 85 Ohio St. 349 (1912)

Brown v. Kendall, 6 Cush. 292, (Mass. 1850)

Priestly v. Fowler, 3 M.&W. 1, 150 Eng. Rep. 1030 (1837).

Farwell v. Boston & Worcester Railway 4 Metc. 49, (Mass. 1849).

Little Miami R. Co. v. John Stevens, 20 Ohio St. 416, (1856).

Robert Bycraft v. Lakeshore & Michigan Southern Railway Co., 8 Ohio N.P. 588 (1894).

Mansfield Railway v. Barr, 2 Ohio App. 367, (1914).

McWeeny v. Standard Boiler & Plate Co., 210 F. 507, (1914).

Lake Shore & M. S. R. Co. v. Topliff, 6 O.C.D. 23, (Ohio 1895).

Olmstead v. Distilling and Cattle Feeding Co., 9 Ohio F. Dec. 288, (1895).

Interurban Ry. & Terminal Co. v. Beirman, 21 O.C.D. 663, (Ohio 1910).

Greve v. Cincinnati Traction Co., 27 Ohio Dec. 625, (1913).

Wallis v. Moore, 26 Ohio Dec. 250, (1916).

Street Ry. Co. v. Rohner, 6 O.C.D. 706, (Ohio 1895).

Lowry v. Mt. Adams & Eden Park Incline Plane R. Co., 68 F. 827, (Fed. 1895)

Steel v. Kurtz, 28 Ohio St. 191, (1876).

Hall's Adm'x. v. Crain, 2 Dec. Repr. 453, (Ohio 1860).

Ellis & Morton v. Ohio Life Ins. & Trust Co., 4 Ohio St. 628, (1856).

Ewing v. Goode, 78 F. 442, (Fed. 1897).

Quay v. Quay, 4 Nisi Prius N.S. 529, (Ohio 1906).

Hamden Lodge v. Ohio Fuel Gas Co., 127 Ohio St. 469, (1934).

Vany v. R.B.F. Peirce, 8 Ohio Dec. 691, (Fed. 1898).

Swift v. Tyson, 41 U.S. 1, (Fed. 1842).

Baltimore & Ohio Railroad Company v. Baugh, 149 U.S. 368, (Fed. 1893).

Industrial Commission v. Brown, 92 Ohio St. 309, (1915).

Industrial Commission v. McManigal, 11 Ohio App. 384, (1919).

Industrial Commission v. Cross, 104 Ohio St. 561, (1922).

McCamey v. Payer, 135 Ohio St. 660, (1939).

Index

Amalgamated Association of Iron, Steel and Tin Workers, 24
American Steel and Wire Company , xiv, xvi, 3-6, 18, 21-24, 34, 39, 46, 49, 50, 52, 54, 55, 57, 58, 64, 75, 80, 82, 87, 88, 91-93, 98, 111, 112, 119, 121, 123, 132,147, 148, 153, 155, 157-161, 167, 171-176, 190, 201-203, 206, 213-216, 220, 224, 225, 227, 230, 231, 233, 234, 236-238
American Steel and Wire Company (of Illinois), 21, 22
American Wire Company, 21, 155
Americanization Committees, 200
Americanization Council, 174
answer, 4, 40, 48, 50, 56, 59, 160
arsenic, 94
asbestos, 204
assumption of the risk, 37, 39, 40, 50, 62, 184, 239

Baackes Nail Company, 21
Baruch, Bernard, 173
blast furnace, 79, 87, 91
Bourne, Emma Norris, 155
Boyd, William Harrington, 183, 185, 188, 189, 227
Brownell, Abner, 155
Brudno, Ezra, 6, 7, 9-12, 16, 18, 47, 152
burden of proof, 51, 55

Civic League of Cleveland, 125
Clark, Harold Terry, 173, 174

Cleveland Bar Association, 10, 110, 111, 114, 175, 205
Cleveland Chamber of Commerce, 171, 184
Cleveland Foundation, 110, 111, 134
Cleveland, Ohio, xiv, 21, 24, 31, 50, 57 114, 122-124, 134, 140, 155, 159, 168, 171, 213, 215, 217-219, 221-224, 234, 235, 237, 238
Cleveland Rolling Mill Company, 22
Committee of Safety, 83, 85
common law, xiii-xvii, 32-34, 36-38, 42, 45-47, 54, 58-60, 63, 98, 99, 111, 119, 123, 124, 147, 149, 160, 184, 187, 201, 202, 204, 205, 239, 240
Consolidated Steel Company, 20
contingent fee, 49, 80
contributory negligence, 37, 40, 50, 184, 239
Cox, James M., 190
Cuyahoga County, xiv, 3, 4, 44, 57, 58, 82, 87, 88, 91, 93, 98, 110, 112, 113, 117, 120, 125-129, 134, 137, 158, 159, 175, 185, 188, 202, 213, 225, 227, 228, 231
Cuyahoga County Bar Association, 175

damages, 4, 20, 33, 34, 36, 37, 40, 42-49, 51, 52, 57, 58, 61, 99, 110, 111, 122, 131, 140, 148, 158, 185, 201-204, 214,